Sarah Coventry® JEWELRY

Kay Oshel

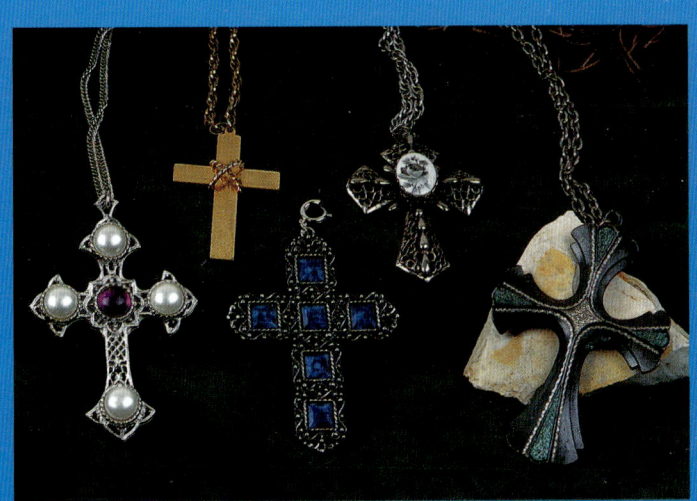

4880 Lower Valley Road, Atglen, PA 19310 USA

"Sarah Coventry" and other associated trademarks are registered trademarks of Sarah Coventry, Inc. Their use herein is for identification purposes only. Sarah Coventry, Inc. did not authorize this book nor furnish or approve of any of the information contained herein. The objects pictured in this book are from the collection of the author of the book or various private collectors. This book is derived from the author's independent research.

Copyright © 2003 by Kay Oshel
Library of Congress Control Number: 2002114577

All rights reserved. No part of this work may be reproduced or used in any form or by any means—graphic, electronic, or mechanical, including photocopying or information storage and retrieval systems—without written permission from the copyright holder.
"Schiffer," "Schiffer Publishing Ltd. & Design," and the "Design of pen and ink well" are registered trademarks of Schiffer Publishing Ltd.

Designed by Bonnie M. Hensley
Cover design by Bruce M. Waters
Type set in BernhardMod BT/Humanist 521 BT

ISBN: 0-7643-1704-0
Printed in China
1 2 3 4

Published by Schiffer Publishing Ltd.
4880 Lower Valley Road
Atglen, PA 19310
Phone: (610) 593-1777; Fax: (610) 593-2002
E-mail: Schifferbk@aol.com
Please visit our web site catalog at **www.schifferbooks.com**
We are always looking for people to write books on new and related subjects. If you have an idea for a book, please contact us at the above address.

This book may be purchased from the publisher.
Include $3.95 for shipping.
Please try your bookstore first.
You may write for a free catalog.

In Europe, Schiffer books are distributed by
Bushwood Books
6 Marksbury Avenue
Kew Gardens
Surrey TW9 4JF England
Phone: 44 (0) 20 8392 8585
Fax: 44 (0) 20 8392 9876
E-mail: Bushwd@aol.com
Free postage in the UK. Europe: air mail at cost.

Dedication

My main dedication is to my family, who helped with this process in a myriad of ways. To my husband, who laughingly states that he knows much more about Sarah Coventry jewelry than he ever wanted to know and recognizes Sarah Coventry pieces when worn by other women. Now that's amazing. And to my two daughters, Denise and Michelle, who looked at me strangely when I said I was collecting even more jewelry and whose mouths dropped open when I said I was writing this book. They have both shared their expertise in design and style by assisting with the photography, so some of their handiwork can be seen throughout the book. And I'm sure they have subconsciously decided what they will do with all this jewelry when it becomes theirs. Hopefully they will wear it and treasure it as many other women before us have done, for truly there is an emotional and historical thread generated by these pieces.

From left: Kay Oshel, Denise Oshel, Michelle and Jon Woods, Alan Oshel.

Acknowledgments

There are many who need to be acknowledged here because of their support, assistance, generosity, and above all, collecting ability. To begin, I would like to acknowledge the efforts of flea market dealers who have searched the Midwestern states for pieces of Sarah Coventry jewelry for my own collection – which started the whole process. Their names are too numerous to mention, but they know who they are. Thank You'all.

More specifically, I would like to thank the following (in alphabetical order): Sara Ayers, Dick Bartges, Wilma Hoth, Nancy Isgrigs, Alynda Kimbrough, Helen Knapp, Dawn Michael, Debbie Warner, and Nona Wilson, who were past Fashion Show Directors on up to the higher management ranks. These folks kept me on the right track with their pieces of jewelry, cardex files, and catalogs to help in identifying names and decades. Dawn Michael shines here with her nearly complete collection of catalogs from 1966 to 1984. Others who assisted were Otheda Smith and her new collection of jewelry, Reba Thompson, Pat Allison, Michelle Kernel, Jenny Wilson, and Jan Koltes, who all assisted with either information, jewelry to photograph, or just inspiration. Jan also had a web site previously that showed many pieces of jewelry and names, but since my initial contact with her this site is no longer available. What a wonderful idea, so check with me if interested. And last, but not least, a special appreciation to my editor, Donna Baker, who was very insightful and kind in working with this novice author.

Contents

Chapter One: Overview — 6
    Introduction — 6
    The Company — 7
    The Parties and the Driving Force — 8
    The Jewelry — 13
    Versatility — 19
    Becoming a Collector — 21
    Using This Book — 22
    An Invitation — 23

Chapter Two: The Early Years: 1949-1965 — 24
    Brooches — 27
    Earrings — 34
    Necklaces — 45
    Bracelets — 50
    Rings and Sets — 53
    1962 and 1963 *Signets* — 56

Chapter Three: The Late 1960s: 1966-1969 — 64
    Brooches — 65
    Earrings — 71
    Necklaces — 76
    Bracelets — 79
    Rings and Sets — 81
    Lady Coventry — 85
    1969 Catalog — 90

Chapter Four: The 1970s — 96
    Brooches — 98
    Earrings — 104
    Necklaces — 111
    Bracelets — 126
    Rings and Sets — 131
    Crosses — 138
    1972 Catalog — 140

Chapter Five: The 1980s — 148
    Necklaces — 149
    Pins, Bracelets, Earrings, and Rings — 152
    1982 Catalog — 154

Chapter Six: Men's Jewelry and Accessories — 164
    Men's Jewelry — 164
    Accessories — 169

Epilogue — 170
Glossary — 171
Bibliography — 173
Appendix: Personal Collection Sheets — 173
Index — 174

Chapter One

Overview

Welcome to what I hope will be a useful and yet personal tool in your quest for collecting jewelry – more specifically, Sarah Coventry jewelry. Although several books have been published regarding Sarah Coventry, many previous books on jewelry have not given this company its due place in the collecting world. My goal for this book is to provide more specific information about Sarah Coventry jewelry, including the decade in which pieces were manufactured and the name attributed to each piece by the company. I hope to also give you more insight into a company highly respected by past employees and bring some of their own words to you directly.

Introduction

Have you ever wondered what your life might be like if you had done just one thing differently? If you had gone just one step in another direction, or if you had met just one different person? Like many baby boomers today, I have had some time to reflect on some of these things. And then I read about Joe Kita, who actually took a year off to try and recapture some of his lost moments and wrote about it in a book called *Another Shot: How I Relived My Life in Less than a Year*.

I, like Joe, have had some thoughts about those lost opportunities, those missed adventures, those unmade memories. However, I am trying to capture some of those "what ifs" in a different way. By authoring this Sarah Coventry book, I feel as if I am going back to an opportunity no longer available, to adventures gained through others' eyes and to the unobtainable memories through photographs and dialogue.

In memory of all those who *did* take the path of Sarah Coventry, I dedicate this book. Their words, memories, and ideals will be the framework into which the many pictures of jewelry are interspersed.

As I embarked upon this project and was encouraged by Nancy Schiffer to indeed proceed, I had no idea how much this book and the directions it led to were truly made for me. With an educational background in the area of guidance, counseling, and substance abuse prevention, I had little expectation of what I would find as I researched Sarah Coventry families involved for ten, fifteen, and even twenty-nine years in the company.

Much of my educational background relied on an understanding of the balance between the affective (or emotional and feeling) side of a person with the cognitive (or factual) learning side. In visiting with and listening to both men and women who had successfully achieved all levels of management or sales at Sarah Coventry, it became evident to me that C. H. Stuart and his family-run business had developed a unique family atmosphere within the ranks. Many of these details and thoughts will be shared throughout the following pages.

My hope for this book is to provide collectors with a perspective on the sense of pride and accomplishment that prevailed in such a remarkable company, a company that cared deeply about its employees/direct sales force and created jewelry that truly has withstood the test of time.

As an invitation would read "You Are Invited!" to travel with me on a journey back through history by way of Sarah Coventry jewelry—1949 through 1984. Relax, enjoy, and begin collecting a costume jewelry that even today is inspiring wearers of all ages.

I also invite you to replicate and use the sample Personal Collection Sheet at the end of the book. Identifying and listing your pieces may just lead you to write a book, much as I have done. Once my 1500 pieces were collected, I needed to catalog them. In so doing, I wanted to learn more about the dates of production and glean some information behind the designs. The result is this book.

The Company

In 1949, The C.H. Stuart, Inc. company had been in business for many years with a variety of offshoot companies including Aquasport, Inc. (a fiberglass boat manufacturer), Artscraft Concepts Inc. (which designed, manufactured, and distributed craft products), a furniture company, and an interior decorating for the home company. In that year, Bill Stuart (C.H. Stuart's son) discussed a new idea with his first employee, Rex Wood. The plan was to begin another company with a direct sales approach similar to that used for other products at the time. This product, however, would be "a glamorous product (fine fashion jewelry)." Through the direct sales approach, a sales force of field representatives would begin the process of creating a national, and hopefully international, organization. In November 1949, Sarah Coventry was born.

The name Sarah has been attributed incorrectly in several other books to a granddaughter of C.H. Stuart. However, a daughter of Jim Beale, Bill's Stuart's brother-in-law, was born in 1949 and named Sarah. Coventry was the location in England where the Stuart family had originated...hence Sarah Coventry.

The offices, located in Newark, New York, soon became the bustling center for the world's largest direct seller of costume jewelry. And, for the next thirty-five years, from 1949 to 1984, Sarah Coventry, Inc. became a very visible and successful company; indeed it was perhaps the most visible and successful of all the Stuart companies. The company did expand to international status with another division, Sarah Coventry International, with offices as well as manufacturing and jewelry distribution plants in the United Kingdom, Canada, Australia, and Belgium.

In 1984 a variety of things happened with the company; each person I've talked to has provided his or her own version so the actual details have been difficult to verify. Ultimately, the company—including its name and perhaps some office space—was sold. The Sarah Coventry jewelry name was continued (see samples in "The Jewelry" section of this Overview), however jewelry manufacturing was moved to China and India and perhaps other countries. During this time, several attempts were made to recreate the party plan concept (see next section) with no success. Some items have been manufactured under the name of Sarah Coventry Accessories. In the late 1980s, Lifestyle Brands, a division of Playboy Enterprises, purchased the name and they are presently still creating jewelry with the Sarah Coventry identification. As a result, the Sarah Coventry name, usually identified on pieces of jewelry with a very small "SC", is still before us—much different, however, from the collectible pieces in this book. The original C.H. Stuart/Sarah Coventry company is now an icon of the past.

20 years, 8 million miles and 100 million pieces of jewelry ago... these men shared a dream.

In 1949, Bill Stuart shared a dream with his first employee, Rex Wood. The dream was to take an infant company, give it a new type of direct sales plan, add a glamorous product (fine fashion jewelry), and build a field sales organization that would be a national and international leader.
As we complete our 20th year in 1969...
One out of every 14 American women will attend or hold a Sarah Coventry Home Jewelry Show.
Every 12 seconds per working day, a Sarah Coventry Home Jewelry Show will be held in the U.S.A.
For the 15th consecutive year, Sarah Coventry will be the world's largest direct seller of fashion jewelry.
Every 2.59 minutes, a new person will join Sarah's worldwide organization—in the U.S.A., Canada, United Kingdom, Puerto Rico, Norway, Iceland and Australia.
Quality...service...ethics...opportunity...progress—these are the keystone blocks upon which Sarah Coventry was built. To the more than 40,000 people who will be a part of our company in 1969, we pledge our continuing dedication to these principles. Sarah Coventry, Inc., Newark, New York State.

Sarah Coventry®
WORLD'S LARGEST
DIRECT SELLER
OF FINE FASHION JEWELRY

An early 1970 catalog, describing the company's past twenty years in business, listed some amazing statistics. It was truly an impressive twenty years for any company, especially one selling costume jewelry. *Courtesy of Pat Allison.*

The Parties and the Driving Force

The growth of Sarah Coventry, Inc. can be attributed to several strategies. The first of these was the company's workforce: the Fashion Show Directors; the Unit Directors; and the Branch, Region, and Area Managers, as well as those who attained Vice President status. There were many women in these positions and many were part of husband and wife teams—in the mid-1970s, these teams totaled nearly one-third of the employees. Former employee Dick Bartges noted that Sarah Coventry had the largest number of men of any such company at that time, and that as Fashion Show Directors, men did very well.

Through the efforts of the managers, Fashion Show Directors (FSDs) utilized the home party plan. Because many women were not employed outside the home in the 1950s and '60s, parties gave them both the opportunity to make some money without leaving children during the day and created social occasions for their friends and neighbors to have a fun-filled evening trying on jewelry and conversing. And the company enthusiastically assisted by providing many tools for the Fashion Show Directors to use—these included clothes to wear and freebies to give as prizes.

These two pieces of jewelry illustrate some of the many incentives that were continually given to employees and Fashion Show Directors who created the frenzy for Sarah Coventry jewelry. On the left is a charm bracelet presented when an employee recruited five people to become a part of the direct sales force. The necklace on the right features a picture of the new facilities in Newark encased in an attractive pendant; it was no doubt given during the open house ceremonies. Other promotional items included watches, service keys with one diamond for five years of service and two diamonds for ten years, plus rings with the Sarah Coventry crest given to the "elite club" of hard workers one year with additional diamonds added each year thereafter.

Sarah Coventry FSDs could wear any fashionable clothes of the day. Many, however, decided to purchase company scarves, t-shirts, or blazers to distinguish themselves at the parties. *Courtesy of an employee.*

These are some of the many items that could be purchased or were provided free for use as promotional gifts or prizes. The tall Fashion Show Director's Guide was created for the convenience of the presenter. It had pictures on one side and what was to be said on the other. *Courtesy of Otheda Smith.*

Fashion Show Directors could host their own shows but usually encouraged friends to host parties, enabling the hostesses to receive points redeemable on jewelry. Recruitment to join the family of Sarah Coventry was another integral part of the company's growth process as well. In speaking to many of the retired employees, I learned that there truly was a family atmosphere throughout the company. Much of this came from the encouragement and support provided by the Newark offices—meetings, trips, scholarships, and jewelry all paid for by the company.

Imagine for a moment, being at one of the parties in a friend's home—or perhaps revisit in your mind an actual party you may have attended. Everyone would be sitting comfortably on sofas, chairs, or perhaps on the floor on cushions. The FSD presented her or himself to the group (men were quite popular in this position) and began displaying the new jewelry for all to see and try on. The early FSDs noted that they used cloth or foam roll-ups for the jewelry; these were then placed in a briefcase-like piece of luggage. Later FSDs were furnished with a blue case specifically designed to carry these roll-up cloths. Eventually, in the mid-1970s, the stacked-kit became the simplified way of carrying large amounts of jewelry from place to place. By shear luck, I was able to purchase one of these blue stack-kits. So be on the lookout for these—which can provide a convenient way to store your collection—or create a similar one from plastic trays and thick foam.

The first official suitcase for carrying jewelry was this blue case, in which the FSDs could carry the many boxes containing jewelry pieces. *Courtesy of Dawn Michael.*

The stack-kit came about later. It had separate trays cushioned both inside and on the bottom to insure care of the jewelry while being transported from party to party. The strap was then secured around all the trays for easy carrying.

Sarah Coventry believed strongly in communicating with the sales force. In the early 1960s, a regular publication entitled *Sarah Coventry's Signet* was sent to FSDs. It identified top sales winners and included promotional boosters, jewelry ideas, and a variety of tidbits to keep FSDs on track. The sales force also received records and holiday cards with messages and enthusiasm builders. As noted earlier, my discussions with past sales representatives and managers attested to the fact that Sarah Coventry cared for its employees and regarded them as family members. This camaraderie kept the sales force constant and dedicated.

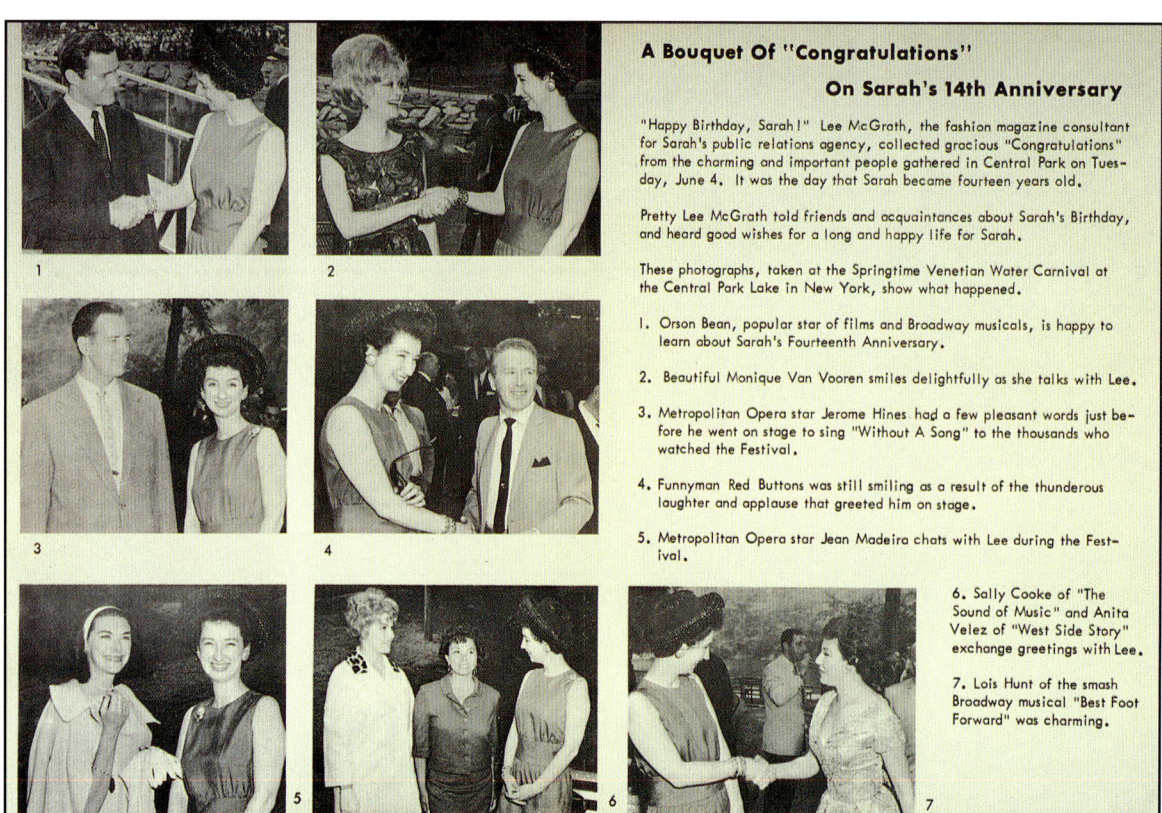

A page from a 1963 *Signet* celebrating Sarah's 14th Anniversary. Sarah's celebrations included top name movie stars and actors. Nothing was spared for the conventions and celebrations. *Courtesy of Jan Koltes.*

Christmas cards for the sales force included 45 rpm records with recorded greetings and boosters designed to make contact with the entire sales force, especially those not able to travel to area or national meetings and conventions—a creative use of the media at that time.

National and regional conventions also fostered this sense of belonging among FSDs. Awards and commemorative gifts were distributed widely to the deserving recipients. These ranged from crowns—donated by the Miss Universe pageant—to charms, trophies, plaques for the wall or desk, and a wide variety of other jewelry pieces for both men and women. Fur coats, trips and cruises, scholarships for children, and home furnishings were some of the additional awards Sarah Coventry employees might receive. Make no mistake, these awards were well deserved but they also served as visual reminders of the many hours of hard work needed for consistent sales and recruitment.

Many promotional awards were displayed in a book called *Dream Book Awards*. This program allowed FSDs of any level to select items based on points earned from recruitment and sales. Points could be accumulated over a period of time for redemption of larger items. The FSD was sent a certificate showing how many points he or she had accumulated. Sometimes part of the credit was retained by the company until the recruit qualified, so it was advantageous for the FSDs to accumulate these certificate points. In the *Dream Book*, points could be redeemed for glass, pewter, and silver items; household items like card tables, coffee pots, and chairs; or jewelry and watches.

Awards in recognition of the FSDs' efforts as well as those of Sarah Coventry's management employees were plentiful and varied. These are just a few of the kinds of gifts presented by the company. *Courtesy of Dawn Michael and Helen Knapp.*

Former FSD Dawn Michael believes this coffee pot was one of the items selected by an FSD from Texas in 1975 (the name and date was still on the original box). Many promotional items were designed with the Sarah Coventry crest, as shown here. Such gifts demonstrate the degree to which Sarah Coventry valued its direct sales force and provided items of great value accordingly.

This goldentone gilded plastic wall case is velvet lined with a mirror in the center—a fashionable way to display one's jewelry. One of two removable trays at the bottom is embossed in gold "Sarah Coventry" in cursive. The plastic back is marked with raised letters "© SARAH COVENTRY, Inc. 1973 NEWARK, NEW YORK." The cardboard backing of the case is stamped "SARAH / TRADE MARK / SARAH COVENTRY, Inc. / NEWARK, NEW YORK." This may have been an item from the employees' *Dream Book*, purchased through certificate points earned. Because of its rarity, current value is $150-200.

The Jewelry

When I look at some of my older pieces of Sarah Coventry, I am awed by their condition and beauty and only wish they could share their stories—who wore them, what events they were admired at, and how many other facets of people's past lives they were a part of.

The success of Sarah Coventry may have resulted from the human factor of managing the large direct sales force, but ultimately I believe the company wouldn't have been what it was without the magnificent costume jewelry that was created just for the party plan sales. Sally Edgett was a Vice-President within the corporate office and became a part of the jewelry selection committee. She noted that suppliers and the Sarah Coventry factory would bring in samples of jewelry for the committee to consider. Once decisions were made, the manufacturer would use a variety of identifying marks on the jewelry, ranging from "SARAH COVENTRY" to "SARAH COV" to "SC" to "SAC" to "COVENTRY." I believe the company's intent was to secure and use a variety of markings in order to discourage duplication by other companies.

The committee then named the pieces. Sometimes the name was in honor of someone's relative or an employee. **Kathleen** was such a piece; it was named in honor of an upper-management employee's wife. Through my research, I discovered that many of the names are very specific to the design. **Papillion**, for example, was the name given to a butterfly pendant. Pronounced pap-e-(y)on (long e), this French word means butterfly. Several names were used more than once, sometimes with a variation in one or two words (as in **Starburst** vs. **Star Burst**) or sometimes just duplicated in different decades.

Variety was very important to Sarah Coventry as the company identified and stayed in tune with their varied customers. The following photos demonstrate some of this variety, from children's jewelry, to a variety of necklaces, to jewelry with a *Wizard of Oz* theme. In addition, former employee Helen Knapp shared a bracelet that was reproduced from an antique bracelet which had belonged to a representative's grandmother. In speaking with these past employees, I deduced that with respect to the designs of the jewelry, every opportunity was taken to be creative and unique.

"For the young at heart" was a descriptive phrase used in advertising jewelry for children, teens, or young adults. These pins and pendants were just a few of the jewelry items created for this age group; anyone, of course, could purchase and wear these pieces. *All courtesy of Alynda Kimbrough.*

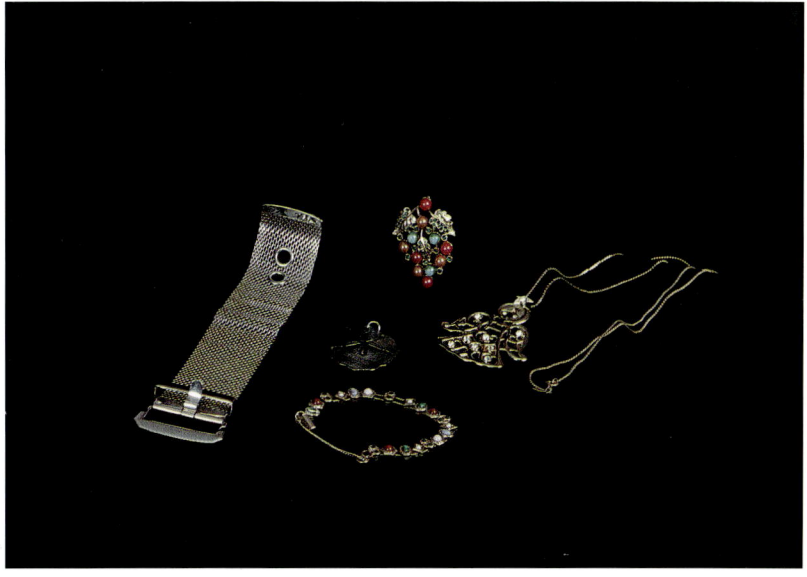

Here are some of the unique pieces of Sarah Coventry jewelry, ranging from a sand dollar, to a mesh bracelet, to Christmas pieces. The center bracelet on the bottom was reproduced from an antique bracelet belonging to the grandmother of a Sarah Coventry representative. *All courtesy of Helen Knapp.*

These necklaces show more of the company's diversity and the desire to provide a fashion look for everyone through the decades. You'll find more of these in the various sections of the book, from personal initial jewelry to crosses. *All courtesy of Alynda Kimbrough.*

Left to right: *Patches* pin is a colorful scarecrow created for the "young at heart." What adult wouldn't like wearing this catchy pin today on a t-shirt, jacket with jeans, or denim dress? The other three pins replicate figures from *The Wizard of Oz* and could be worn singly or in combination. *All courtesy of Dawn Michael*

These photos both show unidentified pieces, although I believe the beaded sets are from the early years. Contrast these with the very simple chain designs utilized later in the 1970s and early '80s.

Many pieces manufactured in other countries, such as Canada and the United Kingdom, have also been identified. They are marked on the back with "SARAH COV" and also with the country name. There are some similarities to those pieces manufactured in the United States, as shown in the following pictures.

Pieces in this picture have been identified as from Canada and United Kingdom. The names of the top two sets are not known, but they are marked with the country name. The left pendant on a card has the same name as a U.S. pendant with a variation of color. See similar piece on page 101. The Crusader Pendant Cross on the far right is also similar to the cross with the same name shown in the cross section on pages 138-139. *All courtesy of Dawn Michael.*

This is a Canadian set of jewelry, identified only on the back with a Sarah Coventry mark and Canada name. *Courtesy of Dawn Michael.*

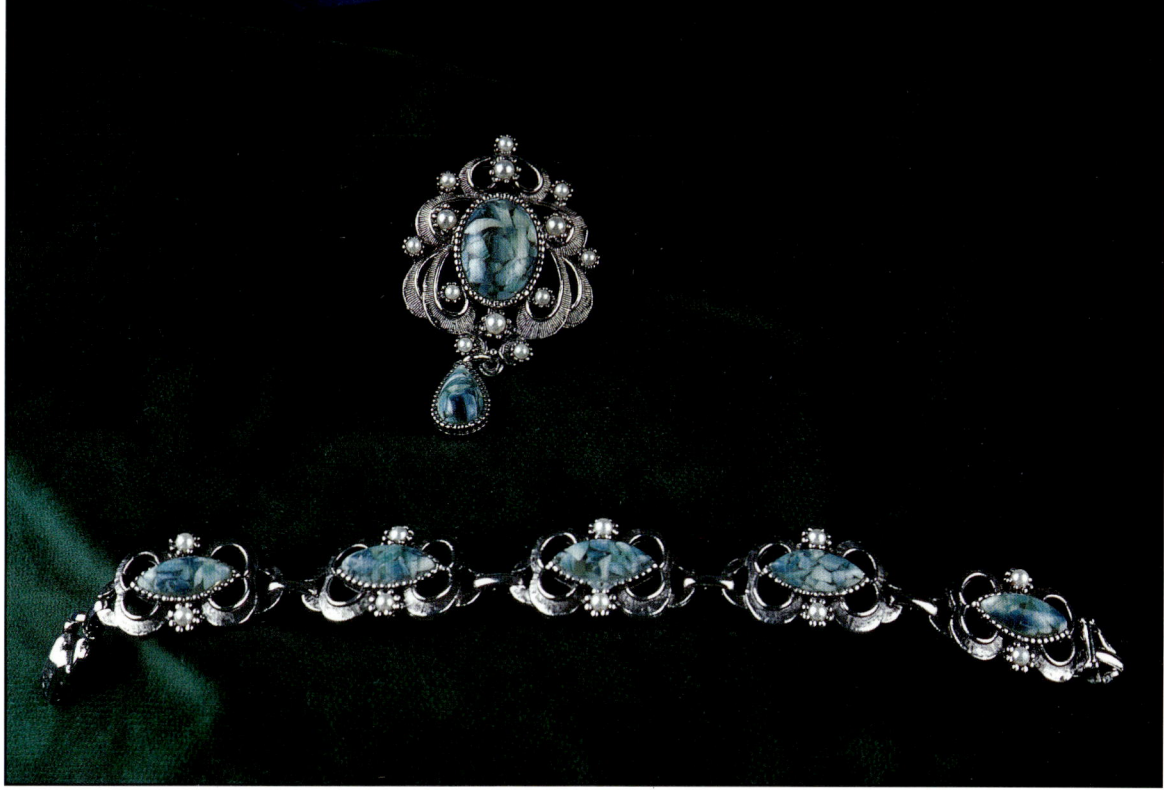

Emmons was a sister company started in the early part of 1949 by the C. H. Stuart, Inc. company. There were many similarities between the two companies—the party plan for direct sales, the style of jewelry, the markings on the jewelry itself, and the appeal to collectors. Emmons did not continue as long as Sarah Coventry, however. Many of the upper level management of Sarah Coventry at that time had little or no knowledge of this sister company. My research has indicated that Sarah Coventry was much more successful, continued longer, and, therefore, manufactured and sold more pieces.

Sets of Emmons jewelry, which are marked on the back similarly to Sarah Coventry. Notice some of the common elements with Sarah jewelry.

I initially began collecting Sarah because it seemed to be easily identified by the marking on the back. I then became rather confused when I found some pieces with no mark, or other marks such as "SAC", "SC", "Coventry," etc. My research in other jewelry books just complicated the issue. Several authors believed that many of these markings were not Sarah Coventry. However, as shown in the following picture, Sarah Coventry was utilizing a variety of markings throughout the years, most likely in order to keep other manufacturers and companies from copying and using similar markings.

The full set on the left is *Dazzling Aurora*, identified from cardex file pre 66. The two sets of earrings are identical matches to the pin and each other. However, you can see the difference in the markings on the back. The one on the left is marked "SAC" in < > (diamond shape), while the second reads "SARAH COV"—both are marked on the back of the clip. The far right pair of earrings also has two markings—one has "SAC" engraved within the < > shape on the clip and one has "©SARAH COV" in raised lettering on the back of the earring itself. The matching pin has "©SARAH COV" marked on its back Proof that "SAC" is Sarah.

I have also tried to categorize the various markings into time frames, but have been only semi-successful in this endeavor. By matching pieces according to the catalogs and their dates, it appears that many pieces were held over for three, five, or even seven years, and that the continuation of manufacturing may have led to a change in the markings or even the name. I have found only three pieces of jewelry that have the full name "SARAH COVENTRY" on the back and am inclined to believe that these pieces are truly some of the very first. I have also located the same pieces with different markings. **Confetti** and **Color Spray** both have "SARAH COV" and "SAC" on the back. The majority of pieces I have located from the pre-1966 time frame used "SARAH COV." I have also found early pieces with marks ranging from "SAC" to "SC" to "COVENTRY" to "SARAH," as well a combination of these as shown in the picture on the previous page.

Sarah Coventry manufacturers and designers displayed a great deal of creativity and spirit. For instance, one charm was uniquely created with the Sarah crest embedded within a Swarovski Austrian birthstone crystal. What a dazzling and eye-catching piece of jewelry! The creators went from very plain and inexpensive jewelry to Ultra-Fashion pieces in a very expensive collection. All were made with a variety of costume jewelry customers in mind.

This unique charm demonstrates some of the amazing twists to creating jewelry at Sarah Coventry. Set within this Swarovski birthstone crystal is the Sarah crest. *Courtesy of Dawn Michael.*

The left set of jewelry shows some of the very plain, simple, and inexpensive earrings that were created by Sarah Coventry. These earrings do not have room for an identifying mark on the back. On the flip side of the costume jewelry spectrum is the Ultra-Fashion collection. These pins are examples of some of the very expensive Sarah Coventry pieces designed for those wishing to purchase better jewelry with the "real look." *Courtesy of Dawn Michael.*

Versatility

From my various resources, I am convinced that one of the main principles followed by Sarah Coventry designers was versatility—making pieces as adaptable as possible to a variety of costumes, situations, and wearers. During the company's thirty-five years of existence, this versatility could be seen in pins that also doubled as pendants with a simple hook on the back; in pendants and necklaces that could be taken apart, worn together, or separately; in tassels or dangles that could be worn with chains, beads, or in combination; in full sets that could be colorfully interchanged; and in some sets with a wide variety of colors to choose for any costume change. My favorites are the interchangeable beads for rings and earrings.

Top row, left: *Inca Fire* is this combination pin and pendant that can be worn alone or with the rest of this pendant. Matching pendant on page 117. **Bottom row, left to right**: *Old Vienna* pin and pendant is a glamorous hand painted oval stone surrounded by antiqued goldentone mounting. Matching ring on page 135. *Pompeii* pendant is a simulated pearl on a unique goldentone large clasp. It could be worn simply on chains or elegantly on beads, as shown on page 121. *Tassel Magic* is a simple tassel of goldentone chains and striking cap attached to a clasp ring. It could be attached to a chain or chains, other pieces of jewelry, or beads.

Convertible is the key word here. **Top row, left to right**: *Fiesta* are goldentone bamboo shaped earrings with interchangeable drops of blue, white, red, and pearlized. From the 1960s. *Holiday Circles* are goldentone mountings with removable lifesaver colored plastic circles to pop into the mounting frame. From the 1970s. *Pastel Parfait* earrings are open ovals of plastic colors that hook into a textured hoop. Matching necklaces on pages 115 and 125. **Bottom row, left to right**: *Spangle-Bangles* pendant is convertible at its best: "The many solid colors of plastic circles attach from the back overlaying a goldentone circle and behind the circle…Remove the plastic circles to wear as bangle bracelets." *Triple Treat* is a 27" pendant with an attached goldentone eyelet hoop to which the interchangeable pendants can be attached. Pictured are burnt orange and Bermuda blue. *All courtesy of Dawn Michael.*

Top row, left to right: *Unidentified* earrings I call Jukebox because they are very similar to the necklace by that name created in the late '50s. I have seen no connection between the two items other than the similarity in design and small beads. Similar pendant on page 47. $15-30. *Unidentified* earrings illustrate some of the many colorful and diversified sets that Sarah created in the late '50s and early '60s. $8-20. **Bottom row, left to right**: *Carnival* earrings came in various colors as well as red, white, and blue. There were usually five dangle beads (the red, white and blue one is missing a red bead). Identified as "carnival of color." From the early 1970s. B; $8-20. *Hulabaloo* earrings are plastic disks dangling from a length of chain. "Swing into Summer…These striking 'fun 'n fashion' earrings are Sarah's answer to the demand for high-fashion baubles that swing and sway at your ears and give you a feeling of up-to-the-minute fashion." This information was from a promotional flyer for 1966. *All courtesy of Dawn Michael*

As noted earlier, the bi-monthly *Signet* newsletter was sent to Fashion Show Directors during the early years of the 1960s. These newsletters provided a written way of keeping the sales people in the field up to date about promotions, award winners, and the versatility of the jewelry. The *Signets* also provided a way for FSDs to share ideas and it is evident that many of the versatility ideas came from customers. In the sample pages shown here, you can see how many of the pieces were not originally designed for versatility, but *became* versatile because of a creative wearer.

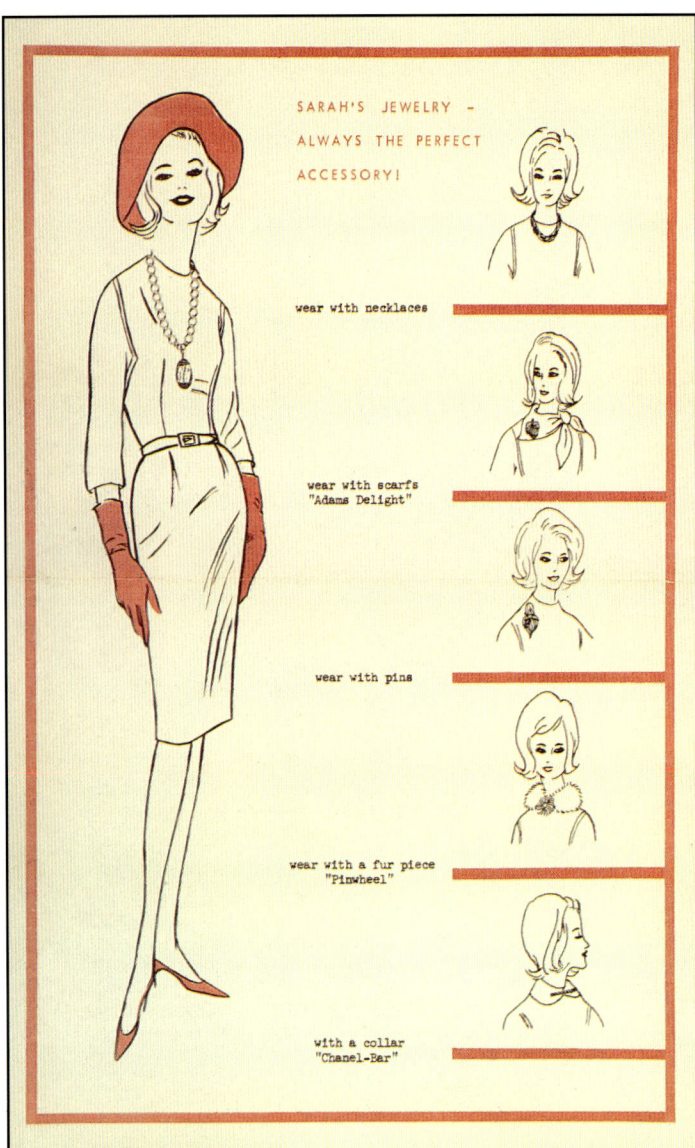

This sheet taken from a *Signet* sent to FSDs in the early 1960s shows the various ways that Sarah Coventry envisioned the pieces of jewelry to be worn. Again, versatility was very important, giving the wearer a wide range of options. *Courtesy of Jan Koltex.*

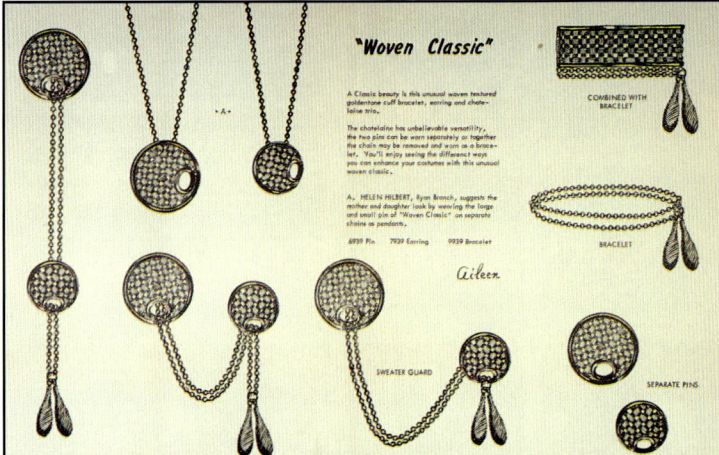

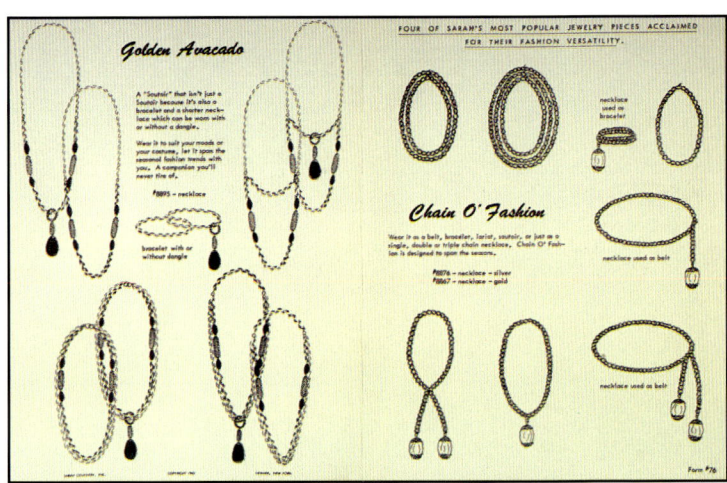

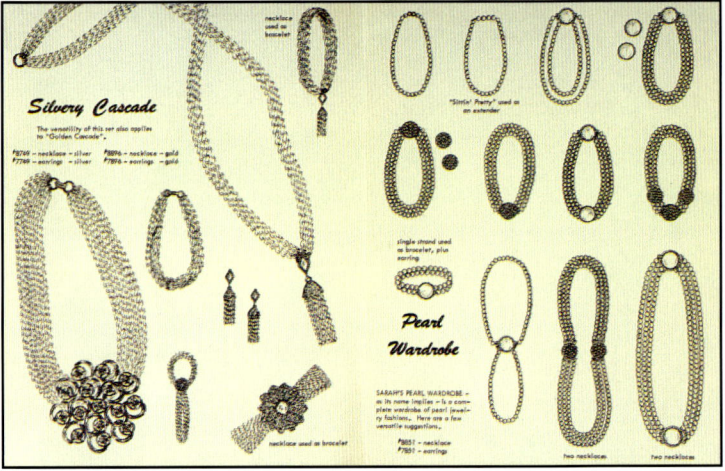

These additional examples of company versatility ideas were sent to each of the FSDs in the early 1960s. This information gave presenters more opportunities for selling various pieces because of the different ways they could be worn. Women purchasing these pieces were working women or women with limited budgets, so buying something that could be worn in a wide variety of ways made the piece more desirable. *Courtesy of Jan Koltes.*

Becoming a Collector

When I began my collection, I had many questions regarding how to go about it. With Beanie Babies, my first real collecting frenzy, I knew that many people just collected the bears. As I purchased each Beanie Baby that was made, I wondered what these collectors did about the beautiful butterfly or the just too darling elephant. I had the same notion with collecting Sarah Coventry jewelry. I had intended to just collect rings and brooches. Then it occurred to me that I might pass up a mint condition necklace still in the box for just a few dollars. I decided that I was *not* going to pass up any piece that was in good condition and priced just right. Hence, I now have some duplicates to trade or sell. Do what is in your best interest…just begin today.

One of my goals for this book is to give you some information I was wishing for when I started my collection in January of 2000. Although I was a person who already had lots of jewelry, the jump into the new millennium found me purposely and doggedly adding over 1500 more pieces.

Instead of cataloging my pieces by pictures or computer, I ventured into book authorship to enhance my own collection and to encourage others to become collectors of Sarah Coventry jewelry as well. Many pre-2000 jewelry book authors had been encouraging jewelry collectors to add Sarah pieces to their collections, stating that they were numerous, easily affordable, and would only gain in value. Since starting in 2000, I have located many others who are seriously collecting and have discovered that there are indeed a lot of Sarah Coventry pieces to be found.

Here is a note of warning as you begin your collection. The following picture shows very clearly two collectible sets (**Wisteria** from the late 1950s and early '60s and **Leading Lady** from the early 1970s) along with some of the current Sarah Coventry jewelry you can purchase. Information about exactly who purchased the original company and/or name varies from person to person. Whoever did purchase the name rights, however, has changed the original concept by selling these pieces in department stores from Wal-Mart to Dillards; has them manufactured in China and India (as with the two lower examples); and has dramatically changed the design and content of the jewelry. Don't be confused by these current pieces. Go for the originals.

Top, left to right: Original pieces of Sarah Coventry—**Wisteria** set from the late 1950s and early '60s, and **Leading Lady** from the early 1970s. At lower left are two cards of Sarah Coventry jewelry manufactured after 1984 when the name/company was sold. These pieces of jewelry can be found in department stores and are made in China and India. They are very different from the collectible Sarah Coventry pieces.

Also be very careful of jewelry items that may have been glued together with one piece Sarah Coventry and the rest some other findings. I am almost embarrassed to say that just recently I located a pin in which only the back was Sarah Coventry and a bright green set had been expertly placed in the center (hot glued at closer glance). This piece was ready for some of the Christmas tree designers who place these pieces of jewelry on velvet in a tree shape, glamorously frame them, add lights, and hang them attractively on the wall. I have conversed with women who admit to taking the unique Sarah hang tags off necklaces because they were bothersome at the back of the neck. Some people have also combined several findings, giving a piece the look of Sarah Coventry when in fact only one part may be—like the clasp. Some pieces have been painted and even pearls have had fingernail polish added to give a different look or to match a costume (I am presuming). So BEWARE. Hopefully, my book and the other Schiffer books will help you to recognize these.

Using This Book

As you begin viewing the jewelry yet to come, you will notice the letters A, B, C, D, or E following each of the descriptions. These letters denote the original pricing: A=$1.00-4.99, B=$5.00-9.99, C=$10.00-14.99, D=$15.00-19.99, E=over $20.00. Following this original pricing information is the current value for each item, expressed as a range from low to high. These values can be affected by several factors:

1) the quality of the jewelry—no missing sets, no discoloration of metal, no replacement of pin back, hooks, or sets.
2) the region where the piece is found—the East and West Coast areas seem to be able to get more for items than the Midwest or southern areas.
3) where you are looking—flea markets, antique shops, garage sales, etc., which can also affect how much variation there is in negotiating.
4) how badly you want the piece, which dictates what you will be willing to pay.

The majority of my own collecting has been from flea markets, where I know the dealers are willing to negotiate. Use the value shown here only as a guide and not an absolute pricing. (My fortune telling skills have not yet proven 100% accurate.) Remember, collecting should be fun and exciting. Finding true buys can offset some of the more expensive prices you may have to pay. Purchasing a piece of history that has weathered thirty, forty, or even fifty years gives me a warm feeling and I would much rather pay extra dollars for such a piece than for a brand new piece of jewelry that is equally expensive. Getting compliments on Sarah Coventry jewelry I am wearing is a much greater "high." I owe a big thank you to my Aunt Louise for giving me my first set—the **Pearl Wardrobe**. It started me looking, exploring, collecting, and authoring!

Pearl Wardrobe "is—as its name implies—a wardrobe of pearl (simulated) jewelry fashions that will go the gamut from a single strand choker to a three strand rhinestone ornamented necklace. Typical of our flair for the unusual, our necklace has matching reversible earrings. On one side—quiet pearl and on the other side—sparkling rhinestones. A masterpiece of fashion." The original price was less than $10 in the early to late 1960s. Value now: priceless, because it was a gift from my Aunt Louise.

During the course of my collecting, I discovered a few of the original Sarah catalogs and became driven to learn more about the names and details of each piece. In the captions for this book, I have captured some of the original wording from these catalogs by placing that information in quotation marks " ". Also, please note that jewelry belonging to other individuals is identified as such with a courtesy line; jewelry with no courtesy line is from my own personal collection.

I have also identified matching pieces and where to find them on other pages. Matching pieces not shown in this book but pictured in Jennifer Lindbeck's *Fine Fashion Jewelry From Sarah Coventry* (Schiffer Publishing, 2000) may also be identified in each caption. For brevity, this will be referred to as the Lindbeck book. I've also provided any additional information that I would have wanted to know as collector.

For those pieces whose names or other information could not be determined, I have indicated ***Unidentified*** in place of the title. If you have or locate documentation for some of these pieces, please contact me at this address:

Kay Oshel
1052 E. 345th Road
Flemington, Mo. 65650

In the chapters to follow, each decade of jewelry is introduced by a past employee I had the good fortune and joy of meeting. Perhaps you too can become acquainted with past employees who, while digressing about events and jewelry, will remark that "It's like visiting old friends."

Lastly, at the end of the book, you will find a sample Personal Collection Sheet on which to list your purchased items. Hopefully this will help eliminate the problem I had of remembering which pieces I owned—and perhaps it will also lead to *your* writing a book!

An Invitation...

As in the original catalogs, the request to join a Sarah Coventry party read: *"You Are Invited."* I now invite each of you **to begin your collection**.

And to get that collection started, I have an original award charm for you. Just send a self-addressed stamped envelope to me at the address above and I will send you (as long as quantities last) one of the charms illustrated below. Welcome Aboard!

Sarah's
Sterling Emblem of Achievement

Congratulations to the following people who have become members of Sarah's Charmed Circle of Honor and have received their Sterling Emblem of Achievement – THE STERLING SILVER HONOR BRACELET.

G. D'ARRAS, J. Cline, Mich.
N. ANDERSON, C. Halvorson, Colo.
M. BLACK, L. Conner, Fla.
L. ANDERSON, R. Gottleib, N.Y.
K. KINTNER, C. Martin, Texas
M. WYRICK, J. Grubb, Md.
M. CROCKER, U. Deaton, Miss.
B. SMITH, J. Smith, Md.
M. MEYERS, D. vonKahrs, Calif.
M. SIEGRIST, D. Siegrist, Kans.
C. B. HENSON, J. Chapman, Calif.
G. DIALS, V. Pollard, Ohio
J. WHITT, V. Pollard, Ohio
B. ROY, N. Werner, Minn.
L. JACKSON, S. Sadler, W. Va.
C. STOAK, M. Livermore, N. Y.
H. MUELLER, P. Tollefson, Minn.
A. CARROLL, F. Weidman, D.C.
C. DENNEY, S. Wyatt, Maine
M. MONDELLO, R. Freytag, N. Y.
F. CASSORO, J. Tietelbaum, Ohio
G. OWENS, A. Bain, No. Car.
J. NARODE, P. Murphy, N. J.
H. KOSISKY, D. Cromwell, Penna.
S. BROECKER, K. Fagerstrom, N. Y.
D. SMITH, G. Seifert, Va.
M. STILES, F. J. Firebaugh, Ky.
B. COX, F. J. Firebaugh, Ky.
B. WILROY, E. Moore, Va.
L. BODIKER, E. Moore, Va.
N. WYATT, C. Shinderman, Va.
J. ROBERTSON, E. Dickerson, Va.
R. FOX, J. Grubb, Md.
D. VARTORELLA, N. Wunderlich, Ohio
G. FURDA, W. Hernandez, Md.
R. ANDREWS, Z. DeFede, Penna.
M. HEILMAN, Z. DeFede, Penna.
S. BROOKS, C. M. Patterson, Ind.
L. KIMBROUGH, B. Clickner, Texas
M. RUPP, E. Foster, Wash.
E. I. FISCHER, A. Haller, Oreg.
R. W. BAUER, J. Knapp, Dela.
M. BELL, N. Wunderlich, Ohio
E. HARRISON, J. Dent, Ga.
W. CLIFTON, A. M. Nagley, Wash.
P. CORCORAN, C. Thompson, Nebr.

L. ZIMMERMAN, E. Moore, Va.
M. GIBBS, E. Moore, Va.
N. BROWN, C. M. Patterson, Ind.
N. ANDREWS, Penna.
H. TIERNEY, V. Hamman, Okla.
E. GIBSON, A. Oliver, Nev.
J. GRAHAM, B. Brumley, Okla.
N. FENNELL, K. Jackson, N. Y.
P. DeNOFIO, K. Jackson, N. Y.
H. SAPP, Idaho
C. HENDRICKS, F. Lancaster, Ind.
L. LAUBENSTEIN, L. Watson, Texas
E. O'DELL, L. C. Ward, No. Car.
W. LAKE, W. Correll, Penna.
M. WOLF, W. Correll, Penna.
J. WITTERS, W. Correll, Penna.
J. GRAVES, R. Kitch, N. M.
D. FLICK, D. Agens, Penna.
B. RAFFEL, E. Walton, Iowa
E. FAUST, A. Bain, No. Car.
I. MACON, H. Oakes, Fla.
H. MEYER, K. Gaffney, Ariz.
M. LANG, Minn.
D. DUNLAP, F. Lancaster, Ind.
M. HOFFMAN, R. Gottlieb, N. Y.
A. LIQUORI, P. Owens, Conn.
C. GOTTA, K. Owens, Conn.
E. BRINEGAR, P. Owens, Conn.
M. PICKENS, A. E. Hergett, Ind.
R. BENYON, F. Weidman, D. C.
M. J. WALL, L. R. Moore, N. Y.
B. MINNICH, W. Correll, Penna.
M. BEARER, N. Andrews, Penna.
N. J. GEORGE, Penna.
M. LOVING, S. Ayers, W. Va.
J. STASH, N. Wunderlich, Ohio
P. DAUGAARD, G. Dickey, Iowa
E. KAIN, J. Jackson, N. Y.
A. WOOD, C. Edwards, Colo.
P. BROADRICK, P. Smith, Tenn.
J. KNIGHT, E. Hoots, No. Car.
E. ESPOSITO, S. Yannucci, N. Y.
M. MIDALEY, E. Sweeney, Calif.
G. BEST, B. Brumley, Okla.
D. MUSKOWSKI, J. McDonald, Ohio
J. SCHIMAN, C. Thompson, Nebr.

THE HONOR BRACELET is one of the high honors you can earn as a member of Sarah Coventry. This Bracelet is earned on the basis of five (5) Qualified Recruits.

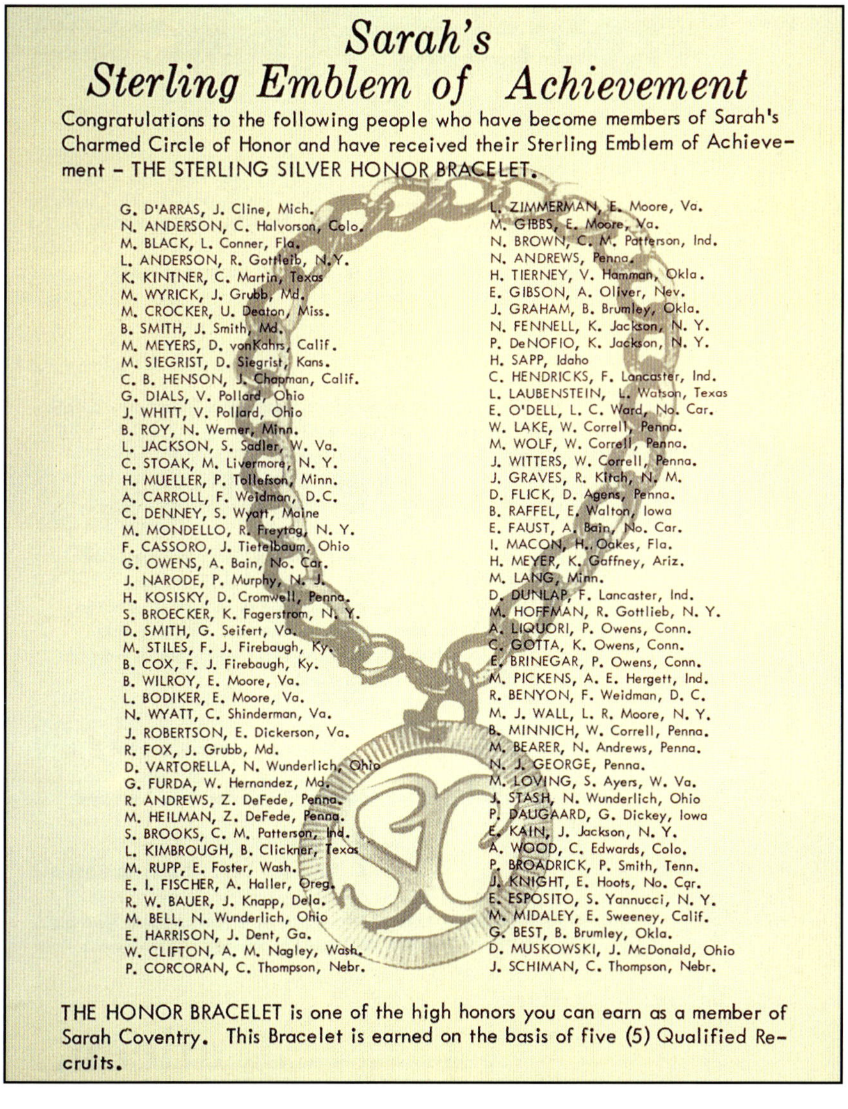

This page from a 1963 *Signet* identifies "Sarah's Sterling Emblem of Achievement"—a charm bracelet with a charm highlighting "5" for a management level employee obtaining five qualified recruits for Fashion Show Directors. You can have one of these too—see information at the end of this chapter! *Signet courtesy of Jan Koltes.*

Chapter Two

The Early Years: 1949-1965

From the very beginning—November of 1949—the Sarah Coventry name and its accompanying jewelry was destined to be a success. Helen Knapp, an early employee who began in January of 1956, was one of the many employees who made such success possible by grasping this business opportunity and making it work. Helen's husband John became a part of the company in 1960—making them one of the many teams of couples involved. They continued till the end in 1984, having achieved the status of Area Managers. Helen and her daughter Sue were very emotional when sharing their memories of Sarah Coventry. They both indicated that many wonderful possessions and events in their family were a direct benefit of working with this company. Helen even described her home as "The House that Sarah Built." One of her first bonuses was also used to purchase a houseboat named "The Knapp-Kin," leading her family to a love of water.

Helen told me that the company was built on the "ethos" or guiding belief of positive thinking. A contemporary of hers, Dick Bartges—also part of a husband and wife team—provided a quote that seemed to be the watchword: "Attitudes are Stronger Than Facts." Both of these former employees indicated that the early Sarah Coventry company was much stronger because of moving people up through the ranks rather than appointing outsiders to the higher management positions. Encouraging husband and wife teams helped to instill the "family feeling" that is a constant refrain when talking with former Fashion Show Directors, even those who were with the company for as little as two years.

Helen Knapp was one of the early Fashion Show Directors who moved through the ranks to an upper management level. She and her late husband comprised one of the many husband and wife teams. She has several display cases filled with trophies, plaques, and other awards earned while working with Sarah Coventry for nearly thirty years.

Discussion with Helen leaves one with a very upbeat feeling about Sarah Coventry and life in general. She speaks about the quality merchandise sold at a good price and how as a Fashion Show Director you had to have a "love of people"—commissions were the only form of payment and selling yourself was as important as selling the product. Helen quips that her mother often commented about some children being born with "a silver spoon in their mouth" while Helen apparently was born with "a door knob in her hand." She comments about originally not having any real interest in sales, however, being part of a very honest company such as Sarah Coventry changed her mind and her creativity subsequently shined through. Still today, Helen is very proud of the company and cherishes the many memories and pieces of jewelry she has, still in perfect condition. She is truly amazed at the party plan companies now in existence—selling candles to baskets to home decorations to cooking utensils—and the amount of money being spent at each show versus the smaller amount required in the 1950s, '60s and '70s. Times do change.

Dick Bartges explained that in the early years, information was handed down verbally from a manager to the FSDs. Then a black and white card file, called a "cardex," was created; later the cardex was printed in color. The picture of a piece or set was on one side of the card and a most flowery description on the other. Despite their length, these descriptions sometimes didn't give the most basic information as to the kind of stones or metals used. Where available, however, I have used cardex descriptions in the captions, identifying them by quotation marks. Prices were given on individual sheets called the "Shopping Guide." The cards all explained about the hostess credit program and about the 2 for 1 plan, which gave customers a chance to purchase a third item for half price.

One of the cards mentions the importance of keeping the cardex up to date, discarding old cards and adding new ones. It appears that many of the FSDs did exactly that and therefore, some of the very early jewelry may not be identifiable. The cards also do not have the years printed on them, adding to the difficulty of pinpointing the exact years of production for pieces up through 1965.

Given that I haven't been able to locate catalogs prior to 1966, I believe that the cardex files were probably used through 1965; at that time the catalog books came into being with years indicated on each.

These cards were some of the first tools distributed to FSDs for describing and picturing new pieces of jewelry at the parties. The cards were held together by a chain allowing the FSD to carry them together or break apart for displaying. FSDs carried mirrors with them to assist customers in viewing the jewelry on themselves; a small hand mirror is pictured with one set of cards. Necklaces were also identified with similar small hand mirror tags. *Courtesy of Helen Knapp and Sara Ayers.*

Jewelry in the 1950s was greatly influenced by the historical events of the time. Space exploration, for example, was one of the major themes replicated in jewelry. Rhinestone jewelry was still a major component of the manufacturers and was greatly sought after by customers. As the mid-1960s emerged, young people began rebelling against "the establishment" and a whole new set of guidelines for clothing, jewelry, and behavior began. Jewelry was being fashioned from plastics with fewer rhinestones used.

Costume jewelry made of quality materials to last decades—such as that made and sold by Sarah Coventry through the party plan—is a collector's fantasy. Unfortunately, Helen Knapp indicated that the very early pieces (up till 1958 or 1959) were not labeled on the back and consequently many may be missed by today's collectors. However, as the company progressed, some of these same pieces were no doubt remanufactured *with* some markings, such as "SAC" or "SARAH COV" (see Introduction for more information on some of these identified markings). In this chapter, you will find several pieces marked on the back of the clasp with an engraved "SARAH COVENTRY®" that are unidentified pieces. If you find documentation on any of them, please let me know.

These are some of the unmarked pieces in Helen Knapp's collection. The top set with the multi-colored stones is **Carousel**, identified from some of the cards. The rest are unidentifiable. *Courtesy of Helen Knapp.*

Brooches

Top row, left to right: A goldentone textured flower comprises this *Splendor* pin. The center is a simulated pearl and the stamens end in tiny green Austrian rhinestones. Matching earrings on page 40. A; $15-35. **Designer's Choice** has small clear Austrian rhinestones overlaying an open-weave leaf covered with larger chaton cut brown stones. Matching earrings on page 40. A; $15-45. **Spring Bouquet** features an artfully done bouquet of leaves and flowers of textured and satin goldentone. A sprinkling of cultured pearls and emerald green beads for flowers brings the bouquet to life. B; $10-25. **Bottom row, left to right**: *Snow Flower* pin is an emerging flower of white enamel with gold ball center. The curved overlapping white petals form a deep pin secured to an intricate goldentone lace background. Matching earrings on page 40. A; $15-35. *Golden Maple* pin is "delicately designed, expertly crafted, let it add its golden splash to your new Fall suit. Its touch is good with tailored or afternoon casuals, handsome with furs and suedes, best with tweeds and flannels." This pin is marked with raised "SAC" initials. Matching earrings on page 40. A; $8-15.

Clockwise, from far left: *Kathleen* is described as "sparkling, fiery rhinestones paved in a sunburst design and centered around a brilliant emerald-type stone making a truly glamorous piece." Matching earrings on page 84, matching ring on page 153. B; $20-55. **"Stunning** is what people will say when they see you in this pin. Great luster combined with a design of grace and simplicity" makes this pin "good fortune and good taste." Matching earrings on page 34. A; $8-25. *Evening Snowflake* pin is "fascinating and sparkling as a falling snowflake on a bright and moonlit night. A man-designed snowflake paved with tiny twinkling rhinestones swirling around a large black diamond (simulated). Truly a Sarah set of great beauty and dignity" of SarahSheen silvertone. B; $25-45. *Frosted Leaves* pin of "lacy design in brilliant silver tone gives a look of early morning frost to the beautiful and graceful stylized leaves. Always in Season!" A; $10-25. *Pinwheel* has a "design in textured glistening silver tone and in the center a cabochon pearl (simulated)—a perennial favorite with fashion minded women. An important pin for your suit, dress or coat. An accent of fashion wherever you wear it." This is a favorite of many and easy to locate. Marked "©SARAH COV" in raised letters on back. Matching earrings on page 34. A; $10-30.

Top row, left to right: *Sea Whispers* pin reflects "the height of fashion this season is the underwater motif. Fish, coral, algae—echoes the romance of underwater flora with its coral design—all created in textured and gleaming goldentone." SarahGlo goldentone. Matching earrings on page 35. A; $10-25. *Precious* is "cultured pearls reflecting all the warmth and flattering luster of the true pearl in an exquisite design from nature. For the woman who likes the finer things either to wear or to give." Made of SarahGlo goldentone. Matching earrings on page 34. A; $10-25. *Nature's Choice* "will be your choice when you see Sarah's unusual maple leaf design. The two-tone look gives the goldentone textured leaf a frosty edge of gleaming silvertone." This popular pin was sold in the early 1960s and continued as hostess credit in the early '70s. Matching earrings on page 35. A; $10-25. **Center**: *Autumn Haze* pin features "a beautiful Autumn Haze glass stone, magnificently cut and polished to pick up and reflect all the lights in an autumn sky at sunset." A goldentone flower motif is attached to the narrow tip of the teardrop. This design is repeated in the matching earrings on page 36. B; $15-35.
Bottom row, left to right: *Pearl Bloom* is a "small delicate pin with the look of real jewelry…this baroque pearl (simulated)" is nestled among three goldentone gleaming leaves and stem. Matching earrings on page 34. A; $10-25. *Amber-Jet* is "the most important pin of the year…and Sarah's designers have created one of unusual and great beauty in this stone set bar pin." The prong set stones are amber and jet black from the late 1950s. A; $13-28.

Top row, left to right: *Wind Flower* is the name given this unique SarahGlo goldentone pin inspired by nature. Think of "fields of flowering golden wheat bending and swaying with the wind" and created from stippling textured goldentone. Matching earring on page 41. A; $10-25. The description for *Peta-Lure* noted that "The lovely design of this textured goldentone pin belies its piggy bank price and proves Sarah's slogan that 'the priceless look of beauty is seldom a matter of price.'" Matching earrings on page 35. A; $8-20. *Lotus Blossom*: "From the romantic past of ancient Japan with its feminine but stately beauty comes the simple elegance of simulated pearls and textured goldentone." Matching earrings on page 34. A; $8-20. **Bottom row, left to right**: *Bittersweet* featured "an exciting fashion color to flatter your whites in the summer or your brown shades come fall or winter. The new slender look in pins so smart, so chic, combined with the ever popular leaf design that knows no age or season barrier." The pin has three bittersweet-orange teardrop shaped cabochon beads. Matching earrings on page 36. A; $10-25. *Fashion Flower*, as its name implies, is a flower stem pin. The "beautifully cut, scarlet aurora stones glisten in bud-like fashion from the full bloom design artfully created in a gleaming golden finish. A long stem rose lifts its patrician head to bloom in beauty on your lapel." Matching "dainty" earrings on page 35, matching "daring" earrings on page 35. B; $15-40.

Clockwise, from top: One of the most beautiful silvertone pins also doubles as a pendant and totes the name of *Celebrity*. "A truly beautiful smoky black stone nestled in an antique frame of unbelievable beauty and surrounded by sparkling rhinestones making an ensemble as captivating and intriguing as romance itself. The pendent necklace unhooks from the silvertone chain and doubles as the large pin accent." Matching earrings on page 35, matching bracelet on page 50, and matching ring on page 53. B; $25-50. **Adam's Delight** is "a perfect fashion accent for that suit or dress. As smooth as satin is this unusual goldentone pin in apple design. Summer or winter, apples are always in season and a design from nature is always in good taste." The detailing includes the core stem at the bottom of the apple. This popular design by the early Sarah designers also doubled as a pendant when worn on a chain. Matching earrings on page 36. A; $10-25. **Golden Cherries** is "a real conversation piece…with its design from nature. A perfect lapel pin for summer or winter, for dress or suit, for country or city." Matching earrings on page 72. B; $10-25. **Adam's Delight** also came in a glistening silvertone with the same three-dimensional textured elegance. Matching earrings on page 36. A; $10-25. **Tropicana** has "all the glamour, beauty and mystery of underwater life in the tropics captured in this darling angel fish pin. All the colors in the rainbow flash from his electra stone body which is nestled in glistening goldentone. A real conversation piece of charm and beauty." B; $15-35. **Silvery Splendor** is a "dashing and dramatic and at the same time cool and elegant" textured silvertone leaf pin. "Its beauty is enhanced by dew-drop-like pearls (simulated) nestled on the glistening leaves." Matching earrings on page 34. B; $12-35.

Top row, left to right: *Bird of Paradise* is this bird in flight pin. "Crystal aurora stones add brilliance to this fashionable silvertone piece…so fashion right on the shoulder of a suit or dress for those extra-special occasions." Matching earrings on page 71. B; $15-45. **Black Beauty**: "A typical Sarah design is the flower motif…textured silvertone petals surrounding a center disc of black. A piece for night or day and any season. The tailored look for night or day in Silvertone." There is another set also called Black Beauty from earlier years—look for it and compare. This pin was late 1960s. Matching earrings on page 75. A; $8-25. **Mini Fleur** is this five petal bedazzled mini flower pin appropriately named and part of Sarah's "Sparkling After-5" collection. The chaton cut rhinestones give the "touch of evening elegance to this dainty and striking flower" pin. A; $10-30. **Bottom**: **Blue Note** has "robin's egg blue stones nestled in gleaming silvertone to make this pin hit a high note in fashion. Mix and match with other pieces for versatility. Around-the-Clock tailored jewelry designs in silvertone." A; $8-20.

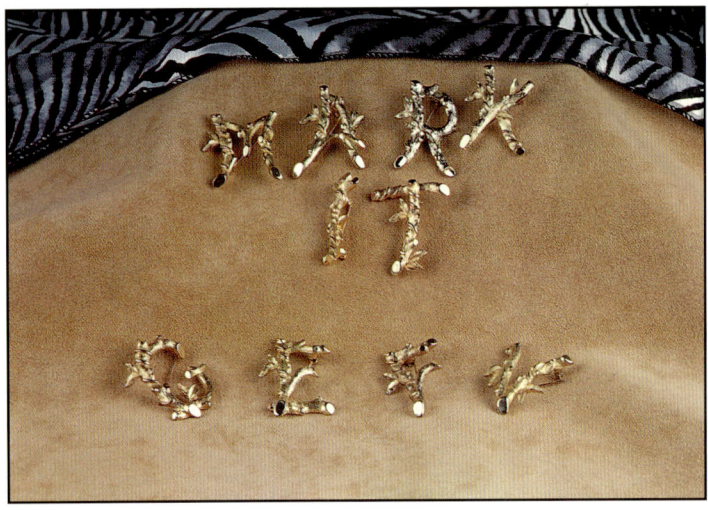

Sarah's A.B.C.'s were pins whose lives began in the late 1950s and continued through the '60s. They must have been very popular as many are out there. "Each of the 26 letters of the alphabet is an original and exclusive design of great beauty. Wear them in groups of three, a pair or even single—on your scarf, sweater, suit, or pocketbook." A; $5-20.

Top row, left to right: *Harvest Time* is the name given to this early dainty pin resembling three heads of wheat tied together with a ribbon of goldentone and accented with an open prong large clear rhinestone and one smaller rhinestone. A; $10-30. **Pearl Elegance (simulated)** identifies this "baroque simulated pearl rose with its lustrous bloom and twisted goldentone stem." Matching earrings on page 71 A; $10-35. **Raspberry Ice** is a glamorous pin. The branch of lavender flower blooms with hot pink chaton cut rhinestones adding to the colorful contrast. Matching earrings on page 37. A; $10-25. **Primrose** has "enameled yellow primrose flowers to grace your linens in summer and woolens in winter. A fresh bouquet all year long. The latest fashion color for summer and cruise wear is this exotic yellow. So sharp and clear, so smart and new." A; $10-25. **Bottom:** *Unidentified* pin is a very striking bow shaped goldentone with sprays of slender stems that end in crystal Austrian rhinestones. $20-35. *All courtesy of Dawn Michael.*

Left to right: *Summer Magic* is a striking white enameled flower blossom on silvertone leaves. It was a part of an early ensemble including a rope chain and a beaded chain that together created a summer wardrobe accent. In 1970 this pin was called "New Summer Magic." Ensemble necklaces and chain on page 46. A; $15-35. **Camellia** is also an enameled white flower pin with petals edged in goldentone. "The huge important pin is the biggest fashion news in jewelry and Sarah's Camellia is the height of fashion. Bound to span the seasons from spring to fall with equal graciousness." A black cabochon bead was used to accent this piece. A; $12-30.

Top row, left to right: *Fantasy* has a "large baroque pearl (simulated) blooming on the goldentone flower stem. Its design knows no barriers for a design from nature is always appropriate with the current trend for gold color combined with the large baroque pearl (simulated). A natural attention getter." This piece was one of the first I located and helped me realize the uniqueness and the startling beauty of Sarah Coventry costume jewelry. A; $10-25. **High Fashion** is "a pin designed not for the person who likes conservative fashions, but instead is created for the woman who loves to dress in the height of fashion. A long slender pin in the shape of a flower with a beautifully cut amber color stone blossom surrounded by tiny dew-like rhinestones." B; $20-45. **Bottom row, left to right:** *Black Beauty* pin is "designed to keep pace with your busy schedule. Sleek as only black can be, delicate in design and destined to go everywhere you go. The type of set you can wear from dawn 'til dark.'" This is the second set of jewelry with this name. These were found on cardex files. Matching earrings on page 35. A; $10-25. **Galaxy** has "color and beauty is this multi-colored square pin. Ceramic red, jade green, lapis blue and turquoise colors surrounded by sparkling aurora stones and lustrous pearls (simulated) that will go with any costume regardless of colored beauty." Same pin on page 68, matching earrings on page 35. A; $15-35. *All courtesy of Otheda Smith.*

Left to right: *Evening Accent* is an elongated star shape pin of silvertone with a large Austrian rhinestone in the center surrounded by smaller Austrian sets. A shooting star effect is achieved by a tail of six petal shapes paved with the same Austrian rhinestones. Throughout this book, you will find at least six different sets beginning with "evening," making for a great deal of confusion in collecting. Matching earrings on page 44. B; $20-45. *Fashion Leaf* pin is a highly textured and detailed goldentone leaf with folded lower edge. Tiny clear rhinestones pave the folded over part, giving a brilliant two-tone effect. Matching earrings on page 40. B; $20-45. *Scepter Pin with Stick Pin* is an exquisite rhinestone flower of convex double layered leaves paved with tiny rhinestones surrounding a large chaton cut emerald rhinestone. The stick pin repeats the petal shape of the rhinestones and attaches in a casing on the back of the pin to be worn separately or together for an elongated effect. This is an excellent example of how versatile much of Sarah Coventry jewelry was and how it resisted looking like costume jewelry. C; $20-45. *Lime-light* is an open-weave circle of goldentone with medium-sized chaton cut iridescent rhinestone sets of lime-green/yellow creating a rainbow of pale colors in the light. A magnificent piece by the Sarah Coventry designers in the late 1950s, early '60s. B; $20-45.

Left to right: *Black Saturn* pin, "Take the black from the night and the brilliance of the stars plus the mystery of the unusual and combine them to create this 'out of this world' pin." This is "as unusual as it is lovely and so expensive looking you can't believe it's costume jewelry at its finest." Matching earrings on page 38. A; $10-25. *Satin Flame* is "a contrast of startling beauty…contrasting the gleam of satin with the richly-textured look. The perfect note of fashion for that basic dress, the lapel of your suit, or even hung on a chain. A flame of fashion, for the fashion-conscious woman." Matching earrings on page 40. A; $10-25. *Daisy Mae* is a large daisy with petals made of satin goldentone alternating with textured goldentone. The center of antiqued gold balls gives an elaborate effect on a simple design. Matching earrings on page 38. A; $10-25.

Left: *Woven Classic* is a chatelaine duo. "The chatelaine has unbelievable versatility, the two pins can be worn separately or together, the chain may be removed and worn as a bracelet. You'll enjoy seeing the different ways you can enhance your costumes with this unusual woven classic." Matching earrings on page 40, matching bracelet on page 51. B; $10-25. **Center to below rock**: *Honey Bunch* pin is, as its name suggests, a honey comb shaped goldentone pin. The mauve colored tear-shaped cabochon beads add to this unique and subtle Sarah Coventry design. B; $15-35. *Zebra* pin is an open-weave zebra shaped pin identified as "jewelry designed especially for the young at heart." A; $8-25. *Pink Ice* is a colorful shamrock shaped pin elegantly made from a large chaton cut deep pink rhinestone with matching smaller rhinestones covering the four leaves of the clover of goldentone. Matching earrings on page 43. B; $20-45. *Feather Fantasy* is the "ultimate in luxury and yet with a price to fit your pocketbook. For fashion is a look, not a price and this pin has a look of elegance, beauty, and graceful design." Gray/green cabochon beads outline the spine length of the silvertone feather. Matching earrings on page 43. A; $15-35. **On rock, left to right**: *Lady Bug* "will charm and delight her…she'll love getting it, she'll love wearing it. The 'sweater set' is pinning it everywhere a pin can go—even on the beau of the moment!" The enameled wings surround a simulated pearl. Sarah Coventry kept the young people in mind when designing jewelry and this is one of those "for the young at heart." A; $8-15. *Polynesian* pin is a white enameled flower with gold/yellow center and mint green leaves. This is truly a tropical look, "beautiful and romantic." B; $12-30. *All courtesy of Otheda Smith.*

Left to right: ***Chit-Chat*** is "one of Sarah's more versatile pieces of jewelry, for each pin can be worn separately or combined with the chain to become a sweater guard or chatelaine." Chit-Chat will "cause chatter wherever you wear it." Earrings were of two sizes, dainty or daring. Matching earrings on page 42. A; $10-25. ***Unidentified*** goldentone diamond shaped open criss-cross pin has square multi-faceted red rhinestones surrounding the perimeter. The pin is accented with small and medium-size simulated pearls and is marked "©SARAH COV." $15-35. ***Daisy*** "has a very definite personality in spite of her classic design. Her richly textured and satin-smooth petals give her an air of distinction." The large gold ball at the center of the convex design closely duplicates the flower in nature, which seems to be a pattern by the designers for Sarah Coventry jewelry. Matching earrings on page 42. A; $10-25.

Top row, left to right: Blues were popular with Sarah, as shown with these three pieces of jewelry. ***Blue Champagne***, "exciting, glamorous, outstandingly beautiful, exquisite, striking, and heavenly are only a few of the adjectives it would take to describe this breathtakingly beautiful pin designed by Sarah's master designers." The sapphire blue stones on silvertone leaves are quite bedazzling. Matching necklace on page 48. B; $15-35. ***Cameo Lace*** is a "delicately carved profile against a sky blue background. The intricate design of gold filigree makes a perfect frame for an ever charming picture." An "heirloom type pin" with matching earring is on page 38. A; $15-35. ***Royal Plumage*** is a large, royal blue grooved set surrounded by silvertone open-weave feathering giving it a triangular shape plumage—hence the name. Matching earrings on page 38. A; $20-45. **Bottom:** ***Celestial Ice*** is an appropriate name for this large circle pin formed from small open circles of silvertone, layered and tilted to give depth. All circles are attractively decorated with a medium-sized chaton cut rhinestone set on one edge of the small circle. Matching earrings on page 41. B; $20-45.

Top row, left to right: ***Golden Brocade*** is a striking pin in a question mark shape. The solid goldentone overlaid with vein-like goldentone enriches and embellishes the brocade. A; $10-25. ***Pearl Flight*** is "inspired by the design of a bird's wing, and embodies an airyness and grace seldom, if ever, seen in a piece of costume jewelry. Its delicate wire work, contrasted by the boldness of a softly gleaming simulated pearl, completes the picture of one of this season's most unusual pieces of fashion jewelry." Same pin on page 55, matching earrings on page 55. B; $15-30. ***Golden Swirl*** is a textured goldentone pin in open swirl. The swirling effect and alternating texture and satin gives the illusion of a spinning windmill. Simple, but eye-catching. A; $10-25. **Bottom:** ***Amber-lites*** is a delicate flower shaped pin of goldentone textured petals with Austrian amber stones nestled among the leaves; it would be worn by the most fashion conscious woman of the 1950s to early '60s. The circle shape gives an interesting raised effect. B; $15-35.

Left to right: *Silvery Nile* has "all the romance and splendor of ancient Egypt with its Pyramids and Kings…reflected in this unusual design by Sarah. The heavy look of fashion and yet feather light to wear. You'll have to try it on to believe it." *Courtesy of Nancy Isgrigs*. Matching earrings on page 110. B; $15-35. ***Windsong*** is the appropriate name for this pin, which gives the effect of wind blowing through the leaves with their turned up ends. *Courtesy of Nancy Isgrigs*. Matching earrings on page 37. A; $15-35. ***Unidentified*** pin is a rather unique looking flat goldentone leaf shape with open weave on one side and solid on the other. The markings on the back are "MADE IN CANADA" and "©SARAH COV." $8-15. ***Unidentified*** pin resembles a sailor knot. The knot is comprised of four braids of goldentone with dark colored rhinestones in the spaces around the braiding. While I'm not certain of the dating, I have added it to this section. Marking on the back is an oval raised shape with "SC" in raised lettering. $10-25.

Left to right: ***Unidentified*** pin is shaped like a starfish with curved goldentone petals. A medium-sized simulated pearl commands the center and makes a simple pin very elegant looking. Marked on the back is "SARAH COVENTRY®" $8-20. ***Siam*** pin is created from "an imitation of jade agate and imported from Germany. According to superstition, this type of stone is supposed to bring the wearer good luck. Regardless of superstition, this pin will certainly bring its wearer a look of up-to-the-minute fashion." SarahSheen goldentone. Matching earrings on page 36. A; $10-25. *Courtesy of Otheda Smith*. ***Sun Flower*** pin is a large multi-textured goldentone design duplicating the sunflower. There are several pieces with similar name and similar design. Matching earrings on page 41. A; $10-30. *Courtesy of Otheda Smith*. ***American Beauty*** pin features "beauty and luster in this SarahSheen goldentone rose. Notice its delicate petal design and gleaming finish. A design as durable as nature itself." Matching earrings on page 41. A; $10-35. *Courtesy of Otheda Smith*. ***Unidentified*** pin resembles some of the other goldentone leaf pins. This one is a solid leaf attached to a stem with a red and black lady bug on the leaf. The pin is marked "©SARAH COV." A; $10-25.

StarLit Trio is shown here in two ways it can be worn. "Sarah's ingenuity has really come to the fore in this glamorous three-way pin. Wear each pin separately or combine them for a large, more sparkling trio. First a textured goldentone circle-type pin, for more glittering occasions a rhinestone scatter pin and—for all-out glamour—the combination StarLit Trio." There is a metal sleeve tube on the back of the center pin in which the pin of the outside piece slips through to secure the two together. True versatility on the part of Sarah designers in the late 1950s and early '60s. B; $25-50. *Courtesy of Nancy Isgrigs*.

Earrings

Top to bottom: *Stunning* "is what people say when they see...these earrings." A SarahSheen silvertone textured and satin smooth design both graceful and simple. Matching pin on page 27. A; $5-15. *Pinwheel* earrings are truly a pinwheel design of textured glistening silvertone with a center of cabochon pearl (simulated). Marking on back of earrings reads "©SARAH COV" in raised lettering, and on back of earrings' clip is "©SARAH COV" engraved. Matching pin on page 27. A; $8-20. *Summer Magic* earrings are small white enameled flower petals on a silvertone base with center accent of silvertone stamens and a white cabochon bead. In 1970 this set of earrings was called "New Summer Magic." Matching pin on page 30, matching necklace on page 46. A; $8-20. *Silvery Splendor* earrings are two textured glistening silvertone leaves accented with two "dew-drop-like" pearls (simulated) in decreasing sizes. Matching pin on page 29. A; $10-25.

Top row, left to right: *Precious* earrings are small goldentone leaves with cultured pearls reflecting all the "warmth and flattering luster of the true pearl in an exquisite design from nature." Matching pin on page 28. A; $8-20. *Hidden Pearl* (simulated) earrings have "the look of 'real' jewelry—the design thought portrayed in this blossom-like earrings—a lustrous imitation baroque pearl peeking out from under goldentone petals. Young and old alike will admire this classic design." A; $10-25. *Pearl Bloom* earrings are another baroque pearl (simulated). Supporting the pearl are the stem and leaves of goldentone, making this earring set a "must for every woman's wardrobe." Matching pin on page 28. A; $10-25. **Center:** *Lotus Blossom* earrings are two overlaid lotus blossoms of decreasing sizes, accented with a simulated pearl in the center. Note that the left earring has its hidden pearl peeking out from under the petals. The other earring is missing that pearl. Named to remind us of "the romantic past of ancient Japan with its feminine but stately beauty...to be worn with your gay daytime wardrobe or in the romance of shimmering moonlight." Matching pin on page 28. A; $10-25. **Bottom:** *One 'N Only* earrings are very fashionable with the single small ornament of lustrous simulated pearl "encased in a golden cage" dangling from screw backs. A; $8-20.

Top: *Fashion Flower* earrings have "scarlet aurora stones" glistening in "bud-like" artwork nestled in the "full bloom design...of gleaming goldentone finish." This larger set is identified as "daring." A; $10-25. **Center**: *Fashion Flower* earrings much smaller then the daring set above are identified as "dainty." Both have a matching pin on page 28. A; $10-25. **Bottom**: *Galaxy* earrings portray a different flash of color and beauty in a square shape. Multi-colored teardrop shape cabochons of ceramic red, jade green, lapis blue, and turquoise are surrounded by sparkling aurora stones and lustrous simulated pearls. Matching pin on page 30. This set was a very early one and was continued through the 1960s, becoming part of the hostess credit items in the early 1970s. A; $12-30.

Top row, left to right: *Peta-Lure* earrings: the "lovely design of this textured goldentone belies its piggy bank price and proves Sarah's slogan that 'The priceless look of beauty is seldom a matter of price.' A basic accent of fashion to go around the clock with your wardrobe." Matching pin on page 28. A; $8-20. *Nature's Choice* earrings "will be your choice when you see Sarah's unusual maple leaf design. The two-tone look gives the goldentone textured leaf a frost edge of gleaming silvertone." This set began in the late 1950s and early '60s and was continued as a hostess credit item in the 1970s. A; $8-20. **Bottom row, left to right**: *Fashion Parade* earrings are a part of a unique set of jewelry developed in the early years of Sarah Coventry. The small earrings replicate the pendant drops with a simulated teardrop pearl nestled in a collar of textured SarahGlo goldentone. Matching necklace on page 45. A; $8-18. *Sea Whispers* earrings are "the height of fashion this season in the underwater motif. Fish, coral, algae echoes the romance of underwater flora with its coral design—all created in textured and gleaming goldentone." Matching pin on page 28. A; $10-25.

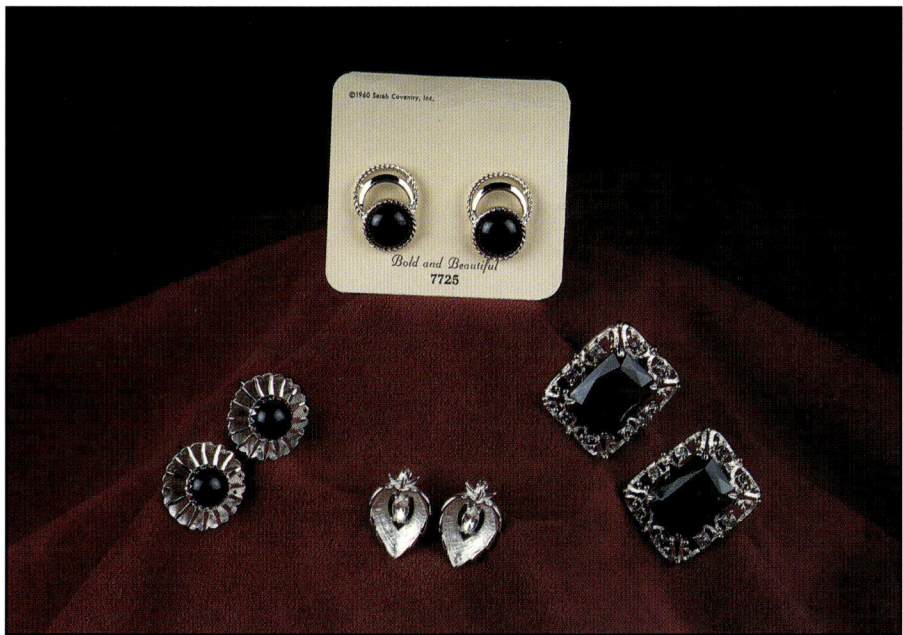

Clockwise, from top: *Bold and Beautiful* is identified on this card as being from 1960. This jewelry "has the elegant feeling of very fine fashion jewelry. Every woman's jewelry wardrobe needs a black ensemble to make it complete. This black and silver...is softly designed and precisely tailored to give you flattery with style perfection." One set of earrings is marked on the back with raised "SAC" in < > (diamond shape) and "SAC" in < > engraved on back of clasp. The other set of earrings has "©SARAH COV" engraved on back of clasp. Matching necklace on page 45. B; $12-30. *Celebrity*, no doubt one of the most beautiful earrings, has "a truly beautiful smoky black stone nestled in an antique frame of unbelievable beauty and surrounded by sparkling rhinestones making an ensemble as captivating and intriguing as romance itself." Matching pin on page 29, matching bracelet on page 50, and matching ring on page 53. B; $20-45. *Crystal Navette* earrings are strikingly simple with their "well-cut navette shaped rhinestone placed in the center of a textured leaf." Beautiful miniatures of the matching pendant shown on page 46. B; $15-35. On *Black Beauty*, the prong set black cabochon set is surrounded by a wheel rim effect of silvertone with raised spirals thinning at the edge of the rim. There are two different pins called Black Beauty. These button like earrings match the pin on page 30. A; $10-25.

Top: *Adam's Delight* earrings are smaller replicas of the larger pin. "As smooth as satin is this unusual goldentone apple design. Summer or winter, apples are always in season and a design from nature is always in good taste." Matching pin/pendant on page 29. A; $10-25. **Center, left to right**: *Siam* earrings are "an imitation of jade agate and imported from Germany. According to superstition, this type stone is supposed to bring the wearer good luck. Regardless of superstition, this will certainly bring its wearer a look of up-to-the-minute fashion." Matching pin on page 33. $A; $10-25. *Matinee Elegance* (not pierced) earrings are "slim and svelte to please milady. Any season is the right season for these fine fashion earrings that add the look of elegance." Matching necklace on page 48. A; $10-25. *Autumn Haze* earrings are "a beautiful Autumn Haze glass stone, magnificently cut and polished to pick up and reflect all the lights in an autumn sky at sunset. The goldentone flower motif is echoed again at the ears." Matching pin on page 28. A; $10-25. **Bottom**: *Bittersweet* earrings have "an exciting fashion color to flatter your whites in the summer or your brown shades come fall or winter," created from a dark orange teardrop cabochon. Matching pin on page 28. A; $10-35.

Left to right: *Adam's Delight* silvertone earrings are smaller replicas of the larger pin. "As smooth as satin is this unusual silvertone apple design. Summer or winter, apples are always in season and a design from nature is always in good taste." Matching pin/pendant on page 29. A; $10-25. *Young and Gay* earrings (only one shown): "petite button earrings that repeat the delicate coin design of the necklace and bracelet." These earrings along with the rest of the ensemble were available from the 1950s through the mid-70s. They are plentiful and easy to find in goldentone and silvertone. (In the early days, FSDs received only one earring of a set, thus jewelry went farther among the sales force and many times customers would purchase only one earring to be worn as a pendant on a chain.) Matching necklace on page 46, matching bracelet on page 50. A; $8-20. *Blue Hawaii* earrings reflect "all the romance of the Blue Hawaiian waters in these pieces of glistening silvertone and imitation stones of Lapis Blue." Matching bracelet on page 50. A; $10-30.

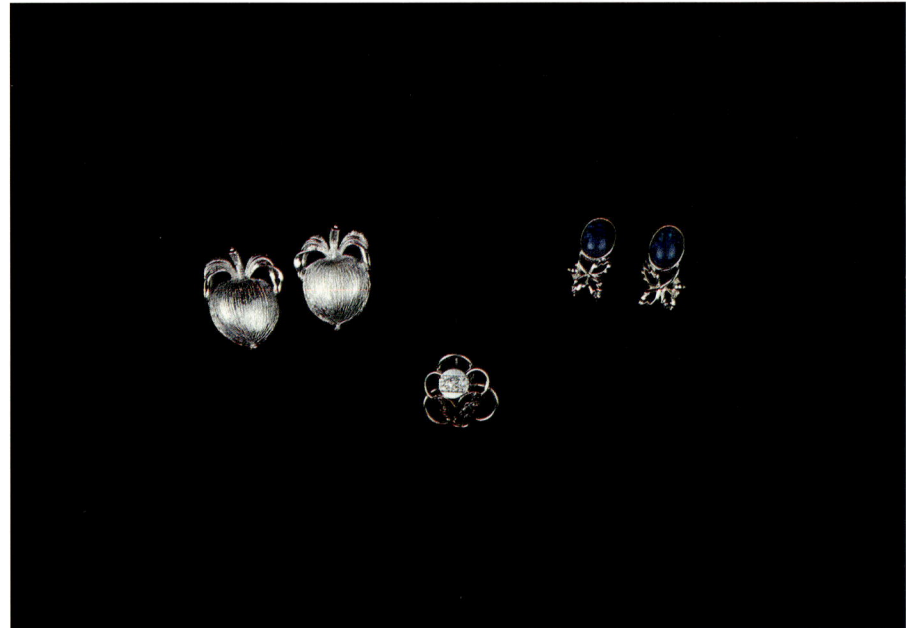

Many jewelry sets were found in the early cardex files and then continued throughout the 1960s and into the '70s—this is true of the pieces shown here. Such pieces may have been continued because there was an overabundance of them or because they were very popular and held over to satisfy the customers. **Top row, left to right**: *Cool Surrender* earrings are "hard to tell from the real thing" with the "three costume black diamonds twinkling and sparkling in a setting of glistening SarahSheen Silvertone." This set was a part of the cardex jewelry of early Sarah Coventry but kept as a hostess credit gift in the late 1960s and early to mid-70s. Matching necklace on page 46. B; $15-35. *Summer Frost* earrings are "maple leaves frosted in gleaming silvertone. Once more a design from nature, ageless in beauty with unlimited appeal. Summer frost can enhance your summer cottons or your winter wools with equal ease." This is one of two pairs of earrings with this same name. The other one is completely different and perhaps was in the '50s, while the maple leaves were early to late '60s. A; $10-35. *Starburst* earrings have "a deep amber stone catching and reflecting the light in the starburst design. A perfect fashion accent for those beige to brown tones and lovely with most any color." This set was continued through the late 1960s and into the '70s as hostess credit items. The name also was used for other pieces of jewelry, some using two words. Watch for those. Matching pin on page 67. A; $10-30. **Bottom row, left to right**: *Allusion* earrings are sparkling Austrian crystals clustered in the center of open-weave serrated edge goldentone overlapping leaves. "Truly an allusion for any fashion-minded person." Matching pin on page 69. B; $15-35. *Strawberry Ice* earrings illustrate another of the designs from nature with their replication of small strawberries. Versatility was an important part of Sarah's jewelry and these strawberries could be coupled with the silvery cascade necklace and earrings for a totally different look. Matching pin on page 66. A; $10-25. *Lady of Spain* earrings are identified from a card as produced in 1961. These rather large silvertone open-weave rotating blocks with center spokes of silvertone balls are certainly eye-catching. Matching bracelet on page 51. B; $15-45.

Top row, left to right: *Endearing* earrings are "dainty and delicate" with the "graceful contour leaf design…accented with soft white pretend pearls." One set of earrings had engraved "©SARAH COV" in large letters and the other set had "©SARAH COV" in smaller lettering. Matching pin on page 67. A; $15-30. *Serene* earrings are shown in both pierced and dangle hook versions. "The perfect name for the soft and quiet look of these delicate earrings. A lovely simulated pearl caught in a web of fine goldentone lace makes a design of ageless beauty." SarahGlo goldentone. As stated in the 1960s, these are "a classic type of jewelry that is never out of fashion" and truly could be worn today. Matching necklace on page 78. A; $10-25. *Tailored Swirl* earrings are, as the name implies, swirls of textured goldentone and satin overlapping in a three-dimensional open-weave effect. These earrings were also pictured with a versatility chain and pin, giving a totally different effect. Same earrings on page 73, matching pin on page 66. A; $8-25. **Bottom row, left to right**: Spectacular *New York* earrings have Austrian crystal rhinestones in each of the three inverted "v" shapes hooked together with a three petal flower at the bottom. The nearly 2" length gives these earrings a glamorous effect, which is no doubt why they were identified as "Continental Sparkled by Sarah Coventry." B; $15-45. *Ivy* earrings are silvertone satin and textured leaves with open-weave and ball centers. This small pair of earrings could be coupled with other silvertone pieces of jewelry. Matching pin on page 66. A; $10-25. *Night 'N Day* earrings are identified as "After-5 Sparkle. Sarah's versatility at its best is shown in this detachable dangle earring. Start out the day in a tailored silvertone leaf dangle and add a cluster of rhinestones at five for added glamour." The leaves are paved with sparkling Austrian crystals "exclusive design to make a more glamorous you." A ring with the same name, but not necessarily a match is shown on page 82. B; $15-35.

Top row, left to right: *Petite* earrings: "tiny, but elegant, simple in style, but classic in design is this darling three leaf in gleaming silvertone perfect for anyone and will go with anything." Matching pin on page 68. A; $8-20. *Evening Star* earrings (in box) have "a cluster of rhinestones surrounding the elegance of a charcoal rhinestone. At the setting of the sun, you'll want Evening Star to enhance the evening ensemble." Matching pin on page 68. B; $20-45. *Raspberry Ice* earrings are striking lavender enameled four and five petal flowers clustered as an elongated branch. The chaton cut hot pink rhinestone centers create wonderful contrast with the satin smooth silvertone background and stem. Matching pin on page 30. A; $10-35. **Bottom row, left to right**: *Fantasy* earrings are another "design from nature carried out in lovely colorful cabochon matrix of stones and simulated pearls. A dash of fashion color to enhance any costume regardless of the season." The star shape is accented by silvertone with smaller simulated pearls at each of the petal tips. Matching pin on page 68. B; $15-45. *Modern Leaf* earrings are shiny silvertone open-weave leaves with a turned-up edge on the end of the leaf. The sparkling silvertone is accented by the textured open-weave convex leaf shape. B; $12-35.

Left to right: *Windsong* earrings have a golden leaf shape with turned-up silver edges. The image of them blowing in the wind certainly reflects the name. Matching pin on page 33. A; $10-35. *Turn-a-bout* earrings are oval in shape with a band of shiny goldentone through the center and textured goldentone on the outer moon shapes. These earrings are similar to the necklace on page 48, which is reversible, or "turns about." A; $10-25. *Exotic* earrings have three layers of textured leaves in between large and very small leaves. In the center of the flower is a red cabochon bead. A; $10-30. *Slim Line* earrings are an unusual pair in the shape of a solid goldentone tulip. Outlining the petals is a shiny open framework with a golden ball at the base of the leaves. A; $10-30. *All courtesy of Otheda Smith.*

Left to right: ***Town and Country*** is the name, not "Pizzazz" as listed on the card. This illustrates the common problem of jewelry getting into the wrong box or on the wrong card. Be careful! These earrings are an open weave of four large intertwining loops with texture on one side and shiny goldentone on the other. A; $10-30. ***Whispering Leaves*** earrings: "Extravagant in everything but the price is this design by nature, duplicated in smart white enamel on metal. This new treatment of fashion jewelry has become increasingly popular because of the elegance of design and its clean cool look. Country bound or off to the city with equal ease is this leaf and grape design by Sarah's master craftsman." SarahSheen silvertone. Matching bracelet on page 80. There is also a set called Whispering Leaf, so be careful with these two very similar, but different, sets. A; $10-35. ***Ultima*** is the name of this exquisite pair of earrings. A large simulated pearl is set among leaves and points of silvertone, accented by tiny rhinestones. A; $12-30. *All courtesy of Otheda Smith.*

Top row, left to right: ***Cameo Lace*** are simple but elegant "heirloom type" earrings "with their delicately carved profile against a sky blue background. The intricate design of gold filigree" outlined in silvertone makes "a perfect frame for an ever charming picture." Matching pin on page 32. A; $10-30. ***Royal Plumage*** is a silvertone set with open-weave feathered plumage offset by a large royal blue rippled oval set. Matching pin on page 32. A; $10-35. **Bottom, left to right**: ***Powder Puff*** earrings are circles of metal with a crumpled look. The white enamel is recessed among the silvertone edges. A; $8-25. ***Summer Frost*** are "dainty floral circles fresh, appealing, and feminine enough to please the man in your life…Clip a spring bouquet on your ears and the romantic feeling of a woman loved, will be yours." The dainty petals are white enamel centered with a variety of chaton cut pastel sets. Marked only on the clip with a vertical "SC". A; $10-30.

Left to right: On ***Indian Princess***, the "look of Indian Craft daringly mixes yellow, orange, green and black in a woven…subtle beauty" design. These goldentone earrings were noted as appropriate to wear in any season. A; $8-25. ***Daisy Mae*** are rather large earrings of textured and satin goldentone. The antiqued center seed pocket is another example of a design from nature used by Sarah Coventry manufacturers, which delighted customers in the 1950s and '60s. Matching large pin on page 31. A; $10-25. ***Black Saturn*** are simplistic goldentone earrings. "Take the black from the night and the brilliance of the stars plus the mystery of the unusual and combine them to create this 'out of this world'" earring set with a teardrop shaped simple cut stone. Matching pin on page 31. A; $10-25.

Left to right: **Ebb Tide** has a goldentone shell of white enamel with goldentone highlights, encrusted with golden balls along the edge. There is an Ebb Tide ring, but it is not a part of this set. The set did come with a matching pin. A; $10-25. **Snow Princess** is the elegant name given to this single earring. The large center white cabochon bead is encircled by small crowns of goldentone topped by clear chaton cut rhinestone sets surrounded by faux prongs. B; $10-30 for two piece set. **Slim 'N' Trim** are "not too dressy to wear to the supermarket and yet smart enough for shopping and dining in the city. Sleek, chic and uncluttered is this snow-white earring by Sarah." A; $8-25. **Snow White** are white petal earrings made from two layers of overlapping petals surrounding a gold ball centered in a fluted cup. A; $10-25.

Left to right: **Light N' Bright** are appropriately named, with their "cool feel of light weight fashionable jewelry to brighten your costume any season of the year." One earring is marked on the back clasp with "SARAH COV" engraved, the other earring is not marked. Same earrings on page 73, matching pin on page 69. A; $8-20. **Radiance** denotes these chaton cut, prong set rhinestones on a sleek stem nestled on a wider goldentone leaf. They are miniature corn shapes of the matching pin on page 99. This set was continued through the early 1970s as hostess credit. A; $15-35. **Royal Highness** is a "masterpiece of such unusual beauty you can't believe it's costume jewelry." The five simulated pearls surrounding a chaton cut, prong set rhinestone and the dangling stems below do give the earrings a royal appearance. Matching necklace on page 47, matching bracelet on page 51. A; $12-35. **Demure** is "just what its name implies, shy, delicate and delightfully bashful." The "petite flower-like" earrings of goldentone have alternating solid and open petals. A; $8-20.

Left to right: With **Monte Carlo**, "all the excitement and glamour of Monte Carlo is reflected in these sparkling special occasion" earrings. "Sparkling jonquil rhinestones surrounded by gleaming gold and crystal rhinestones make…unbelievable beauty." Matching necklace on page 48, matching bracelet on page 52. B; $15-35. **Plain and Fancy** are "Unusual and striking. A masterpiece of design and craftsmanship as different looking as it is daring and as striking as it is distinctive. This brilliance and use of two tones is a new and daring technique developed for your admiration and can be worn with either PLAIN or FANCY clothes." Same earrings on page 43. Matching bracelet on page 52. A; $8-20. **Versaille** is a large multi-faceted green stone set in goldentone prongs and encircled by a square shape of goldentone rope. This set is one of my favorites and may be hard to locate. Matching bracelet on page 52. B; $12-35.

Top row, left to right: *Fan-fare* is the appropriate name for these "large, but light and airy" SarahSheen silvertone earrings. "Light as a feather and yet giving you the cover-the-ear look you've requested. An earring tailored enough to go with your suit and yet designed to complement your costume on more elaborate occasions. Try Fan-fare for fun and flattery." A; $10-25. *Camellia* earrings are "fashion in its lovelier form" with their white enameled leaves alternating with goldentone leaves creating a nest for the black pearl centers. Matching pin on page 30. A; $10-30. **Bottom row, left to right**: *Mystic* is this single earring that "dances, flirts, glimmers, glows." The large dark hematite (simulated) stone is surrounded by offset silvertone rippled for dramatic effect. "Mystic reflects the mood of its wearer from summer silks to winter wools." As this is a single earring, it may have been purchased singly to be secured to a necklace or lapel. In the early years, only one earring was sent to the FSDs rather than a whole set, so that may account for its single status as well. A; $10-25 for complete pair. *Woven Classic* is aptly named because of its unusual woven textured goldentone circles. Matching bracelet on page 51, matching pin on page 31. A; $10-25. *Pearl Flattery* features a combination of gold and seven simulated pearls hanging from hinged goldentone loops and rings. A simulated pearl secures the earring to the ear. Matching bracelet on page 51. A; $10-25.

Top row, left to right: *Splendor* earrings are textured goldentone four leaf flowers. Inside the smaller satin petals is a simulated pearl center with stamens ending in tiny green Austrian stones. Matching pin on page 27. A; $12-30. *Designer's Choice* is an unassuming name for a what I think is a spectacular set of earrings. The solid oak leaves are studded with small clear rhinestones. Matching pin on page 27. $A; $10-25. *Golden Maple* is "delicately designed, expertly crafted, let it add its golden splash to your new Fall suit. Its touch is good with tailored or afternoon casuals, handsome with furs and suedes, best with tweeds and flannels." The gold ball at the center base point gives a 3-D effect to an otherwise flat earring. The identifying mark on the earring clasp is "SAC" in a < > shape. Matching pin on page 27. A; $8-20. **Bottom row, left to right**: *Snow Flower* earrings are white enamel petals surrounded by goldentone open-weave petal shapes. The depth created by the petals hides a gold ball in the center. A flower looks like it is peeking through the snow, as suggested by the name. Matching pin on page 27. A; $10-25. *Fashion Leaf* earrings are created from a textured goldentone leaf with a folded edge of rhinestones. The effect gives a brilliant two tone effect. Matching pin on page 31. A; $10-30.

Top row, left to right: *Fancy Free* are open-weave circles of silvertone with a free form leaf design in the open center. As with most pieces of Sarah Coventry, the name closely reflects the design—these are fancy and yet free in form! There are several sets of jewelry with this name. Matching bracelet on page 126. A; $10-25. *Feathered Fashion* is another kind of feather design from Sarah. The comma shaped feather of open silvertone textured with an overlay of silvertone at the base provides the fashionable look. A; $10-25. *Satin Flame* features "a contrast of startling beauty…flame design…contrasting the gleam of satin with the richly-textured look. The perfect note of fashion for that basic look…A flame of fashion, for the fashion-conscious woman." SarahGlo silvertone. Matching pin on page 31. A; $10-25. **Center**: *Rhapsody in Blue*: "typical of our flair for the unusual, our designers have created an ensemble anciently reminiscent of Cleopatra and yet with a look of the modern and the abstract. Textured silvertone coupled with stones of exquisite beauty. A masterpiece of fashion is this delightful" earring set. A; $10-30. **Bottom**: *Frosted Feathers* single earring has an open feather effect of goldentone with three textured silvertone teardrop shapes at the base. Matching earrings on page 41, matching necklace on page 47. A; $10-20 for pair.

Necklaces

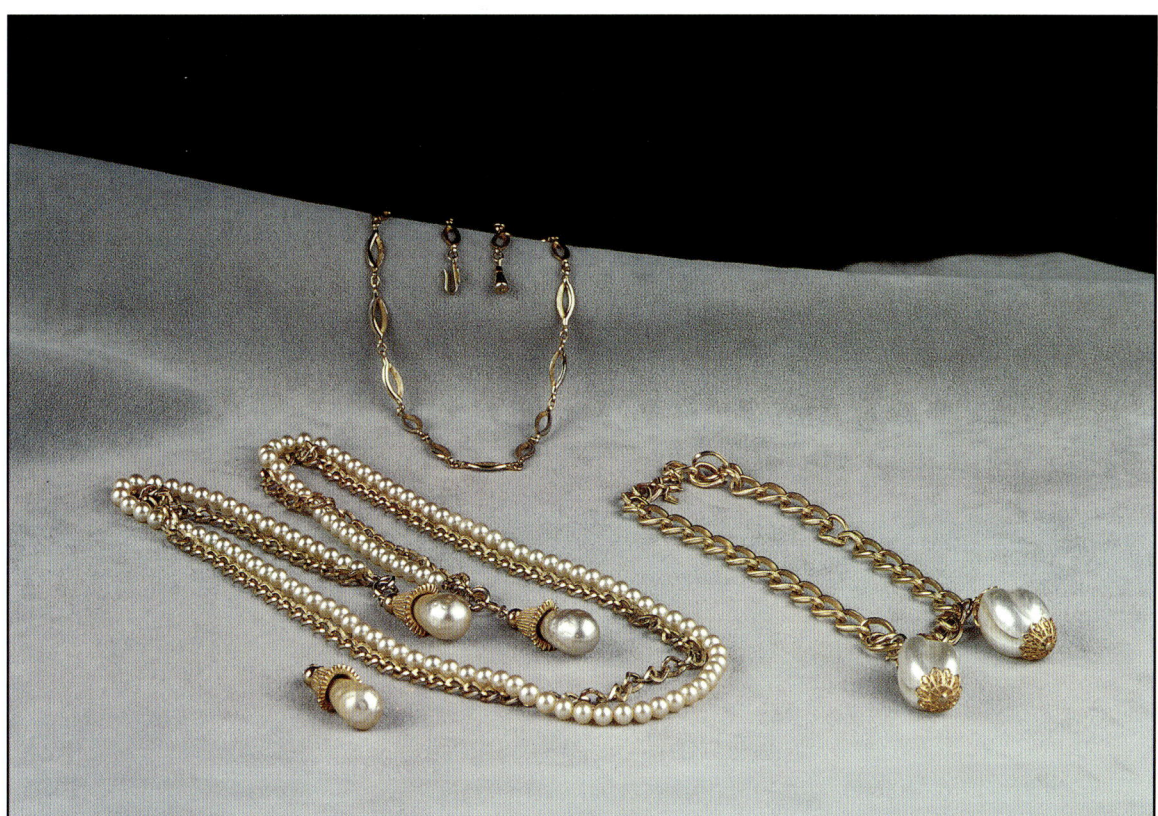

Top: **Delightful** necklace is created from goldentone links of open teardrop shaped metals. "It's delightful, it's delicious, it's delovely, this dainty and darling chain necklace. Designed for the young lady or the petite woman. Delightful has a very expensive look but can be purchased for very little." This design was shown on very early cards and continued through the early 1970s catalogs. It must have been a very popular piece and will be easy to find. Matching bracelet on page 50. A; $8-20. **Bottom row, left to right**: **Fashion Parade** necklace is given the opportunity of making a basic dress "into a Fashion Parade." This picture shows the open ended chain and pearl string with baroque pearl and goldentone capped pendants on each end. "Wear your pearl (simulated) separately, wear the golden chain separately, or combine the two in a parade of different fashions." This versatile set could be worn with the opening in front or (with pendants removed) worn with hooks in the back. Matching stick pin on page 67, matching earrings on page 35, matching ring on page 82. B; $10-35. **Chain O' Fashion** is identified as "the ultimate in versatility." This is a single chain, but the original included three lengths of chain plus the detachable pearlized dangles. With the three lengths it could also be worn as a belt, bracelets, lariat, sautoir, or just as a single, double, or triple chain necklace. This necklace was made in silvertone as well. B; $10-35.

In sharp contrast to the chains previously shown, these two exquisite necklaces made it very difficult to distinguish between costume jewelry and the "real" thing. **Left to right**: **Celebrity** is a very appropriate name for the set of jewelry that includes this versatile pin/pendant. It has a large rectangular or emerald cut "beautiful smoky black stone...nestled in an antique frame of unbelievable beauty and surrounded by sparkling rhinestones." As a pendant attached to a silvertone chain and worn against black or dark clothes, it would have made an expensive statement. Matching earrings on page 35, matching bracelet on page 50, and matching ring on page 53. B; $35-55.
Bold and Beautiful is equally as breathtaking in a more simplistic way. This necklace "has the elegant feeling of very fine fashion jewelry." The rather large round black cabochon sets are captured among both satin and textured silvertone links fastened together with silvertone loops. (**Bold and Beautiful** also came in white cabochon sets on goldentone.) A card was dated 1960. Matching earrings on page 35. B; $20-45.

Left to right on stand: *Young and Gay* necklace has alternating coin and open chain links sturdily connected to form a "feminine yet tailored" piece of jewelry. Many times several bracelets were connected together to form a longer necklace, or just a few were used for a choker. This piece was identified with "SAC" while others I have found say "SARAHCOV." Same necklace on page 78, matching bracelet on page 50, matching earring on page 36. A; $10-25. *Crystal Navette* necklace has a "well-cut navette shaped rhinestone placed in the center of a textured silvertone leaf. Gently swaying on a sparkling chain and you have a pendant of great fashion and beauty." Matching earrings on page 35. A; $15-40. *Silvery Cascade* necklace: "you'll never wear a light, more luxurious necklace than this aluminum of feather light chain by Sarah Coventry. Your jewelry wardrobe won't be complete without Silvery Cascade." Many different pendants could be worn with this necklace—customers sometimes purchased an extra earring so one could be worn as a pendant while the other two served as earrings. These necklaces were very popular—women felt their wardrobe wouldn't be complete without one—and can be found easily. The necklace also came in golden cascade. Same necklace on page 113, matching earrings on page 75. B; $8-20. *Summer Magic* is the name given this necklace of beads and silver chain. "First I'm a matinee length necklace, then 'Presto-Chango' I'm a rope, another sleight of hand and I turn from just silver color to a two-strand white and silvertone necklace attractively pinned with a striking flower pin. 'Tis really magic." In 1970 this necklace was renamed "New Summer Magic." Matching pin on page 30, matching earrings on page 34. B; $10-25.

Top to bottom: *Dancing Magic* appropriately denotes this necklace. Medium-sized chaton cut Austrian aurora borealis rhinestones set in a goldentone rope setting form the pendant ball. The ball's movement and light hitting the stones create a striking piece of jewelry. Matching earrings on page 75. B; $10-35. *Cool Surrender* necklace makes it "hard to tell from the real thing…these costume black diamonds twinkling and sparkling in a setting of glistening SarahSheen Silvertone." This was an early piece and the set was continued through the early 1970s as hostess credit. The marking on the back is "SC" raised within an oval raised shape. Matching earrings on page 36. B; $15-40. *Sultana* is a solid teardrop shaped pendant on an equally heavy linked chain. Its sunken tiny pastel rhinestones and raised geometric goldentone shapes add to the elegance. "Designed to enhance your jewel tone wools, your tailored blouses, even your sweaters and to add fashion color to your blacks and whites, summer or winter." This set was carried over to later years as hostess credit. Matching earrings on page 73. B; $10-25. *World's Fair* necklace was inspired by "the New York City World's Fair with all its glamour, gaiety, international flavor and romance. You'll feel like a woman of mystery and glamour in this sparkling necklace inspired by the city lights and its world famous World's Fair." The three petal flowers of silvertone encrusted with rhinestones are linked together. Matching bracelet on page 51, matching earrings on page 84. B; $25-50.

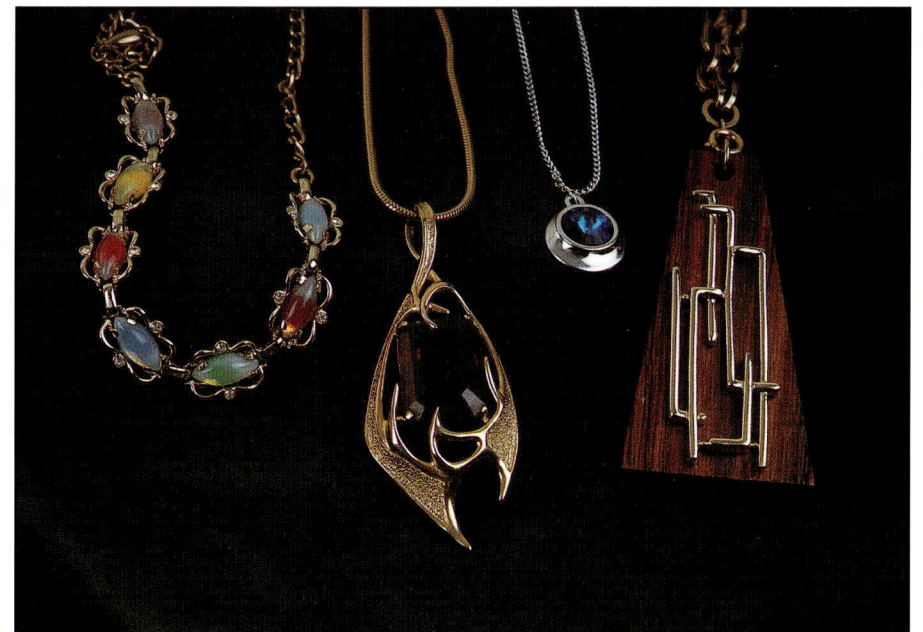

Left to right: ***Sabrina Fair*** necklace is a "rare collection of Sabrina stones assembled" to create this "appealing and feminine" piece of jewelry, with "each Sabrina stone tenderly guarded by sparkling chatons." A very dainty and delicate design. Matching ring on page 53. B; $10-25. ***Molten Topaz*** is a high fashion pendant necklace, "daring in both size and design. This deep amber colored stone is artfully set in a golden flame design giving reflections as warm as a burning flame." Matching earrings on page 42. B; $15-35. *Courtesy of Nancy Isgrigs.* ***Liquid Lites*** necklace has a large dark blue Austrian glass stone surrounded by a silvertone band dangling from a silvertone chain. Located in the 1970 and 1971 catalogs. B; $10-35. ***Classic*** features goldentone wire shaped in various cross-like shapes backed by a dark walnut wooden triangle and attached to a heavy, open link chain. B; $12-25. *Courtesy of Nancy Isgrigs.*

Top to bottom: ***Star Shower*** necklace is a glamorous 7-8" display of prong set clear chaton cut rhinestones alternating with a dangling three spray goldentone shower effect ending in additional clear rhinestones. This piece of jewelry is one I could have missed because it doesn't look like costume jewelry and does not have the characteristics of other Sarah pieces. B; $15-30. ***Frosted Feathers*** necklace has a two-tone effect of the late 1950s and 1960s. The two-tone design is created by the open feather effect of goldentone combined with two textured silvertone teardrop shapes at the base. Matching earrings on page 41. A; $10-20. *Courtesy of Otheda Smith.* ***Royal Highness*** necklace is a "masterpiece of such unusual beauty you can't believe it's costume jewelry." A royal appearance is indeed achieved with this glamorous look fit for a "Queen." Matching earrings on page 39. B; $20-45.

Left to right: ***Stunning Plus*** pendant is a triangular shape of jet black stone suspended within a double-ringed teardrop shape of SarahSheen silvertone. B; $15-30. *Courtesy of Otheda Smith.* ***Jukebox*** necklace is a 1950s pendant of unique design. The double ringed goldentone frame encircles an artfully done jukebox and two dancing figures. Small red, light and dark blue beads create the heads and front of the jukebox. Little information about this pendant was found, but I can imagine that many teen-agers and young adults in the '50s were thrilled to own this imaginative and colorful necklace. I was delighted when I found it, as again it strayed from the typical characteristics of other Sarah pieces. This necklace shows how diversified and sensitive to the customers Sarah Coventry was. Marking on the back of the pendant is "©SARAH COV" in raised letters. A; $15-30.

Left to right: ***Matinee Elegance*** chain and pendant has five textured beads attached to gold cylinders, all grouped together to form the dangling pendant. The dangling links are the same as the shorter chain links. This SarahGlo goldentone necklace is another prime example of Sarah's ability to create diversity in costume jewelry—there was something for everyone. Matching earrings on page 36. A; $8-20. ***Simply Elegant*** necklace is another example of how diversified Sarah designers could be. It is created from small textured curves showering five spears of silvertone linked together. Matching bracelet on page 51, matching earrings on page 42. B; $15-35. ***Acorn Treasures*** pendant necklace "will be one of the most treasured possessions in your jewelry wardrobe. This pendant has the look of 'real gold.' You'll be amazed at the tiny price of this expensive looking set." A; $10-25.

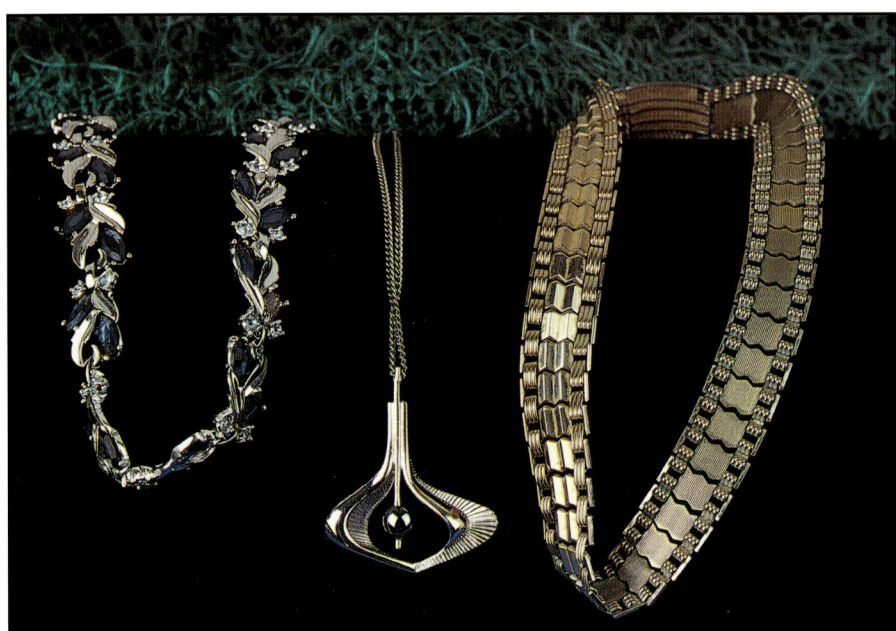

Left to right: ***Blue Champagne*** necklace is created from SarahSheen silvertone. "Exciting, glamorous, outstandingly beautiful, exquisite, striking, and heavenly are only a few of the adjectives it would take to describe this breathtakingly beautiful necklace designed by Sarah's master designers. It's 'Perfection.'" It has dark blue navette stones nestled among silvertone leaves and smaller light blue chaton cut rhinestones. One location I found this set identified it as "Blue Mystery," with the same description. More frequently, however, "Champagne" was used. Matching pin on page 32. B; $15-35. ***Danish Modern*** has a pendant shaped like a squashed circle. It is fashioned from textured and satin silvertone with a hematite drop suspended from the silvertone pendulum. Drop is marked "©SARAH COV" in raised lettering. A; $10-25. ***Turn-a-bout*** necklace is a goldentone 1" wide choker with textured finish on one side and satin finish on the other, allowing for wearing either side out. A unique clasp also provides for the "turn-about," reversible effect. Matching earrings on page 37. A; $12-35.

Left to right: ***Fashion Circle*** necklace was described as the "height of fashion, elegant sautoir. A chalk white ball encased in a gleaming golden cage and hanging from a slim line chain. The fashionable ornament is detachable allowing the dangle to be used on a bracelet and the chain to be used with other dangles or pins as a pendant necklace. A real circle of fashion." B; $10-25. ***Rain Flower*** necklace was actually produced in the early 1970s. The six independent petals attached to the chain are clear rhinestones surrounded by a four petal goldentone wire frame. B; $12-25. ***Monte Carlo*** necklace is a cluster of "sparkling jonquil rhinestones surrounded by gleaming gold and crystal rhinestones, making an ensemble of unbelievable beauty. All the excitement and glamour of Monte Carlo is reflected in this sparkling special occasion piece." Matching earrings on page 39, matching bracelet on page 52. B; $30-55. ***Instant Fashion*** goldentone necklace of the late 1960s has versatile chains combined with simulated pearls. This combination made instant fashion changes possible. B; $10-25. *Courtesy of Nancy Isgrigs.*

Left to right: *Personalized Pearls* necklace is a "versatile pearl (simulated) rope necklace designed to be worn many ways to suit you and your wardrobe." The three drops can be removed and the three strands of pearls can be attached to an accompanying clasp (not pictured here). This is from the late 1960s. C; $15-30. With *Dawn to Dusk*, "Sarah's versatility at its best is displayed in this unusual pendant. Quiet pearl (simulated) on one side for before 5:00, reverses to sparkling rhinestones at dusk." Matching earrings on page 71. A; $10-25. *Color Spray* necklace is "pastel and dainty, tiny enough for a young teen-ager, lovely enough for a bride and designed so that even grandma would love to own it. This pinwheel design with its sparkling pastel stars encased in antiqued white swirls will be a favorite for all ages for years to come." SarahSheen goldentone. Matching earrings on page 41. A; $10-25. *Courtesy of Harriette Oshel.* On the *Golden Braid* necklace, "soft textured swirls fall caressingly around your neck forming a collar of fashion and beauty." This is a dark goldentone-bronze color necklace. B; $15-35. *Whispering Leaves* necklace: "extravagant in everything but the price is this design by nature, duplicated in smart white enamel on metal. This new treatment of fashion jewelry has become increasingly popular because of the elegance of design and its clean cool look. Country bound or off to the city with equal ease is this leaf and grape design by Sarah's master craftsman." Matching earrings on page 38, matching bracelet on page 80. B; $15-30. *White Satin*: "as smooth and silky as White Satin and just as luxurious is this beautiful and versatile rope that leads many lives." Matching earrings on page 74. B; $15-30. *Courtesy of Nancy Isgrigs.*

One of the early necklaces was this *Golden Wardrobe*, similar to the *Pearl Wardrobe* shown on page 22. This three strand necklace of golden beads can be changed to one or two strands for variation. A; $20-35. *Courtesy of Alynda Kimbrough.*

Bracelets

The **Celebrity** bracelet pictured here with the corresponding cardex is one of the most exquisite pieces of jewelry Sarah Coventry made. The five large and beautiful smoky black stones are "nestled in an antique frame" of glistening silvertone. Each silvertone frame delicately hides tiny sparkling rhinestones, making the bracelet shimmer while being worn with the other pieces of the ensemble or separately. Matching pin/pendant on page 29, matching ring on page 53, matching earrings on page 35. C; $20-45.

Left to right: *Blue Hawaii* bracelet has "all the romance of the Blue Hawaiian waters." The imitation stones of Lapis Blue stand out against the glistening silvertone leaves and links. Matching earrings on page 36. A; $15-30. *Young and Gay* silvertone bracelet of small solid coins alternating with silvertone circle links gives a "sturdy and yet feminine, tailored and yet appropriate to wear with your Sunday best" look. This very inexpensive bracelet was quite popular and several bracelets can be clasped together to form a choker or necklace. Identifying marks vary. Goldentone has "SARAH COV©"engraved, silvertone has "©SARAH COV" engraved, and others have "SAC" engraved in < > shape on the clasp. Matching necklace on page 78, matching earring on page 36. A; $8-15. The description for *Multi-Swirl* bracelet notes that "current fashion sportswear calls for exotic colors and the look of bulk." This was certainly achieved by Sarah with the exotic colored glass stones centered in each of the textured silvertone swirls. A; $10-35. *Indian Treasures* bracelet has the "look of molded silver." Turquoise color stones are offset in the silvertone coin shapes. A; $10-25.

Left to right: *Young and Gay* goldentone bracelet is the same as the silvertone version. Many pieces of Sarah Coventry jewelry came in either silvertone or goldentone. Matching necklace on page 46. A; $8-15. *Harmony* bracelet is delicate and beautiful and was created to blend and harmonize with whatever it was worn with, including other goldentone bracelets—"harmony loves company." This design was continued from the 1950s through the late '60s. A; $10-25. *Delightful* bracelet features "dainty and darling" open teardrop shaped metal links connected with "o" rings. Though designed for the young lady or petite woman, it was very inexpensive and therefore popular with many customers. I am not sure whether they also made ankle bracelets, but I found one that is much too large for my wrist so I choose to wear it on my ankle. Interesting. Again, this bracelet continued to be offered through the 1950s, '60s and early '70s. Matching necklace on page 45. A; $8-15.

Left to right: *Egyptian Temptress* is a unique bracelet of vertical goldentone teardrop shapes slightly scored and separated with goldentone satin. Small gold balls dot the inside of each shape and accent the ends of each of the connecting pieces. This artfully done design gives an Egyptian effect. Matching earrings on page 41. A; $15-30. *Unidentified* bracelet looks like miniature ladders hinged together, giving a textured and satin-smooth silvertone effect. Marked "©SARAH COV" engraved on clasp only. Matching earrings on page 44. $10-25. *Harvest Wheat* bracelet is identified with that name in *Fifty Years of Collectible Fashion Jewelry: 1925-1975* by Lillian Baker, pages 44-45. It has no other documentation, so for now we'll use this name. Marked "©SARAH COV" engraved on clasp and also marked "©SARAH COV" in raised letters on the back of the bracelet itself. Matching earrings on page 75. $10-25. *Pearl Flattery* bracelet: "One of the most popular combinations in fashion jewelry today is the combining of gold and pearls. Sarah's designers have created a…bracelet that can be worn by sunlight or candlelight with equal beauty." Matching earrings on page 40. B; $12-35. *Lady of Spain* bracelet has a glamorous silvertone scroll design reminiscent of Spanish wrought iron work. The large center section with decreasing sizes makes for a handsome piece of costume jewelry. Identified as made in 1960. B; $15-35.

Top row, left to right: *Woven Classic* is a 1" wide solid hinged, cuff bracelet of an unusual woven textured goldentone. Matching earrings on page 40, matching pins on page 31. B; $10-25. *Simply Elegant* is the extravagant name given to this textured and satin-smooth silvertone bracelet created in a pineapple design with satin sprigs of silvertone extending from both ends of the pineapple shape. Matching earrings on page 42, matching necklace on page 48. A; $15-35. *Unidentified* bracelet of three strands of golden beads with a rhinestone clasp. Since it isn't identified but is no doubt from the '60s, I placed it in this section. $10-25. *World's Fair* is a bracelet inspired by the New York City World's Fair. The "glamour, gaiety, international flavor and romance" of the World's Fair is duplicated through the sparkling rhinestones encrusted in the leaf designs. Matching necklace on page 46, matching earrings on page 84. B; $20-45. **Bottom left**: *Mademoiselle* is a cuff bracelet of chalk white and gleaming goldentone. The textured fabric design was created "for the smart young woman" and coincided with the *Mademoiselle* magazine issue targeting young women and their fashions. Matching earrings on page 41. B; $10-25.

Left to right: *Hearts and Flowers* bracelet with an enameled heart "in daughter's favorite colors of pink and blue…will sweeten every young wardrobe." A; $8-25. *Royal Highness* bracelet has twin simulated pearls alternating with a single, chaton cut clear rhinestone. Off setting each pearl or rhinestone are small goldentone leaves hinged to create a snug-fitting bracelet. Matching necklace on page 47, matching earrings on page 39. B; $15-45. Another *Simply Elegant* bracelet (see description above). A; $15-35. *Happy Holiday* is comprised of "color charms linked together in a delicate silvertone design creating a bracelet you can wear anywhere, anytime. Wear with sweaters and tailored clothes or combine with pearls on dressier occasions. Multi-color charms know no season and are fashion right from morn 'til night." This bracelet has a variety of shapes and stones, ranging from baroque pearl to jet black, giving it a festive look. Matching earrings on page 72. A; $10-25. *All courtesy of Otheda Smith.*

Left to right: *Parisienne Nights* has "all the glamour and romance of an evening in Paris...Hundreds of sparkling rhinestones create this piece befitting a queen." Matching ring on page 81. B; $15-40. ***Monte Carlo*** bracelet features sparkling jonquil rhinestones surrounded by satin and textured teardrop shape goldentone and prong set crystal rhinestones. Matching necklace on page 48, matching earrings on page 39. B; $15-40. ***Versaille*** bracelet is a large cuff of dazzling goldentone. It has a very large, green/yellow multi-faceted square jewel encapsulated in a prong set twisted rope frame. The rest of the band is engraved with leaves and flowers, enhancing and accenting the large stone. Matching earrings on page 39. B; $15-50. *Courtesy of Otheda Smith.*

Left to right: *Gracious Lady* bracelet is a combination of golden chain and simulated pearls. The unusual magnetic clasp creates a gracious piece of jewelry, hence its name. A; $10-25. ***Plain and Fancy*** bracelet looks like a grapevine of leaves intertwined together. The use of both silvertone and goldentone gave this bracelet a striking appearance. Matching earrings on page 39, matching bracelet on page 52, A; $10-25.

Rings and Sets

Left to right: Here are two rings from the 1950s and early '60s that stand out. **Celebrity** has "a truly beautiful smoky black stone nestled in an antique frame of unbelievable beauty and surrounded by sparkling rhinestones, making it captivating and intriguing as romance itself." The ring has adjustable sizing. Matching pin/pendant on page 29, matching earrings on page 35, matching bracelet on page 50. A; $15-40. **Sabrina Fair** ring is a Sabrina glass stone imported from Europe. "You asked for it! Sarah's designers have created it! A delicate ring…A touch of delicate color on your finger." Marked on inside of ring is "SARAH COV" engraved. Matching necklace on page 47. A; $10-25.

Left to right: **Alaskan Summer** bracelet, pin, and earrings set with simulated pearls nestled among satin-smooth and textured silvertone leaves and stems. Tiny sky blue beads are placed strategically among the pearls and leaves. C; $30-55. **Wisteria** set includes silvertone pin and earrings decorated with Austrian glass chaton cut crystals in hot pink and lavender. The crystals are highlighted by textured and satin-smooth blossom caps along with slender stems delicately meshed to form a glamorous bouquet. The name "Wisteria" was given to another set in later years; it was similar in color but very different in style. Watch for it. B; $25-50. *All courtesy of Alynda Kimbrough.*

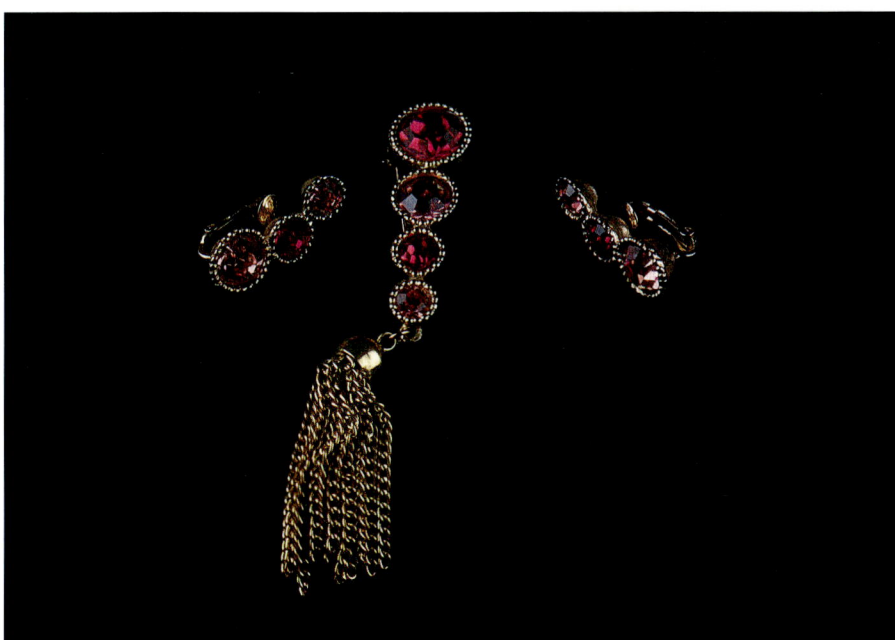

Saucy set of earrings and pin with tassel. "Pert 'n' Saucy is this petite Paris-inspired pin with its provocative chain tassel and matching earrings. Vogue pink to magenta rhinestones make up this design that can be worn horizontally or vertically, depending on the need of your costume." SarahGlo goldentone. A; $20-45. *Courtesy of Alynda Kimbrough.*

Royal Ballet set includes necklace, earrings, and bracelet. "Just as a fine ballet group are dancing in perfect unison, so is every pearl (simulated) dancing and sparkling in delicate and precise fashion in this royal necklace, bracelet and earring group by Sarah's regal designers. A sparkling vision of grace and line combined to give you an ensemble of breathtaking beauty" in SarahSheen goldentone. This was another set that gave costume jewelry the look of "real jewelry." C; $35-60.

Frozen Lace is "delicate, graceful patterns, a spectacular ornament of baroque styling, distinctively yours to wear and wear and wear. The giant earrings double as clips; the bracelet, on black velvet ribbon, makes a stunning choker." C; $25-45. *Courtesy of Otheda Smith.*

Chantilly Lace set of earrings, bracelet, and necklace represent goldentone at its best. The goldentone lace in square and rectangular shapes makes this set a designer's dream. The earrings were designed by overlapping three squares of lace with their points down, for an ear covering result. The bracelet and necklace are made from rectangular lace pieces; on the necklace, the pieces fan out from the neckline creating a solid golden bib. Magnificent and so goldenly rich. C; $35-60. *Courtesy of Otheda Smith.*

Moonlight Madness set includes necklace pendant, earrings, and shoe clips. The necklace pendant is a unique tree design using alternating rows of simulated pearls and prong set clear rhinestones. The earrings and shoe clips are identical, with two rows of clear rhinestones surrounding a row of simulated pearls in a contour shape. A very striking and sparkling set of costume jewelry for evening wear. Note that the earrings are stamped "© SARAH COV" on the back clasp, while the shoe clips are marked with raised "©SARAH COV." C; $25-55. *Courtesy of Otheda Smith.*

Left to right: *Pearl Flight* pin and earrings: "inspired by the design of a bird's wing, this set embodies an airyness and grace seldom, if ever, seen in a piece of costume jewelry. Its delicate wire work, contrasted by the boldness of a softly gleaming simulated pearl, completes the picture of one of this season's most unusual pieces of fashion jewelry." Earrings were of two sizes of the same design. C; $20-45 *Unidentified* set of pendant/pin and earrings are solid goldentone with raised hatchwork of goldentone, giving a simple but elegant appearance. $20-45. *Courtesy of Otheda Smith.*

Clockwise, from left: *Unidentified* set is a glamorous necklace and earrings created from an open weave of goldentone scattered with clear rhinestones. Three sections are hinged, creating a bib-like effect. The earrings are smaller replicas of a section of the necklace. Marked on earring backs is "©SARAH COV" engraved and also a raised "L" and "R" to indicate left or right ear. The necklace is marked only with a hand mirror tag "SC" on one side and "©SARAH COV" engraved on the other. $30-55. *Tawny Shadows* set of necklace and earrings has large, light brown stones nestled in swirls of goldentone and accented with clear, smaller rhinestones. I have seen two sets and quickly realized that the brown stones come out easily so in some cases may have been replaced with other colored stones. Marking on earrings is "©SARAH COV" in small letters engraved and on necklace itself "©SARAH COV" in raised letters. Matching bracelet on page 91 of Lindbeck book. $18-35. *Celestial Fire* set of necklace and bracelet has "flashing, multi-faceted rhinestones, framed in whirling golden loops, with all the grace and magnificence of custom-made jewelry. You will sparkle. You will glow. You will wear Celestial Fire forever!" The description identified Celestial Fire as "the most popular and cherished ensemble in Sarah's collection." It certainly is a sparkling and shimmering set of jewelry. There were matching earrings as well. Markings on bracelet are "SAC" engraved in < > shape while the necklace had < > on the hang tag with "SAC" in raised letters inside. B; $20-45. *Courtesy of Otheda Smith.*

Aurora Swirl earrings are made from large aurora borealis glass stones that are chaton cut and prong set in wide goldentone swirls. The bracelet is created from the same swirls, with each set hinged together to form a close fit. B; $20-45. *Courtesy of Otheda Smith.*

1962 and 1963 *Signets*

I was fortunate in being able to locate Jan Koltes, one of the many non-employee collectors, who graciously loaned some of her *Signets* to me for this book. These were sent out bi-monthly for a short period of time in the early 1960s (and possibly in the late 1950s) to keep all of the FSDs updated about promotions, commissions, awards, and jewelry items. Here are some pages from one issued in 1962.

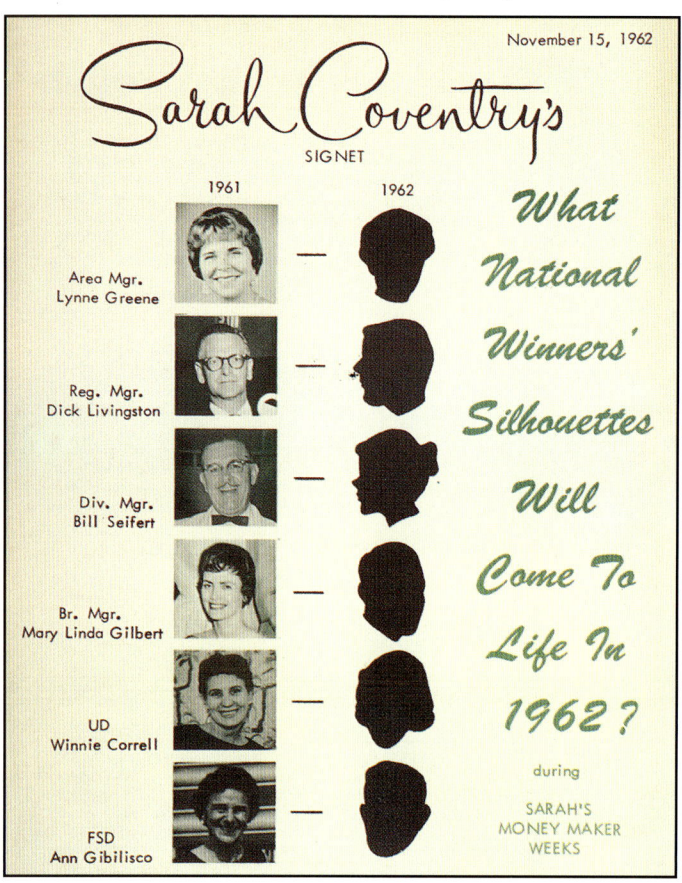

DON'T WONDER, ASK US!

QUESTION: Could Sarah bring us earrings to match the "Fantasy" pin?
— LINA BRYANT
C. Hays Branch, Virginia

ANSWER: I doubt that we will. Have you tried the "Chain O' Fashion" earring with "Fantasy"?

QUESTION: Would it be possible for Sarah to put a hook similar to those on the "Galaxy" and "Starburst" pins on the "Adam's Delight" pins?
— JOY BOONE
Davidson Branch, Oklahoma

ANSWER: Sorry, no - but they both hang well on chains.

QUESTION: 1. Will you ever have a "Sabrina Fair" pin?

2. Will you ever have a smaller earring to match "Silvery Cascade"?
— LINDA CARL
D. Schieman Region, Ohio

ANSWER: No to both.

QUESTION: There is a notation on our shopping guides that links may be added or taken from bracelets at $1.00 per link. Does this mean that every bracelet issued may be adjusted in this way?
— ELEANOR KOVATS
Evichan Branch, New Jersey

ANSWER: No, only those designated - "Twirling Pearls" and "Celebrity".

Your questions are answered by **aileen**.

A Glimpse of Sarah's 1963 Dream Book

(COMING SOON)

- and better yet -

Now available in sizes 8 to 18

for

2 RECRUITS - - -

A BEAUTIFUL

BASIC LEATHER

EXQUISITELY TAILORED

JACKET

in white or beige.

Christmas BOOSTERS

FSD DIANNE SPOTTS, Griffin Branch, Pennsylvania has these two Christmas ideas to pass along: "Keep Christmas foremost in the minds of guests at shows from now on by using a small plastic Christmas tree with earrings clipped on the branches; bracelets and necklaces hung as ornaments. It looks very attractive and is very effective.

"A similar idea for the coming season is an inexpensive wreath - preferably a homemade one - hung right on your 'show table' - on which you can clip earrings and drape bracelets and necklaces. An appealing way to keep your show guests aware of Christmas."

UD BONNIE SMITH, Hamilton Branch, Ohio, submits this Christmas Booster: "I am receiving nice compliments, larger orders and most important, more bookings by using this idea. I took RSVP and wrapped it in Christmas paper with red and green streamers taped to each one. I put the packages down in a red net Christmas stocking with the streamers hanging over the top. I then cut a Christmas tree out of art paper and put this poem on it:

"Christmastime isn't far away,

So hurry up now, don't delay,

Just pull a streamer form my Christmas stocking

By booking a show you can do some

FREE Christmas Shopping!"

Beloved Star Loves Sarah

Beloved stage, screen and television star, Lillian Gish, will be wearing Sarah Coventry jewelry when she attends the American Academy of Dramatic Arts' Annual Dinner Dance at the new Americana Hotel in New York on November 18. Miss Gish is honorary chairman of the benefit at which Rosalind Russell will receive the Academy's Seventh Annual Award of Achievement for Alumni. The gracious Miss Gish will model the smart black linen-weave ensemble she is wearing here, accented by "Sea Whispers", Sarah's exciting underwater flora and coral design.

Sarah Coventry jewelry will be an award at the very social American Academy of Dramatic Arts' dance. Founded 78 years ago, the AADA is the oldest dramatic training school in the English speaking world. The roster of Academy graduates boasts many stars including, among others, Cecil B. DeMille, Spencer Tracy, William Powell, Edward G. Robinson, Rosalind Russell, Grace Kelly, Anne Bancroft and Jason Robards, Jr.

Miss Gish has not yet formulated her plans for the 1963 season. But an actress of her calibre and renown, sought by television, Broadway and Hollywood producers, will sign when the right vehicle comes along. So watch for her. You will be seeing her soon.

CARDEX WINNERS

REMEMBER - don't use Cardex *instead of* a regular Fashion Show, but rather *in addition to*. Let your Cardex be a plus for you.

CARDEX - A TRAVELING STORE - "Recently I forgot my Cardex and left it after a show. About a week later, my hostess called saying she had some orders and would I pick them up. There was my extra show. She asked to keep the Cardex a while longer as she had more friends to contact so I re-booked her! She is now working for items she couldn't afford otherwise. My Cardex is my traveling store as well as a friend of my hostess," writes FSD LOIS ANDERSON, McClurkin Branch, California.

CARDEX IN THE GREENHOUSE - "Thanks, Sarah, for the wonderful, most useful Cardex. I had my first show last week for my sister-in-law. She called and wanted the Cardex for two outside orders. I sent it to the greenhouse with my mother-in-law. She happened to give it to her daughter when she was eating lunch around the table with the rest of the girls. They asked her what it was. She told them it was a Cardex for Sarah Coventry Jewelry. They looked at it and every lady ordered something. That night I had a century show - $107.00. Thank you for the Cardex," writes FSD DIANE MOORE, Coliechio Branch, Ohio.

HOORAY FOR THE CARDEX - "The Cardex worked wonders for me! I asked the girl in the grocery store to have a show and when she told me she really couldn't I asked her to take the Cardex and show it to some of the other girls in the store. Very reluctantly she took the Cardex and I could see doubt written all over her face. When I went back she gave me a $100.00 order and told me how much fun she had doing it. She also said there were a few more people she wanted to see and asked if she could keep the Cardex a while longer. I told her of course and when I went back the second time she had another $100.00 show for me. She was thrilled with all her free jewelry and the extra nice RSVP I gave her. She then informed me she'd like to do it again. So hooray for the Cardex and all Sarah's lovely jewelry," writes UD JOY SMITH, Ayers Branch, West Virginia.

New Issue Comes To Life!

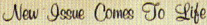

Unit Manager, IRENE WEITZEIL (Phillips Branch), California in sending these pictures along of the New Issue adds that "It's just wonderful". The beautiful lines of High Fashion, the elegance of Sea Whispers are really outstanding. Simply Elegant is just like its name. All the pieces are terrific. On the left - Br. Mgr. Dorothy Phillips presents the Fall issue while on the right we see High Fashion adding the finishing touch to a french twist.

District Manager, "Johnnie" Williams of the Cannon Region, Nevada introduces new jewelry issue as members of her group join in modelling and admiring the new issue.

DON'T WONDER, ASK US!

QUESTION: Will "Golden Avocado" earrings be available for pierced ears?
— CHRISTINE COLE
Burchardt Branch, N.Y.

ANSWER: Sorry, we have no plans for them at this time.

QUESTION: Will "Pearl Wardrobe" ever be available in a longer length?
— LUCILLE RYAN
Owens Branch, Mass.

ANSWER: Probably in the near future.

QUESTION: Do you think "Designer's Choice" earrings will ever be made into scatter pins?
— UD G. LIVENSPIRE
Schiemann Reg., Ohio

ANSWER: I doubt it.

QUESTION: 1. Will it be possible to have earrings that match our "High Fashion" pin?

2. Will it be possible to get "Simply Elegant" in goldentone?
— UD ANNA LOPEZ
Reich Br., N.Y.

ANSWER: 1. Not at this time.

2. Sorry, no.

Your questions are answered by **aileen**.

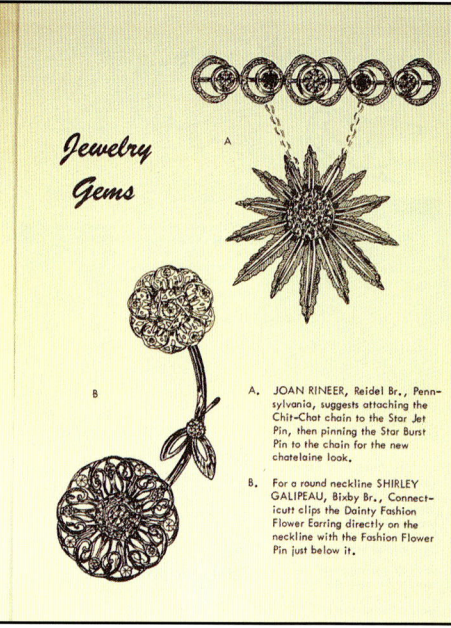

Jewelry Gems

A. JOAN RINEER, Reidel Br., Pennsylvania, suggests attaching the Chit-Chat chain to the Star Jet Pin, then pinning the Star Burst Pin to the chain for the new chatelaine look.

B. For a round neckline SHIRLEY GALIPEAU, Bixby Br., Connecticutt clips the Dainty Fashion Flower Earring directly on the neckline with the Fashion Flower Pin just below it.

Here Comes Santa Claus!

This is the first time I've been asked to write a fashion column, but being a typical little girl of "three" plus I love clothes and jewelry, I think it will be kinda fun to tell you what jewelry I like to wear with what.

When I'm playing around the house in the morning or going to toy school I wear my plaid wool slacks and white orlon sweater, I like to wear just a bracelet and my favorite is "Playmate". Notice I'm holding my Santa Claus to remind you that little girls like to get jewelry from Santa.

When I'm going to wear a blouse and skirt and my knee socks, I still don't like to wear too much jewelry, so I just have Mom put on my "Funny Face" necklace.

Now I'm getting dressed to go to a party, so I put on my blue velveteen jumper with the white blouse with embroidery blue hearts and pink roses and my "Hearts and Flowers" necklace and bracelet. This set looks real pretty with my outfit, and any little girl would like to get it for Christmas.

When Sundays here and I'm putting on my favorite organdy dress with a stick out slip, (my dress is aqua with pink rose embroidery at the waist) "Party Time" necklace and bracelet looks just right with this dress for either Sunday school or parties. Besides they wiggle.

I'm not wearing jewelry now, cause I must put my jewelry away carefully in a cotton lined box, if I want it to last and look nice.

Good night,
Patty

P.S. Don't forget little girls like to get fashion jewelry for Christmas.

THINGS WE LOVE TO HEAR

Dear Sarah:
I am writing a letter of praise and gratitude for my Branch Manager Maxine A. Miller. She is always there when we girls need her, and is willing to drop everything and help us when we run into trouble. In the last promotion, "Fashions In Orbit", I had quite a few bookings and most of them in the third week of the promotion. I worked the first two weeks, then was unexpectedly rushed to the hospital very sick with a staph infection.
Maxine held my shows for me and left them in my name so I wouldn't lose the prizes I was working for. One was a "century show" and two others were over $75.00. So thanks to a wonderful and thoughtful Manager I am the winner of the lovely prizes.
I think my Manager can't be beat.
— FSD GAY GIARDINI
Miller Branch, North Dakota

Dear Sir:
Enclosed is a money order in the amount of $132.01 which is the total payment of the jewelry I received.
The jewelry arrived safely at my home and is now in the hands of the girls who placed the orders. They are all completely satisfied and very well pleased with their jewelry. I would like to add 16 more satisfied customers to your great list.
Marlene Teal, Fashion Show Director, is a very pleasant person and all of the girls liked her.
— ROSEMARY CAPUANO, Ohio
A Sarah Coventry Hostess

Editor's note: FSD MARLENE TEAL is from the D. Schiemann Region, Ohio

Dear Signet Editor:
I want the whole Sarah Family to know about the most outstanding group of FSD's in Sarah – The Maraden Branch. I should know – I'm their proud Manager Jean Maraden. September 3rd I was admitted to the hospital for 4 weeks. My UD Nancy Babyak and my FSD's took over. They not only did the job of selling, booking and recruiting, interviews, meetings and training classes – they made it a spectacular. Thanks, girls, I'll make it up by being a better, healthier Manager.
— BR JEAN MARADEN, Pennsylvania

J. D. & Olive Buchanan Branches
SAN DIEGO, CALIFORNIA

Left above:
UD LEONOR DELANO (rt.) of San Diego with two of her Spanish-speaking FSDs at recent Anaheim, California Seminar.
Right above:
Gold Key Winners: FSD Mrs. Parks of Los Angeles, Leonor Delano and Dorothy Nothwang.
Presentations made by Executive Vice President Dan O'Farrell Zermeno.
Left below:
FSD Betty Scott being presented awards for an outstanding job during recent "Fashions in Orbit" promotion.
Right below:
FSDs and UDs of both J.D. and Olive's Branch promote lay-a-way idea for Christmas with the aid of RSVP and such props as Christmas stockings, styrofoam snowmen, sleighs, angels and the like. Reg. Mgr. Ruthe Angelo (2nd from right) shows her approval of the idea.

SARAH SALUTES THE STARS!

TOP TEN UNIT DIRECTORS		PERSONAL SALES
Lois B. Widmer	C. Briggs	$572.31
Billie Hildebrande	D. McDonald	$552.09
Connie Hoellerich	J. Chapman	$545.97
Joy Williams	J. Maddux	$468.74
Mary Zeigler	J. Zeigler	$429.87
Evelyn Mette	R. Bedell	$424.02
Shirley Cote	R. Roy	$410.50
LaVonne Jones	R. Denny	$405.41
Charlotte Styles	A. Cozzolino	$400.70
Anne M. Carroll	F. Weidman	$395.97

TOP TEN FASHION SHOW DIRECTORS		PERSONAL SALES
Alvin Magedoff	P. Magedoff	$716.96
Ann Gibilisco	K. G. Snyder	$594.56
Carol Heidel	M. Skilling	$570.85
Elinore Barnett	R. Sallee	$524.05
Ruth Pfeffer	R. Gilbert, Jr.	$503.18
Darlene C. Reimer	M. D. Millward	$482.88
F. Stubblefield	J. Rehders	$469.79
Patricia Laporto	J. Pietrofesa	$464.14
Jane Siford	D. Burnap, Sr.	$457.73
Audrey Lieving	P. Koranza	$456.38

IBM Dated 10/17/62

EXPLANATION OF COMPUTATION FOR TOP NATIONAL MANAGER...
1 point for each $100 volume, plus 100 points for each start, plus 50 points for each % of activity.

HERE AND THERE WITH SARAH

FSD PATRICIA HERMAN was presented with a Lady Buxton jewel chest by Br. Mgr. Rita Tarquino, right, and Div. Mgr. Richard O'Donnell, left. Pat was high FSD in the Hecker Region, New York for the "Fashions in Orbit" contest.

At left is JOYCE GORGON, newest UD in the T. Tipton Branch, Texas. Joyce, a Fashions in Orbit winner, was queen of the Branch her last week as FSD. Joyce attributes her success to the fact that her Unit Manager Mildred Gorsie encouraged and helped her so much. At the middle of the fourth week of Fall recruiting she had half her goal made for the Del Coronado. Joyce's husband Rick, an Army man, helps her with the children. A part-time FSD, he also helps by holding shows and recruiting.

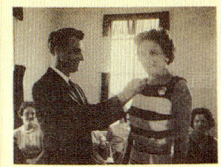

Pictured at right is UD JOAN SOVINSKY, McFadden Branch, Louisiana. Awarding her Gold Key with pearls is Division Manager Jack Reed.

ALL MEMBERS OF SARAH'S FAMILY

UD ELAINE HERALD and UD DOTTIE REYNOLDS, shown at right with Regional Manager Bill Seifert, shared a birthday cake presented to them recently at a Unit Meeting of the Gwen Seifert Branch, Virginia.

New recruits in the Randy Mink Area, Lou Gigi Region, during the Fall Recruiting Drive really got "the red carpet treatment". When due to a shipping strike in New York their kits were delayed, Randy and Lou (pictured here) sought the warehouse where kits were stored and took it upon themselves to deliver same.

Sarah's Fashion Coordinator Aileen VanTyle proudly displays the Mead Citation, awarded to Case-Hoyt (the company that prints our Cardex) and Sarah Coventry for outstanding color photography and printing in regard to Sarah's Cardex.

Around the towns with Sarah!

The Burnap Branch, Indiana, congratulates their Queen, JANE SILFORD, with sales of $380.78. Also to be complimented are SALLY WENZEL with $291.45, NANCY BECKWITH with $247.72, L. SOMMER $210.47 and ALMA GARDNER $203.04. Top honors for recruiting go to RUTH GRABNER who had 4 starts and to SELMA BOWERS with 3 starts.

THERESA BASSETT is Queen of the Crupi Branch, New Jersey. Her sales - $396.46.

Sales of $403.39 qualified GISELE GIBSON as Queen of the Gregware Branch, New York. Runner up is FLORENCE PRAIRIE with $357.19.

Again Queen of the Cline Branch, Michigan is able BESSIE DAUGHARTY who scored this time with $354.10 in sales. Following close behind, as she did before is PHYLLIS POLING. Newcomers JUNE MOYLE and BONNIE MILLER are to be congratulated, too.

High in sales in the Wessels Branch, Illinois, is MILDRED LAUK with 5 shows and sales of $418.00. Also high were HELEN EBERT, DONNA HOBBS, ALICE CASAZZA, MAY ROMANCK and JANE BOWLING.

CHARLOTTE GENTILE walked off with the honors in the Nolan Branch, New York. Two evenings - two shows - one of $295.99 and one of $196.70 - gave Charlotte a total of $492.69. Congratulations, too, go to JOAN THOMPSON whose total was $240.46.

The Hammock Branch, Ohio is cheering FLORENCE SCHANK with one top volume show of $296.66. We're cheering, too.

AROUND THE TOWNS (continued)

Hats off to the Queen of the LaGrange Branch, Missouri! She's CHLOE BEHLING whose sales totaled $463.84 plus 10 Bookings and 1 recruit.

Top honors in the Bedell Branch, California, this week go to EVELYN METTE with $503.97 and runner-up JANICE GAGE with $439.12. Both had two century shows.

The Egdall Branch, Massachusetts, congratulates RALPH COSTA who had a "really big show" of $518.66 followed by another that quickly brought his total volume to $581.87.

Sales of $258.28 qualified DOROTHY HANSEN as Queen of the Agens Branch, Pennsylvania.

LINDA LUX of the Pugh Branch, New York reigns as Queen in her group with sales of over $200.00 while HELEN HOST took top honors for her high show of $165.00.

Congratulations to newly promoted Unit Manager HELEN TURNEY of the Hamman Branch, Oklahoma for her sales of $251.04 plus ten bookings.

Queen of the Nelson Branch, Michigan is MONA KACZUK with $212.63 in sales. New FSD MARGARET STANLEY is winning laurels already with a starter show of $106.27 volume and six bookings.

Another newcomer, FRANCES SCHWIERKING, of the Schiemann Branch, Ohio, is off to a fine start with $183.94 in sales and 9 bookings.

High sales honors in the Birney Branch, Ohio go to SUE ROGERS who in her second week of business had $295.32. Century shows were held by Sue and by BETTY CUZZONE.

Volume star in the M. Riedel Branch, Pennsylvania this week is NORMA RUTTKAY with $257.98, followed closely by BETTY FISHER with $251.43.

NOT "SITTIN' PRETTY"
"Sittin' Pretty" is a service piece on which no commission is paid and is not considered an item on the 2 & 1 plan.

Fashion Newsy Notes

PASSED ON TO US BY......

.....FSD Sandra Laughinghouse, B. Evigan Branch, N. J. - "I find that the PEARL WARDROBE earrings on the rhinestone side look very lovely with the NITE LITES ring."

.....FSD Alpha Trammell, G. Seifert Br., Va. - "My high school teen-ager likes to use her YOUNG AND GAY bracelet for a friendship bracelet. They put charms on it - in the rings."

.....FSD Joan Lannaye, M. Skilling Br., Wisc. - "I wear LUCKY PENNY or YOUNG AND GAY bracelet around my ponytail to hide the rubber band. They can be brightened up by a single earring attached to the center of the bracelet."

.....FSD Shirley Heine, N. Diak Br., N. J. - "Last evening I was rushing to go out. As luck would have it the handle on my purse broke. I used the smallest section of CHAIN O' FASHION as the handle and attached one bauble to each end. I had loads of compliments. Needless to say Sarah Coventry Jewelry is truly versatile."

.....UD Pamela Kohnhorst, A. Capps Br., No. Car. - "Just have to let you know what teen-agers here are doing with the SITTIN' PRETTY pins. They are buying 3 or 4 of them and wearing them 'step style' on sweaters and dresses."

.....FSD Marilyn A. Baker, D. Chrysler Br., N. Y. - "I frequently combine SILVERY CASCADE and GOLDEN CASCADE into one attractive necklace. This can be worn with the FASHION LEAF, FROSTED FEATHERS or WINDFALL earrings."

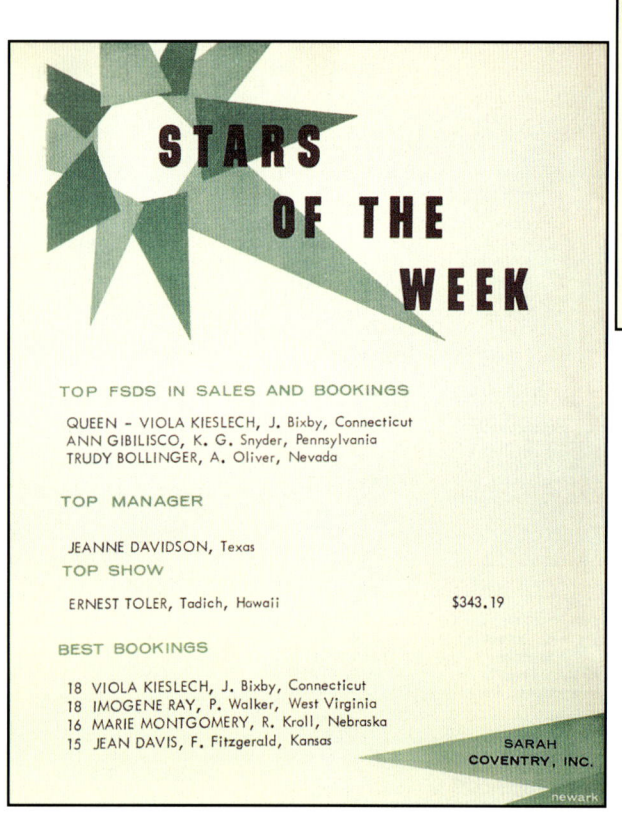

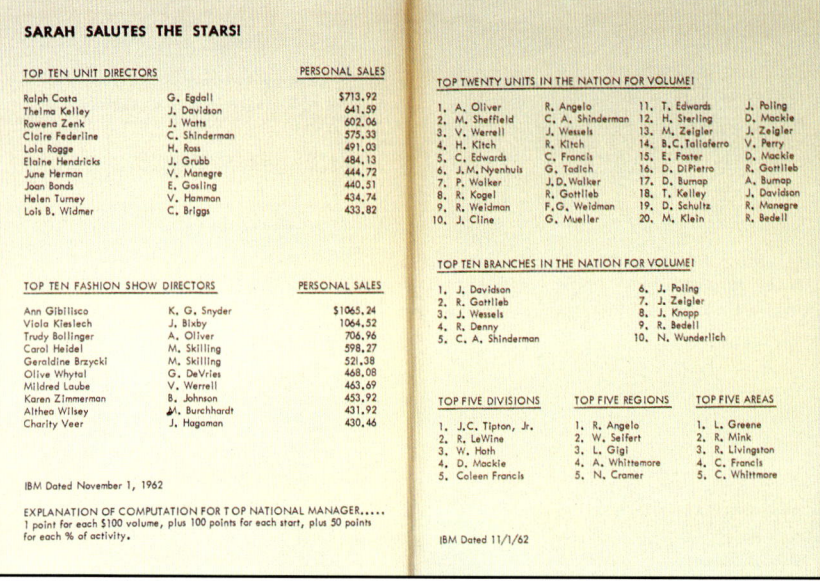

A second *Signet* is included here to show some of the information continuously provided to the field employees by the Sarah Coventry company. *Courtesy of Jan Koltes.*

Know "Your" Right Moment

William Shakespeare, aside from being one of the world's greatest playwrites, also left behind some very quotable quotes, one of which is, "There is a tide in the affairs of men which, taken at the flood, leads on to fortune."

In essence, Shakespeare is saying that there is a time in life when we are offered an opportunity to earn a virtual flood of rewards – IF we recognize and take advantage of the "right moment".

Your "right moment" is NOW – during our current Fashion Bingo program. Just for filling in one row of your Fashion Bingo score card, you have a choice of any one of three exciting gifts – each a very practical and useful gift for you or any member of your family.

Right now, with family vacations out of the way, is an excellent time to book more and more Shows. Very shortly "missy" and "junior" will be in school giving the mother of the house a great deal more free time to think about her personal jewelry wardrobe.

Yes, from now until the first of the year is "your right moment" to BOOK, SELL – and equally important – RECRUIT.

Be sure to take full advantage NOW of the exciting and rewarding Fashion Bingo program by filling in as many rows as you can.

"Know Your Right Moment" by filling row after row and ending in the dough!

GOOD SELLING,

Bernie Marshall
Assistant Promotion Manager

YOUR "SIGNET" IS PUBLISHED WEEKLY IN THE OFFICES OF SARAH COVENTRY, INC., SALES PROMOTION DEPARTMENT. OFFICERS OF THE COMPANY: C. W. "BILL" STUART, PRESIDENT; REX WOOD, EXECUTIVE VICE PRESIDENT IN CHARGE OF SALES; JOHN JOYCE, EXECUTIVE VICE PRESIDENT and GENERAL MANAGER; AL WINFREY, VICE PRESIDENT - SALES PROMOTION.

EDITOR IN CHIEF	ALTHEA SMITH
FASHION EDITOR - - - - JEWELRY GEMS	AILEEN VAN TYLE
RECRUITING RECORDS	GLADYS HODGE
EDITOR OF "THE DIGEST" (FOR MANAGERS ONLY)	BARBARA DEANE
SALES INCENTIVES - - - PREMIUM INFORMATION	GLORIA SCHWEITZ
WEEKLY MEETING GUIDES	BARBARA DEANE
SALES PROMOTION INFORMATION	BERNIE MARSHALL
KIT, PAYROLL and SUPPLIES	BARRY HEATH
SALES COORDINATOR	DICK GOODMAN
ADMINISTRATION, GENERAL INFORMATION	MANDELL COOKE
CREDIT INFORMATION	KEN CODDE
ARTIST	MARLENE WAGEMAKER

SARAH COVENTRY, INC.   COPYRIGHT 1963   NEWARK, NEW YORK

THINGS WE LOVE TO HEAR

Dear Aileen,
Must drop you a line to tell you I think the new issue is beautiful. I thought what we had was terrific, but Sarah really out-did herself.
If this doesn't sell well, nothing will!
Thanks for the great pick-me-up. I was starting to get depressed and thought I would never have a good Show this summer. Well, I sure will now!
– FSD SANDY GERHOLD
Appel Branch, New Jersey

Dear Sarah,
I am a FSD who did not want to be one but thanks to the perseverance of Branch Manager Charles Patterson, I was finally signed up. Mr. Patterson told me I would have fun. Well, I am having a ball! The jewelry grows on you and I found it is easy to sell. I understand I am first in line for the Pioneer pin in my Branch so far.
My son is also a FSD and he is having as much fun as I am. He's 18 and still going to school but intends to continue his work during school days. Mothers take note: get the boys in on this, too, it helps pay for clothes and gives them spending money besides.
– FSD BETTY MUDGE
Patterson Branch

Dear Aileen,
Sarah's new fall line of jewelry is very exciting and simply elegant, and best of all, very versatile!
Thank you for a wonderful opportunity.
– FSD MARY ANN HEILSBERG
F. Wilson Branch

Dear Aileen,
We received the new fall issue yesterday. It's lovely! It really is just right for the new fashion styles in clothing for fall.
– FSD LINDA THURM
Wessels Branch

New Jewelry Fashion Show

AYERS BRANCH HOLDS "CHRISTMAS IN JULY" STYLE SHOW

Two hundred women gathered to view the latest in fall jewelry in the lovely ball room of a local hotel when the Ayers Branch presented their "Christmas in July" style show recently. Door prizes were given and 48 bookings obtained. Modeling Sarah's new jewelry were:

1. FSD BETTY KELLEY wearing "Woven Classic" with a Chanel-style jacket.
2. Hostess Betty Snodgrass chose "Nature's Choice" to accent her basic dress.
3. Hostess Kay Wingrove wearing "Pearl Flattery" – perfect accent with her black dinner dress.
4. FSDs BERTHA SAULTON and DELORAS McVEY showing "Flirtation" and "Sun Flower."
5. FSD MAYDA OLSON showing the Hostess Special and a special for fall, "Molten Topaz."
6. FSD PAULINE TUCKER in popular, pendant style "Stunning-Plus" and "After Five" ring.

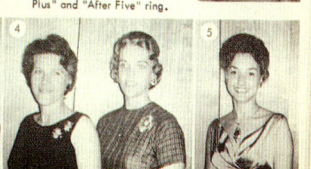

BOOSTERS

SHOW BOOSTER

"I purchased a thirty-cup electric coffee maker to loan to my Hostess," writes FSD JEWEL CRAWFORD, L. Weber Branch. "You'd be surprised how this helps in booking Shows. In most areas, you can get them for trading stamps. I also have folding chairs which I offer. This has been a tremendous booking booster for me!"

FASHION BOOSTER

"Something I find most successful and a real interest-holder during my presentation is a 'Fashion Board'," writes Branch Manager JERI CHAPMAN. "I covered a piece of plasterboard (about 2 feet by 3 feet) with fabric. On this I tack illustrations from fashion magazines showing the variety of places where pins can be worn – in the hair, at the hip, etc. I include many small pictures showing how popular chains and pearls are, and so on, and during my demonstration I refer to this. Right in the center I have 2 center pages from the Signet telling about Sarah jewelry being worn on the US Steel Hour and Garry Moore shows. We know what a prestige Company we are and I want to be sure all the Guests at my Shows know. I have found a visual item such as the fashion board really backs up the presentation. Hope this helps someone else."

PRE-CHRISTMAS BOOSTER

"Last year, after the Christmas Season when the gift wrap and greeting cards went on sale, I bought a considerable amount of these items at very reasonable prices, to be used as gifts at my Fashion Shows," writes FSD SHIRLEY HOACHLANDER, H. Willis Branch.

"With the new line of jewelry out, I intend to have a drawing at each Show for all the Guests who purchase 3 items or more. The person whose name is drawn will receive her choice of a 4-roll pack of Christmas wrap or a box of greeting cards. I have already booked 3 Shows for the new August issue. I believe this will give the Guests an incentive to buy jewelry for Christmas gifts and to do their shopping early."

DON'T WONDER - ASK US!

QUESTION:
1. Will we have identification bracelets for men? for women?
2. Will we have jewelry especially made for hair, shoes, hats or bags?
3. Will we have charm bracelets for children? for women?
4. Will we ever have odd-shaped rings for teen agers?
5. Will "Parisienne Nights" or "Celebrity" come in a smaller size?
6. How about having a section of the Signet for creative booking ideas and hints for oldtimers and newcomers?
– UD BARBARA LISA
Crupi Branch

ANSWER:
1. No, we will not have either.
2. Probably not.
3. Yes, we will probably have them for both.
4. I don't believe I know what you have in mind.
5. No.
6. Excellent! Send in your ideas, won't you!

QUESTION: I believe the earrings to "Fashion Parade" are too small. Do you think we will ever have daring ones?
– UD MARGE UCHWAT
Michaelis Branch

ANSWER: No, but other pearl or pearl and gold earrings can be worn with the necklace such as "Pearl Elegance", "Egyptian Temptress", etc.

QUESTION: Is there any chance of having the jewelry shipped in gift boxes?
– FSD JEAN MELLODY
Marts Branch

ANSWER: We are studying a new box idea at this time.

Your questions are answered by *aileen.*

Shall We Dance?

Meet Swen Swenson, the brilliant young actor-singer-dancer, who has been stopping the show cold at every performance of "Little Me" with his exciting first act song and dance, "I've Got Your Number."

This popular and handsome newcomer tipped his black bowler in appreciation when he was presented with Sarah's fashionable goldentone ON THE SQUARE tie tac and cuff links.

A man with that certain "know-how" about fashions, Swen felt that this design was the perfect complement for this distinguished pin-striped suit, or any other suit in his wardrobe.

Photographs courtesy of Avery Willard

Call-Back Stories

Don't Take "No" For An Answer

"Tell the girls not to take the first 'no' for an answer," writes FSD ROSEMARIE FOSCHIA, R. Bartges Region. "Wait awhile and then call back. It implants the idea in their head and possibly by the time you go back they are ready to have a Show.

"It worked for me; had a $75.00 Show and got another booking from it that I wouldn't have had if I'd taken 'no' the first time."

With Or Without An Excuse

"I am a former FSD who has just returned to work for Sarah after six years. Naturally, some changes have taken place during this time, one of which is the requirement to get credit information from the Hostess. On a recent occasion I had neglected to do this the night of the Show and had to call back the next day. The Hostess rebooked for those unable to attend the first Show. I also booked another girl I hadn't had the opportunity to talk with because she left the Show early. Now I know how important Call-Backs are, with or without a necessary excuse," writes FSD JEWEL CRAWFORD, L. Weber Branch.

Take Time To Call Back

"I have a friend who has given me several good orders and I gave her a pretty item of RSVP," writes FSD SUE BRADY, Moore Branch. She would not give me a Show because she works so hard. I had a delivery I wanted to make to her in person since she did not have a car to come and get it. On the fourth of July I caught her home. She was so pleased with some of the jewelry I brought along to show her she ordered over $19.00 worth. With her family's help we built this into a $25.00 Show with a promise of a booking from her daughter-in-law.

"I was glad that I went in person to see her – this Show made me a Princess for the fourth of July week and helped me win my "Parisienne Nights" bracelet and many other prizes. Take time out to visit your Hostesses and former customers. My friend has a Cardex now and I think she will have other orders for me."

Winners All

IN THE KABISCH BRANCH –

FSD PAT NECHEL, right, happily accepts floral arrangement from Branch Manager MARY LOU KABISCH, left. Pat, who was Branch Queen during every week of the Trader Rex promotion, is a go-getter doing a terrific job in both sales and bookings.

IN THE MARTS BRANCH –

FSD SYLVIA FITE, looking more than pleased, is awarded "Parisienne Nights" bracelet, below, by Branch Manager CHARLES MARTS for her achievement in the 4th of July Special. Sylvia is now training to become a UD.

FSD KEN REUTER, winner of the floral arrangement during the Trader Rex promotion (above right) was also King of Sales in the Marts Branch this week with $210.01 in sales.

In pic at left above Ken's wife Lolly shows him how well she likes "Parisienne Nights" bracelet he won for her during the 4th of July Special.

Fashion Hints

PASSED ON TO US BY . . . . .

. . . FSD IDA DUPIO, Nyenhuis Branch, who suggests that Sarah pins can be worn easily in short hair by simply taking a small piece of hair and making a tiny "pony tail" out of it with a rubber band where the pin is to be positioned. Fastened through the rubber band the pin will not slip as it would if fastened to hair pins or bobby pins.

. . . FSD LOUISE LEGAZ, Sterling Branch, who says, "Lucky Penny" and 'Fashionette' bracelets look lovely with 'Fashion Parade' necklace and earrings."

. . . FSD DELORIS SWINFORD, W. Jernigan Branch. Deloris suggests that it is often well to mention the "Stunning" pin to people who wear glasses. It's the perfect place to hang your glasses and is an especially good idea for nurses, teachers, office workers or even for housewives.

. . . FSD BARBARA SHIMKO, James McDonald Branch, says, "Try wearing one of our earrings in the center of the headbands that are so popular now. They really dress them up."

. . . FSD JANE SIFORD, L. OBrien Region always suggests using the bracelet extender to lengthen "Golden" or "Silvery Cascade" necklace for those who find they need a slightly longer length. She reminds us that it's the bracelet extender not the necklace extender that fits "Cascade" necklaces.

. . . FSD HELEN THOMPSON, A. Baker Branch who uses the "Young N' Gay" bracelet for an easily-adjustable extender for "Golden" or "Silvery Cascade". She then can wear the earrings to either set to complement the necklace.

. . . FSD MARGARET A. BENNETT, Kuna Branch, who comments that the new "After Five" ring is outstanding when paired with "Mystic" earrings.

. . . FSD BEVERLY SCHOFIELD, also of the Kuna Branch. Beverly suggests that the "High Fashion" pin or "Starburst" pin look lovely on a dark fur hat or collar.

. . . FSD SUE BRADY, Ernest Moore Branch, says that a large "Celebrity" earring makes a lovely accent on a white fur hat, while the pin looks equally well on a matching white fur collar. For a simple earring to wear with this combination, Sue suggests "Stunning."

CARDEX WINNERS

REMEMBER – don't use Cardex instead of a regular Fashion Show, but rather in addition to. Let your Cardex be a plus for you.

CARDEX FINDS A WAY – "I'd been creative booking in a small town and having poor results. I was all ready to call it quits when this woman sent me to see a school teacher. School was just out and she was planning to have a relaxed vacation. She didn't think she could do too well with a Cardex Show but she'd try if I'd give her extra time. I made the exception and was I glad I did!

"I went back last Thursday to pick up the order. She had a $75.69 order, seven 2 and 1 orders, she came in for the VP Special and earned $20.00 worth of jewelry for herself, 4 pieces of RSVP from me plus the free pieces she and all her Guests are going to get from the Company – which she knew nothing about.

"She was delighted, her husband was delighted and I was delighted for her. Hats off to the Cardex and such a terrific promotion just when we needed it."
- FSD STELLA SHANK
Warner Branch

CARDEX CROWNS A QUEEN – "I would like to share with you my wonderful experience with Cardex. I held a Show where only 4 Guests showed up, with total orders amounting to $33.83. My Hostess took my Cardex to work with her and two days later called to report additional orders of $100.00!

"Since the VP Special and the Firecracker Special were both on, my Hostess got extra credits, and has promised to have another Show very soon. A happy Hostess and a happy FSD – because the sales helped me to become Queen of the Unit for that week. I have only been with Sarah for two short months, and I must say I am very pleased with the opportunities presented by our Company. Thank you so much!"
- FSD JOANNE BREINING
Bedell Division

BULLETIN BOARD

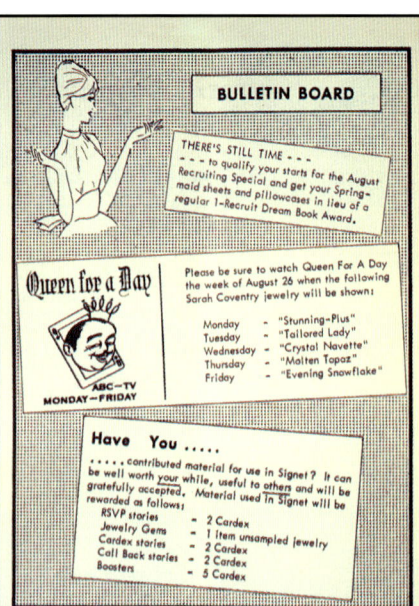

THERE'S STILL TIME - - -
- - - to qualify your starts for the August Recruiting Special and get your Spring-maid sheets and pillowcases in lieu of a regular 1-Recruit Dream Book Award.

Please be sure to watch Queen For A Day the week of August 26 when the following Sarah Coventry jewelry will be shown:

Monday — "Stunning-Plus"
Tuesday — "Tailored Lady"
Wednesday — "Crystal Navette"
Thursday — "Molten Topaz"
Friday — "Evening Snowflake"

Have You .....

. . . . . contributed material for use in Signet? It can be well worth your while, useful to others and will be gratefully accepted. Material used in Signet will be rewarded as follows:

RSVP stories — 2 Cardex
Jewelry Gems — 1 item unsampled jewelry
Cardex stories — 2 Cardex
Call Back stories — 2 Cardex
Boosters — 5 Cardex

New FSDs Praise R.S.V.P. Special

"Six weeks with Sarah Coventry has been 'real pleasure,'" writes FSD LOIS WILKINS, G. Gzechowicz Branch. "The RSVP jewelry given to each buying Guest has boosted sales tremendously.

"So many Cardex orders had been taken in one plant near here that my Hostess was afraid she would receive no orders when she took the Cardex but the RSVP jewelry really worked. The girls working with her gladly gave her orders, even though they had ordered from others the week before.

"Thanks so much for the sales boosters you give us FSDs!"

"Because of the wonderful RSVP offer Sarah made," writes FSD JOAN BLOMQUIST, Cafaro Branch, "I booked 8 Shows for the next two weeks. The Shows were booked at two Fashion Shows held within four days of one another with a total of 13 women attending the 2 Shows. Then, both Hostesses rebooked. Also two past Hostesses booked (making the fourth Show for each) and four people I had never met booked. They were very impressed.

"I am very proud to be part of the Sarah Family."

Have you had an interesting experience with RSVP jewelry? If you have please send us your story. If it can be used in Signet you will receive an award of 2 Cardex.

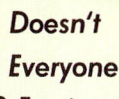

"DOESN'T EVERY woman have lots of earrings?" Mrs. Ada McKellepp asks with surprise.

You see, she thinks there's nothing remarkable about her collection of 130 pairs of them — all of which are worn with as great a regularity as one woman can reasonably wear 260 earrings.

Mrs. McKellepp, who lives at 127 E. Arlington ave., has been accumulating earrings for about 10 years. Most of them are gifts from friends, and none are of great value, she says.

Mrs. McKellepp, a waitress in a downtown restaurant, wears earrings every day. But even at that rate, each of her 130 pairs would get worn only twice a year.

Faced with that fact, Mrs. McKellepp grins and admits: "Okay, I guess you could call it a hobby."

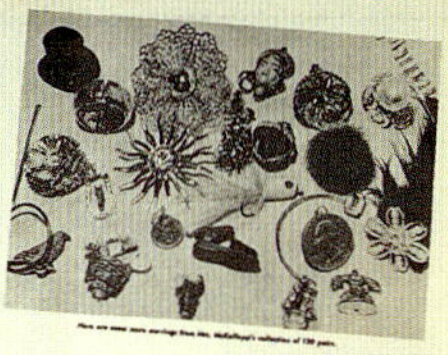

Doesn't Everyone Own 260 Earrings?

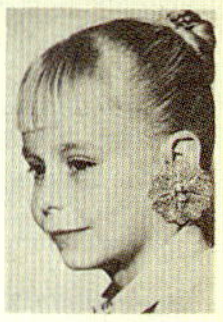

Editor's Comment: You'll notice Mrs. McKellepp has many Sarah Coventry earrings among her favorites.

Article from "St. Paul Sunday Pioneer Press."

Mrs. McKellepp's daughter Gracie, 7, tries on some of her mom's earrings.

UD VISITS SARAH'S HOME

UD NORMA JEAN SIMMONS and her husband are shown at left with Fashion Coordinator Aileen VanTyle.

It was a pleasure to welcome this up-and-coming gal from the M. Hammock Branch to Sarah's Home Office.

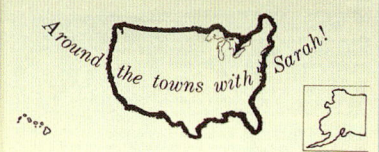

Congratulations to Queen of the E. J. Stoops Branch FSD BETTY FARRAR. Betty topped everyone in the Branch with a grand total of $353.35 in sales last week. No wonder the Branch is so proud of her.

"There's gold in them there hills," says FSD RUTH MOON, and she should know — she's Queen of the Denious Branch for the third week in a row with sales of $334.15. Runner-up is FSD LENA WIGGS.

The Buck Region this week announces that both its Queens are from the Shinderman Branch. FSD Queen is CHRISTINE WILLIAMS. UD Queen is CLAIRE FEDERLINE with personal sales of $311.12.

FSD C. HEIDEL reigns as Queen of the M. Skilling Branch this week. Her volume totaled a neat $310.59 for the week.

UD MARGARET HUGHS, winner of 5 sets each of "Celestial Fire" and "Midnight Magic" in a recent Area contest, is Queen of the H. Warner Branch this week with total sales of $310.10.

Queen of the E. Hicks Branch is FSD LYNORA REEVES with $305.84 in sales which include 2 Century Shows. UD ROSIE SNELL had a Century Show because her Hostess wanted to be eligible to attend the Branch's preview showing of the new issue and built her Show from $65.00.

FSD CHLOE BEHLING reigns as Queen of the M. Clines Unit, E. Thompson Area with sales of $208.19 plus 15 new bookings.

FSD CAROLYN MARKEGENE, B. L. Sitton Branch, visited a nearby Army hospital on August 1. Star total — one baby girl, 6 lbs. 13 ozs. Good show, Carolyn!

AROUND THE TOWNS WITH SARAH (continued)

Queen of the Moskal Branch is FSD JEAN SMITH with a Double Century Show totaling $247.00. Happy Hostess, too, with $52.00 credit. HELEN ROACH had the most advanced bookings in the Branch — a total of 7.

FSD LILY SMITH is Queen and FSD WYNONIA McGLOTHING is runner-up in Acting Division Manager C. Scott's own group. Wynonia celebrated her third week with Sarah with a Century Show.

Queen of the week in the J. Williams Branch is CHRISTINE DUGGER with ETHEL MARSHALL running a close second. Both of these FSDs had a Century Show among their sales for the week.

UD HAZEL SPOTTS scored as Queen of the F. Groover Branch with high personal sales.

The Vaughn Branch this week honors FSD WILMA KOLB as Queen of the Branch with high sales as well as high Show for the week.

FSD JUDY MILLER of the Tucker Branch was a very excited and happy girl when her very first Fashion Show became a Century with 3 bookings. A fine start, Judy!

Three FSDs vied for top spot in the L. Rinehart Branch this week. MITZIE WOOD won out with high sales in the Branch, followed closely by runners-up VEONA SPENCER and MADALINE GASKILL.

FSD DELORA FARISH is Queen of the G. Hopkins Branch, and was winner of the Court of Flags charm and the Sterling Silver State charm during the SCP program.

In the M. Huff Branch, Queen last week was FSD JOAN TRABER with sales of $212.81 while this week FSD FERN FRENTZ took the honors with $204.64 in sales. Joan also won the State charm as well as "Orbie" during SCP.

quickie show pays off in Werrell Branch

Five minutes after leaving a meeting the evening of August 5, the day she received the new issue, FSD SHIRLEY JERO held an unexpected Show at 10:00 P.M. She stopped at an aunt's to show her the new jewelry. The aunt, in turn, called 3 neighbors and from them Shirley received an order for $32.86. Adds Shirley, "this order was on new items only as that was all I had along with me — plus Shopping Guides. Thanks to Sarah for this lovely assortment."

Here & There With Sarah

IN THE NANCE BRANCH — FSD MARIE CAGEL was presented the flower arrangement for top FSD in sales for the Branch during the "Trader Rex" promotion. Branch Manager ANNE NANCE made the presentation (below).

IN THE SMYTH BRANCH — Br. Mgr. MAUD SMYTH (above - center) with members of her Branch who attended a pot-luck dinner and auction examine a replica of Sarah's Court of Flags. Out of town guests included Asst. Prom. Mgr. BERNIE MARSHALL (seated - left) and GLADYS HODGE (seated - right), and Act. Area Mgr. DOCK McDONALD (standing - rear).

SARAH GOES TO THE FAIR

A grand total of 40 bookings, 4 recruits, $180.00 in sales and hundreds of leads resulted when the Faylene Groover Branch took Sarah to the county fair. Below right, is the lovely pink and white display booth occupied by Sarah. At left, FSD DOTTIE ORWIG, one of the many FSDs whose efforts made the display such a big success, writes an order.

SARAH SALUTES THE STARS!

TOP TEN UNIT DIRECTORS

		PERSONAL SALES
Ernestine Provart	E. Thompson	$590.70
Paulette Magedoff	E. Holsman	560.08
Dorothy Hines	E. Moore	544.28
Claire Federline	C. Shinderman	417.18
Edna Foust	R. McNabb	390.36
Keith Dodd	G. Finch	375.87
Cora Kinkead	R. Kinzie	346.44
Jean Woody	B. Denious	333.46
Patricia Stevens	M. Portesi	315.74
Thelma McConnell	S. Hoyt	315.42

TOP TEN FASHION SHOW DIRECTORS

		PERSONAL SALES
Annette Schimming	Judy Howeth	$668.70
Ruth Moon	B. Denious	417.61
Jeannette Hagthrop	F. Wilson	406.95
Geraldine Reed	B. Johnson	404.09
Dorothy Krumpos	A. Nagley	403.13
Gloria King	D. Phillips	397.37
Linda Parker	G. Finch	390.80
Florence Kendall	P. Whitney	390.59
Carol Heidel	M. Skilling	374.65
Edythe Brooks	C. Esposito	370.21

IBM Dated 8/8/63

EXPLANATION OF COMPUTATION FOR TOP NATIONAL MANAGER...
1 point for each $100 volume, plus 100 points for each start, plus 50 points for each % of activity.

SARAH SALUTES THE STARS!

TOP AREA IN EACH ZONE

Zone 1	J. Renick
Zone 2	L. Greene
Zone 3	C. Cramer
Zone 4	South West
Zone 5	Southern California

TOP FIVE AREAS NATIONALLY

1. L. Greene
2. Southern California
3. I. Jessup
4. South West
5. C. Whittemore

TOP TEN DIVISIONS

1. E. Armbrister
2. O. Buchanan
3. R. Bedell
4. D. Reed
5. G. Seifert
6. E. Gosling
7. R. Manegre
8. R. O'Donnell
9. L. Hays
10. D. Chrysler

TOP TEN REGIONS

1. W. Seifert
2. A. Whittemore
3. K. Gosling
4. W. Cannon
5. J. C. Tipton
6. D. Virgil
7. G. Neal
8. C. Francis
9. W. Hoth
10. R. Buck

TOP TEN BRANCHES IN THE NATION FOR VOLUME

1. J. D. Buchanan
2. M. Thompson
3. M. Klein
4. M. L. Gilbert
5. J. D. Walker
6. M. Smyth
7. F. Wilson
8. H. Sterling
9. N. Wunderlich
10. E. Hoots

TOP TWENTY UNITS IN THE NATION FOR VOLUME

1. F. Watts	F. Wilson	11. H. Shaw	M. Spaulding
2. M. Rosengreen	M. Thompson	12. M. Finch	G. Finch
3. E. Miller	B. Miller	13. D. Nelson	J. D. Buchanan
4. O. Whitsel	E. Whitsel	14. Jeff Howeth	Judy Howeth
5. W. Buchanan	E. Akom	15. V. Ladd	M. L. Gilbert
6. E. Provart	E. Thompson	16. M. Saliture	R. Bedell
7. C. Federline	C. Shinderman	17. A. Orazi	L. Orazi
8. J. Lufter	E. Lufter	18. M. Clines	E. Thompson
9. M. J. Weldon	G. Ciaramitaro	19. D. French	A. Denny
10. M. S. Knight	E. Hoots	20. P. Byrd	G. Ciaramitaro

IBM Dated 8/8/63

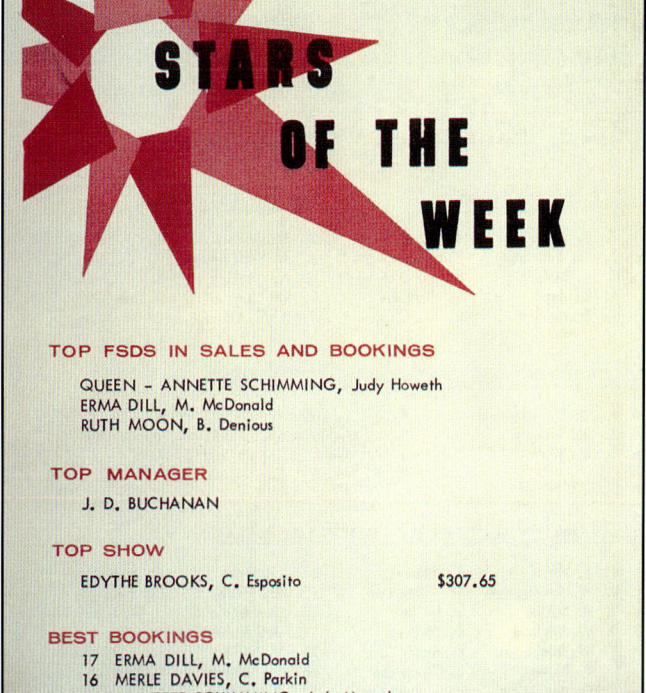

STARS OF THE WEEK

TOP FSDS IN SALES AND BOOKINGS

QUEEN - ANNETTE SCHIMMING, Judy Howeth
ERMA DILL, M. McDonald
RUTH MOON, B. Denious

TOP MANAGER

J. D. BUCHANAN

TOP SHOW

EDYTHE BROOKS, C. Esposito $307.65

BEST BOOKINGS

17 ERMA DILL, M. McDonald
16 MERLE DAVIES, C. Parkin
15 ANNETTE SCHIMMING, Judy Howeth
16 EVELYN RECKART, E. Lufter

SARAH COVENTRY, INC.

IBM Dated 8/8/63

newark

Chapter Three

The Late 1960s: 1966-1969

The mid to late 1960s saw clothing fads change dramatically—from jeans all the way to mini-skirts. With these costumes, jewelry was not considered an accessory necessary for the total wardrobe look. Costume jewelry was changing as well—it had less glitz and was more simplistic, subtle, and wearable with various costumes. As you will see, however, Sarah Coventry kept up and in many cases led the fashion pack.

Fashion Show Directors for Sarah Coventry became even more important to the total picture during this time. One such promoter for you to meet is Dawn Michael. She began with Sarah in 1966, became a regional manager in 1971, and continued with the company through 1984. During the early years, Dawn told me, a perfect show consisted of $100 in sales, two party bookings, and one person recruited as a Fashion Show Director. There were many repeat customers and friends frequently rotated having parties, thereby securing pieces through the hostess credit bonus points.

Dawn Michael became a Fashion Show Director with Sarah Coventry in 1966 and continued with the company through 1984. Look for many pieces of her very large collection featured in this book.

Not pictured here is another Sarah employee I'd like you to meet—a most pleasant individual named Sara Ayers. Sara, who graciously provided me with my first view of the cardex file, started in 1959 and continued through 1981. Both she and her husband John were employees of Sarah Coventry, with Sara reaching the status of Sr. Vice President (the second woman to hold that title). John was an Area/Regional Manager. Sara commented to me that employees were respected by Sarah Coventry and that they could depend on the company standing behind them—as in the case of lost jewelry or kits. Dawn and Sara both described how the company helped the regional and area managers develop their own promotional materials, and also gave them the opportunity to promote others and make their own decisions. This again fostered the "family" feeling and the development of real leaders, helping to create a credible, fast growing, and successful company.

Advertising for Sarah Coventry kept the name continuously before the general public, with pieces of jewelry awarded to contestants and worn by actresses on television shows like *Queen for a Day*, *As The World Turns* and *Stars on Books*. Ads that ran continuously in popular magazines such as *Glamour*, *Red Book*, *Ladies' Home Journal*, *Good Housekeeping*, and many others caught the woman's eye for fashion jewelry. Such advertising techniques gave FSDs the support that made their direct selling much easier.

When Dawn Michael spoke enthusiastically of the company, she mentioned the many award trips that were totally paid for by the company as well as the numerous awards she received—from the plaques on her shelves and walls to the fur coat hanging in her closet. No doubt one of the most important benefits provided by the C.H. Stuart, Inc. company was the scholarship money available to employees' sons and daughters. Each year ten youth were selected to receive an amount ranging from $250 to $2500 a year. Dawn's son was a recipient of one of these scholarships, which assisted with his college program.

It was through Dawn's assistance and her collection of catalogs dating from 1966 through 1984 that I was able to identify much of my jewelry. There were three catalogs published each year—one usually in January, one for the spring/summer season, and one for fall/winter season. The 1966 and 1967 catalogs continued the very descriptive information previously found on the cards. In 1968, this information was drastically reduced, with only minimal information about each piece included in the catalog. Therefore, fewer captions in this section include excerpts from the actual catalog descriptions of the jewelry.

Dawn Michael surpasses anyone I have met to date for number of items in her collection—so many of her pieces have been added to this book. Thank you very much, Dawn, for your time and diligence in collecting through the years and for introducing this section of Sarah Coventry jewelry to the readers.

Brooches

Fashion Petals pins of orange, white, and jet black are three examples of the colorful enameled petals. Other colors were blue, hot pink, and green. These fashion pieces were in the spring catalogs but the information declared that such jewelry could bloom any time of the year. B; $10-20.

Top row, left to right: *Water Lily* pin has "shiny goldentone and white enameled petals making an unbeatable combination in this fresh-looking water lily design. A real three dimension look is achieved in this unusual, but life-like water lily set. Fashionably large but light and airy." SarahGlo goldentone. A; $10-25. ***Deep Burgundy*** pin is made of "gleaming golden petals surrounding a colorful center of deep burgundy glass stones securely held by prongs." Matching earrings on page 71, matching ring on page 81. A; $10-25. *Satin Petals* pin, "designed with sophisticated simplicity goldentone flower pin. So smart when pinned on your dress or coat. Equally as attractive when worn on a chain or pinned to your favorite fabric bag." The satin finish has both a textured and a smooth look and duplicates a very realistic design from nature. Matching earrings on page 73. A; $10-25. **Bottom row, left to right:** *Sunflower* pin is a unique variation of a sunflower design made of goldentone. A tailored effect was achieved by using layers of slender petals with scored edges surrounding a textured center button. This is one of several pieces with the name sunflower or sun flower. Matching earrings on page 74. A; $10-25. *Tailored Swirl* pin is a combination of satin and textured goldentone, creating an open and airy swirling pin. Matching earrings are on page 37. A; $10-25.

Top row, left to right: *Moonflower* pin has "textured silvertone petals surrounding a large high luster pearl (simulated) and giving the effect of a flower kissed by the moonlight." Matching earrings on page 41. B; $12-30. *Strawberry Ice* pin is a striking replica of a strawberry, from the textured surface to the satin strawberry accents, cap, and stem. In the catalog it was coupled with other tailored silvertone jewelry for added versatility—especially with the Silvery Cascade necklace and earrings. Matching earrings on page 36. A; $15-35. *Aurora Blaze* pin is created from a central aurora borealis chaton cut, Austrian crystal stone surrounded by flames of encrusted tiny chaton cut Austrian crystal rhinestones. It was identified as having "After-5 sparkle and glitter designed to make the night more exciting." Same pin on page 83, matching earrings on page 72. C; $20-45. **Bottom row, left to right:** *Nocturne* is "true elegance for either daytime or evening wear…beautifully designed silvertone flower pin with its lustrous center pearl and petals edged with imitation marcasites." The effect is one of moonlight glow. A bracelet with the same name is not a matching piece. B; $15-35. *Star Fire* is a star shaped pin with sparkling blue Austrian crystals surrounded by textured silvertone. It was identified as "After-5 sparkle and glitter designed to make the night more exciting." Matching earrings on page 72. B; $15-35.

Left to right: *Sarah's Circle* pins in both goldentone and silvertone were identified as "just the right gift for the person who likes the very simple design with a look of elegance." The identifying marks read "SARAHCOV" on the back at the top of the outside ring. However, the letters are hard to see and may even be worn off. Matching earrings on page 73. A; $8-20. *Garland* pin is a unique combination of textured silvertone and goldentone leaves attached to a circle wire. It was identified as "the tailored look for night or day." Matching earrings on page 43. A; $8-20. *Ivy* pins in silvertone and goldentone are a combination of textured and satin petals. Catalogs identified them as a way "to enhance your outfit by day or night…and a tailored look for all seasons." Matching earrings on page 37. A; $8-20.

Top row, left to right: *Song of India* is a colorful pin that reminds customers "you don't need to travel to India to see and appreciate the romance and color reflected in their Temples of Worship." The piece "has re-created this look of beauty in this multi-color" pin. Matching earrings on page 73. B; $10-35. *Wooded Beauty* pin is made from two inlaid brown enameled leaves with goldentone satin edges; it looks like inlaid wood finish. The intricate detail is quite amazing in this costume jewelry. Matching earrings on page 72. A; $10-25. *Light of the East* pin has five domes of multi-colored enameled sets. The blue, green, and red are very striking against the goldentone framework. It was identified as "simplicity and elegance." Matching earrings on page 73. Note: I found one of these domes set in a cat pin. Someone had replaced a body set in this cat pin with one of these sets, giving the impression it was Sarah Coventry. Be careful. B; $15-35. **Bottom row, left to right:** On *Jade Garden,* the "sculptured array of golden leaves and a bud-like cultured pearl accent the beauty of this lovely pin with its authentic jade stone." A; $10-25. *Pearlized Perfection*: "as new as tomorrow's sunrise is this unusual Pearlized pin with its classic leaf design. The pearlized finish allows it to be in style all year round and makes it as classic as a string of pearls." Matching earrings on page 72. A; $10-25. *Remembrance* pin was a very popular pin that was continued into the 1970s. The diamond shaped goldentone pin has an antique look and supports a center turquoise stone surrounded by other teardrop shaped matching turquoise sets and simulated pearls. Matching earrings on pages 72. B; $15-35.

Top row, left to right: *Crescent* pin in silvertone was described as "tailored simplicity of a beautiful design crafted in gleaming silvertone." Marked on back in raised letters is "©SARAH COV." Matching bracelet on page 80, matching earrings on page 72. A; $8-20. *Temple-Lites* pin of goldentone has a unique Eastern design. The diamond antiqued shape is made up of four individual diamond shapes with dark red, blue, and green rhinestones on each section plus six dark green oval beads dangling from the bottom corner. I only found it listed in the fall catalog for 1969. Matching earrings on page 75. B; $20-45. *Baroque Goddess* pin in goldentone is a large, flattened simulated baroque pearl surrounded by a large chain link frame. B; $10-35. **Center row, left to right:** *Demi-Flower* pin in silvertone and *Demi-Flower* pin in goldentone. A combination of textured solid and open-weave petals creates the illusion of "half" a flower, hence the name. A; $10-25. **Bottom:** *Mystic Blue* pin completes this array of pins from the fall 1969 catalog. On this fascinating piece of Sarah jewelry, a goldentone reverse application of flower petals encircles a large Austrian iridescent blue crystal set in prongs. Matching earrings on page 75, matching ring on page 81. B; $15-35.

Clockwise, from top left: *Promise* pin is a dainty wire circle with a mesh rose and stem. "The tailored look, simple in design, but with the look of Goldentone Elegance." Marked inconspicuously on the back of one leaf "©SARAH COV" engraved. A; $10-25. *Starburst* pin is a large "deep amber stone catching and reflecting the light in the starburst design. A perfect fashion accent for those beige to brown tones and lovely with most any color." This was a set that carried from the early 1960s to the early 1970s as hostess credit. Matching earrings on page 36. C; $10-25. *Whispering Leaf* pin is a classic flat leaf shape with intricate veining replicating a leaf from nature. It has a simulated pearl accent at the top. Matching earrings on page 72. A; $10-20. *Feather-Brite* pin is a simple curve of solid-textured goldentone: "the tailored look, simple in design, but with the look of Goldentone Elegance." There was also a pin called Feather Bright in the '70s. A; $10-20. *Golden Mum* pin is far from simplistic with its "sparkling Austrian rhinestone centered in Goldentone Flowers for fashion accents, day or night." B; $15-30. *Endearing* pin is a "dainty and delicate lovely wreath type pin with its graceful leaf design accented with soft white pretend pearls." Matching earrings on page 37. A; $10-20. The *Fashion Parade* stick pin, identified as "The latest fashion 'must' for your jabot or scarf," was created from a simulated pearl in a textured cap of goldentone. "Pearls the perennial classic go everywhere and with everything." Matching earrings on page 35, matching necklace on page 45, matching ring on page 82. A; $8-15. As shown by this selection of pins, Sarah's designers planned for a variety of customers and occasions for wearing.

Top row, left to right: *Acapulco* pin uses a kaleidoscope of green and orange beads in a star shaped tailored look of goldentone. Matching bracelet on page 79, matching earrings on page 72. B; $20-45. *Royal Hawaiian* pin has a combination of small orange beads and pearlized dots scattered on a goldentone framework. Matching earrings on page 71. A; $15-35. *Daisy Time* is a daisy shaped pin with teal petals. The flower is set on a silvertone stem and a bold yellow center bead brings the pin alive. B; $15-35. **Bottom row left to right**: *Ocean Star* pin gives "a dash of color combined with gleaming Goldentone for year-round fashion accents." The starfish shape is encrusted with tiny teal and white beads. Matching earrings on page 72. B; $20-35. A *Galaxy* "of color and beauty is this multi-color square pin." It has "ceramic red, jade green, lapis blue and turquoise colors surrounded by sparkling aurora stones and lustrous pearls (simulated)…that will go with any costume regardless of color." This set was also held over as hostess credit after the first pieces were offered for sale. Same pin on page 30, matching earrings on page 35. B; $20-45. *All courtesy of Dawn Michael.*

Top row, left to right: *Petite* pin: "tiny but elegant, simple in style but classic in design is this darling three leaf in gleaming silvertone. Perfect for anyone and with anything." SarahSheen silvertone. Matching earrings on page 37. A; $10-20. *Evening Star* pin is "a cluster of rhinestones surrounding the elegance of a charcoal rhinestone. At the setting of the sun, you'll want EVENING STAR set to enhance your evening ensemble." This is one of the many pieces with "evening" in the name. Matching earrings on page 37. B; $15-40. *Fantasy* pin "a design from nature carried out in lovely colorful cabochon matrix stones and simulated pearls. A dash of fashion color to enhance any costume regardless of the season." Matching earrings on page 37. B; $15-35. **Bottom**: *Scented Traveler* pin is "a beautiful combination of fine fashion jewelry and a hauntingly beautiful fragrance that lingers long after you've left. The perfect gift to give or to receive." This piece of jewelry opens to display perfumed gel and was found in only one catalog in 1969. B; $10-25.

Top row, left to right: *Fashion in Motion* pin in silvertone is true to its name with nine dangling chains and silver beads. The oval pin is an open kaleidoscope of silvertone and beads. This pin was only pictured in one of the catalogs for 1969. B; $15-35. *Tahitian Flower Blue* pin (also comes in white) was described as "the big fashion news of the large enamel flower. Sarah's designers present this colorful group for Spring and summer." B; $10-25. **Bottom row, left to right**: *"Dogwood" White* pin (also comes in hot pink and jet black) is a "colorful enamel flower pin to bloom from your lapel any season of the year." B; $10-25. *Accent* pin (missing one petal) was found in only several catalogs of 1969. It has a solid goldentone five petal flower with a curled outside edge on each petal. A; $8-15.
All courtesy of Otheda Smith.

Left to right: *Evening Splendor* pin achieves a half circle effect with a large hand polished Austrian rhinestone seeming to gather up the silvertone design. "The look of a million rhinestones is achieved through a high luster finish." Matching earrings on page 74. A; $15-35. *Simplicity* is "simple and stunning…The perfect tailored pin to take you 'around the clock' or 'around the world.' Simplicity is at home anywhere." A; $10-25. *Placid Beauty* pin has "soft blue beads nestled in enameled white leaves in an exquisite design from nature." Matching earrings on page 43. A; $10-25.

Top row, left to right: *Sarah's Angel* pin is "jewelry designed for the young at heart with a simulated pearl as head in SarahGlo goldentone." Note the intricate detail of wings, arms, and legs. A; $10-25. *Tic-Tac-Toe* pins are "a happy trio, these three colorful little chick-a-dees. Each a different color and all boasting deep red eyes. Wear these colorful little charm-tacs single, in pairs, or as a trio." B; $10-25. *Silvery Maple* pin is "a design from nature expertly crafted in textured silvertone making a tailored pin you'll never tire of. Silvery Maple is in bloom season after season." Matching earrings on page 73. B; $10-25. **Bottom row, left to right**: *Birds in Flight*: "what is lovelier or more graceful than birds in flight and Sarah's designers have caught this beauty in a gleaming tailored silvertone set." Matching earrings on page 73. B; $8-20. *Strawberry Festival* pin is "as beautiful as a fresh-picked berry and as gay as a strawberry festival. This imported stone is exclusive with Sarah." Made of SarahSheen goldentone. Matching earrings on page 71. B; $15-35. *All courtesy of Dawn Michael.*

Top row, left to right: *Evening Comet* pin: "take the beauty of a star and combine it with all the animation and fire of a comet and you have a design of breathtaking beauty." Identified as an "after-five" kind of pin of SarahSheen silvertone. B; $15-35. *Light N' Bright* pin is "the cool feel of light weight fashionable jewelry to brighten your costume any season of the year." Matching earrings on page 39. A; $8-20. *Fashion Flower* pin is a very attractive goldentone six point flower shape with open-veined petals and a center cluster of small hot pink chaton cut rhinestones surrounding a larger hot pink set. "A dash of color combined with gleaming goldentone for year-round fashion accents." There is also another set with this same name. Matching earrings on page 73. B; $15-35. **Bottom row, left to right**: *Flower Flattery* white pin features "the magic of the daisy captured in metals and hi-gloss enamel. Designed to grow on your lapels any season of the year." The pin and matching earrings also came in pink and yellow. B; $10-25. *Frenchie* pin is "jewelry designed especially for the young in heart." This upright French poodle is a unique pin for any age. A; $8-15. *Allusion* pin has "sparkling Austrian rhinestones centered in goldentone flowers for fashion accents, day or night." Matching earrings on page 36. B; $10-25.

Top row, left to right: *Harvest Wheat* pin has a multi-colored rhinestone center surrounded by wheat-like goldentone sprigs all attached to a goldentone stem, giving the effect of a flower. (Note that the sprigs of wheat match the bracelet and earrings identified on pages 44-45 of *Fifty Years of Collectible Fashion Jewelry 1925-1975* by Lillian Baker.) Matching bracelet on page 51, matching earrings on page 75. $15-30. *Golden Trillium* pin was located in only one 1969 catalog. Trillium defined is a lily-like leaf and a group of three. Matching earrings on page 75. B; $15-30. **Bottom row, left to right**: *Filigree Clover* is a simple four leaf clover in open-weave design identified as filigree. Matching earrings on page 75. B; $10-25. *Sun Flower* pin was found in the cardex files as well as late 1960s catalogs. "The swirl of goldentone will add a simple but elegant touch to your summer shifts or winter sheaths." Matching earrings on page 75. B; $10-25. *Award Pin* features covered wagons surrounding red aurora Austrian crystal rhinestones. This pin was given to top producers during a campaign featuring covered wagons and emphasizing the pioneering spirit. Many of the award pins and other jewelry were very exquisitely designed with cost of little concern. Current value—if lucky enough to find one—$25-40. *All courtesy of Otheda Smith.*

Top row, left to right: *Unidentified* pin is one of the favorites in my collection and I am disappointed that I haven't been able to accurately name it. This circle goldentone pin is quite exquisite. Its red aurora crystals, no doubt imported from Austria or Germany, lie in clusters among the delicate gold leaves. Matching earrings on page 75. $20-45. *Mystic Swirl* pin has "a jet black center surrounded by a swirl of textured and shining silvertone" and "gives a feeling of mystic beauty. In fashion any season." This is from the late 1966 and 1967 catalogs. A; $10-25. *Woodland Flight* pin is from the early '60s. "The grace of the deer in flight was captured in this design of classic beauty. Its clean, simple lines combined with its antique SarahSheen luster make it a once in a lifetime set." Matching earrings on page 74. A; $15-30. **Bottom row, left to right**: *Mountain Flower* pin is a glamorous flower pin with imported Austrian green aurora stones clustered in the center and surrounding petals paved with clear crystals. Matching earrings on page 74. B; $15-30. *Courtesy of Harriette Oshel*. *Fashion Round* pin in silvertone is a circle pin created from textured and shiny ribbon like silver. This was found first in the 1970s. Matching earrings on page 74. B; $10-25. *Black Imitation Diamond* pin has "Exquisite rhodium blossoms with a unique and sparkling tiffany cut stone of deep and lasting beauty." This set began in the early 1960s and continued into the late '60s as hostess credit. Matching earrings on page 74. A; $15-30.

Earrings

Many of these earrings were continued through the early 1970s as either sale items or hostess credit. **Top row, left to right**: *Royal Hawaiian* earrings are swirls of goldentone highlighted with small pearl circle disks and dark orange/red beads. These were found in the cardex with no specific dates. Matching pin on page 68. A; $10-25. *Deep Burgundy* earrings are the matching center cluster of "deep burgundy glass stones securely held by prongs" as on the pin. Matching pin on page 66, matching ring on page 81. A; $10-25. *Pearl Elegance* earrings are "Blossoms of the baroque (simulated) pearl rose set in SarahGlo goldentone." These can "be worn when a costume calls for just a light touch of white." Matching pin on page 30. A; $10-25. **Bottom row, left to right**: *Golden Bangle* are "popular wedding band earrings of SarahGlo goldentone with pierced look clip. Leaf design delicately engraved is flattering and tailored." A; $8-20. *Versaille* earrings are medium to large, with a light green/yellow multi-faceted stone set in prongs of goldentone and surrounded by a rope-like mounting. Matching bracelet on page 52, same set shown on page 39. A; $10-30. *Goddess of Fashion* earrings were described as "the new, the unusual, the eye catching dangle earrings" of SarahGlo goldentone. Matching necklace on page 77. B; $10-25. *All courtesy of Dawn Michael.*

Top row, left to right: *Bird of Paradise* earrings are winged shapes of "crystal aurora stones on...fashionable silvertone." Matching pin on page 29. B; $15-30. *Enchanted Forest* earrings are "truly enchanted moss green leaves veined in gleaming goldentone." Matching pin on page 51 of Lindbeck book. B; $10-25. **Center row, left to right**: *Dawn to Dusk* earrings have "Sarah's versatility at its best displayed in this dangling earring set. Quiet pearl (simulated) on one side for before 5:00, reverses to sparkling Rhinestones at dusk." Matching necklace on page 49, A; $10-25. *Strawberry Festival* earrings "as beautiful as a fresh-picked berry and as gay as a strawberry festival in this strawberry motif. This imported stone is exclusive with Sarah." Matching pin on page 69. B; $10-25. **Bottom row, left to right**: The description for *Fashion Flirt* earrings notes that "flirting is what happens when wearing these baroque pearl (simulated) earrings of goldentone." These were some of the early pieces of jewelry that were continued throughout the late 1960s. Same earrings on page 42. A; $8-20. *Fashion Loops* earrings feature "golden fashion to swing and sway at your ears and give your costume the look of up to the minute fashion." B; $8-15. *Fashionette* earrings are a "single ball drop" of SarahGlo silvertone. These pierced look earrings were referred to as "chicken style." A; $8-20. *Sophisticated* earrings are "slim and sophisticated-looking in this lovely 'chicken' earring designed to look as if it were a pierced style. A sparkling SarahSheen, silvertone finish for town or city wear." A; $10-25. *Courtesy of Dawn Michael.*

Top row, left to right: *On Stage* earrings have simulated rippled effect pearls with SarahGlo goldentone leaf caps holding the pearls secure. B; $10-25. *A-Go-Go* earrings, with large crystal beads attached to long chains, are high-fashion baubles that swing and sway at the ears. A; $10-25. *Saucy Swingers* earrings of goldentone are "swingers for every occasion for that up-to-the-minute fashion feeling." Added intrigue was created by the holes and crevices in each dangle. B; $10-25. *Wooded Beauty* earrings have "the tailored look in this single leaf of goldentone with brown in-laid center." Matching pin on page 67. A; $8-20. **Bottom row, left to right**: *Ocean Star* earrings are "chicken dangle" made of goldentone and encrusted with tiny teal and white beads on one leg of a starfish. "A dash of color combined with gleaming goldentone for year-round fashion accents." Matching pin on page 68. B; $10-25. *Bewitchery* earrings were created with silvertone chain blackened for "the tailored look for night and day." Matching necklace on page 114 of Lindbeck book. A; $8-20. *Gypsy* earrings are open circle loops of SarahGlo goldentone with "chicken dangle" hooks. These are similar to other earrings from the early '60s that matched a belt/necklace. Same earrings on page 42. A; $8-20. *All courtesy of Dawn Michael.*

Top row, left to right: *Acapulco* earrings with orange and green beads have "the tailored look, simple in design but Goldentone elegance." Matching pin on page 68, matching bracelet on page 79. B; $10-30. *Crescent* earrings are made of three overlapping crescent shapes in silvertone with "the tailored simplicity of a beautiful design crafted in gleaming silvertone." Matching pin on page 67, matching bracelet on page 80. B; $10-25. **Bottom row, left to right**: *Valencia* earrings are small goldentone open-weave earrings with a dark coral cabochon in the center. Matching pin on page 64 of Lindbeck book, matching bracelet on page 127. A; $8-20. *Happy Holiday* earrings are multi-colored stones made from the charms of the matching bracelet. The baroque pearl (simulated) in the center surrounded by stones of dark colors along with the silvertone setting make these earrings very striking. Matching bracelet on page 51. A; $10-25. *Chain-o-lites* earrings have a silvertone chain tassel dangling from a dazzling ball of Austrian crystal rhinestones: "Sarah's sparkling After-5 jewelry gives you the touch of evening elegance." Matching necklace on page 77. B; $15-30. *All courtesy of Dawn Michael.*

Top row, left to right: *Aurora Blaze* earrings were identified as "After-5 Sparkle." The chaton cut Austrian crystal in the center is surrounded by flame-like shapes paved with crystals, hence its name. Marked on the earring itself is "©SARAH COV" in raised letters. Same earrings on page 83, matching pin on page 66. B; $15-45. *Star Fire* earrings in a starfish shape have a navette blue Austrian crystal center surrounded by smaller chaton cut lighter blue Austrian chaton cut crystals set in prongs. Matching pin on page 66. B; $20-50. *Whispering Leaf* earrings are simple but elegant earrings with goldentone textured leaf shapes and artfully created details of veins, stems, and sawtooth edges. The addition of a simulated cultured pearl adds the touch of elegance. Matching pin on page 67. A; $15-35. **Bottom row, left to right**: *Golden Cherries*, another design from nature, were identified as "a real conversation piece." The convex textured shape is accented by the satin finish of the leaves and stem. Matching pin on page 29. A; $10-25. *Remembrance* earrings feature a textured, colored turquoise cabochon set in prongs within an antiqued teapot shape background. In 1968 the antique look was the fashion look: "the new look in Fashion is the 'old look.'" A very popular pair of earrings. Marking on earring itself is "©SARAH COV" in raised lettering. Same earrings on page 104, matching pin on page 67. A; $10-25. *Pearlized Perfection* earrings are two white enameled leaves accented with goldentone on the edge and spine. "The pearlized finish allows it to be in style all year round." Marked on clasp is "©SARAH COV" engraved. These earrings also have a raised "L" and "R" to indicate on which ear to wear.

Top row, left to right: *Carousel* (pink and orange) earrings have "vivid fashion colors combined in a light lariat swinger earrings." These also came in combinations of blue and green plus citrus shades of yellow/green/orange. Matching necklace lariats on pages 76 and 77. A; $8-20. *Birds of Flight* earrings: "what is lovelier or more graceful than birds in flight captured in this silvertone circle." Matching pin on page 69. A; $10-25. Tailored *Silvery Maple* earrings are another design from nature in textured SarahSheen silvertone. Matching pin on page 69. A; $8-20. *Sarah's Circle* earrings in silvertone and goldentone textured finish. "Just the right gift for the person who likes the very simple design with a look of elegance. For something that looks lovely again and again try Sarah's Circle" jewelry. Matching pins on pages 66. A; $8-20. **Bottom row, left to right**: *Fashion Swingers* goldentone (*Café Society*) earrings are "for up-to-the-minute feeling of fashion." A; $10-25. *Hi Swinger* earrings were identified as Fashion Swingers for every occasion with their very fashionable dangling effect. B; $10-30. *Café Society* silvertone *Fashion Swingers* are the same as the goldentone but with silvertone textured baubles and chains. *All courtesy of Dawn Michael.*

Top row, left to right: *Tailored Swirl* earrings are identified as "quality fashion accents in Silvertone to mix and match for added versatility." These earrings were shown coupled with other pieces of jewelry for different looks. They also came in goldentone. Same earrings on page 37, matching pin on page 66. A; $8-25. *Light of the East* earrings are clip-ons, though there was also a set of dangles. They feature a colorfully painted oval stone of red, green, and blue with golden highlights. Matching pin on page 67. A; $10-25. *Light N' Bright* earrings have "the cool feel of light weight fashionable jewelry to brighten your costume any season of the year." Same earrings on page 39. A; $10-25. **Bottom row, left to right**: *Holiday* earrings in red and turquoise are button earrings with a goldentone center strip and could be worn with multi-color fashions. Other colors included black, green, and white. There were matching bracelets for all of the colors. A; $8-20. *Summer Magic* single earring was created to contribute to chain and beaded necklaces. "As white as snow, as cool looking as an icicle, and as beautiful as only a design from nature can be." This earring made a very versatile fashion accent and was perhaps purchased singly to wear as a pendant. Same earrings on page 34, matching necklaces on page 46, matching pin on page 30. A; $10-25 (for pair of earrings). *Satin Petals* earrings were "designed with sophisticated simplicity in this goldentone flower set. Notice the lovely satin finish and the realistic look of this design from nature." Matching pin on page 66. A; $10-25.

Top row, left to right: *Holiday Ice* earrings have a large chaton cut imported emerald stone surrounded by tiny clear rhinestones. "Sarah's sparkling After-5 jewelry gives you the touch of evening elegance." Matching necklace on page 83, matching pin on page 83. B; $10-35. *Fashion Petals* earrings (pink): "colorful enameled petals in the very latest fashion colors give you a striking set to be worn now and into winter. Petals may bloom any time of year." Matching pin on page 65. B; $10-25. The description for *Song of India* earrings noted that "You don't need to travel to India to see and appreciate the romance and color reflected in their Temples of Worship." I found several pieces of this set with many of the turquoise sets missing. When all sets are there, they are totally awesome. Matching pin on page 67. B; $15-35. **Bottom row, left to right**: *Garland* earrings with two-tone leaves intertwined at the center with a gold ball have "The tailored look for Night or Day." Matching pin on page 66, and a second pair of earrings on page 43. A; $8-20. *Sultana* earrings are solid goldentone in a slightly curved shape, accented with multi-colored rhinestones and raised geometric shapes of goldentone. This set with necklace was continued as a hostess credit item into the '70s. Matching necklace on page 46. A; $10-35. *Fashion Flower* earrings have "A dash of color combined with gleaming Goldentone for year-round fashion accents." Matching pin on page 69. A; $15-35.

Top row, left to right: *Symphony* earrings are small Austrian crystals secured with silvertone prongs surrounding a larger clear rhinestone also secured by prongs. All the crystals are nestled in shiny silvertone filigree leaves. "Sarah's sparkling After-5 jewelry gives you the touch of evening elegance." Matching ring on page 82. B; $15-35. *White Satin* earrings: "as smooth and silky as White Satin and just as luxurious are these dangle earrings echoing the feeling of fashion at its best." Matching necklace on page 49. A; $8-20. **Bottom:** *Polynesian* earrings made of SarahGlo goldentone enameled metal are "as beautiful and romantic as a tropical flower or a Polynesian Sunset…will add fashion beauty to your costume summer or winter." Matching pin on page 31. B; $12-30.

Top row, left to right: *Dancing Jet* earrings are "the new 'pretend' pierced earrings sweeping the fashion world. Sarah's designers present a faceted-cut jet-colored stone to dangle and dance at your ears day or night." One of the top ornamental goldentone pieces is missing. A; $8-20. *Rain Flower* earrings are in their original box. They are created from a medium-sized clear rhinestone surrounded by a goldentone wire-like frame shaped with four scallops. This set is from the early to mid-1970s but is pictured with the other earrings here. Matching necklace on page 48. C; $10-35. **Bottom row, left to right:** *Golden Embers* earrings have an oval shape "synthetic Topaz Glass stone" set in a bold goldentone rectangular shape. Matching necklace on page 76, matching ring on page 82. A; $10-25. *Pyramid Treasures* earrings have "the fascination of ancient Egypt. Notice its sharp, clear-line design artfully carried out in glistening silvertone…wear from spring through summer and into winter." Matching bracelet on page 80. A; $10-25. *Caged Pearl* earrings are simulated pearls surrounded by a silvertone swirl cage. These earrings are clip with the look of pierced but there were also pierced sets. A; $8-20.

Top row, left to right: *Sunflower* earrings have "the tailored look for all Seasons in Silvertone. These earrings are 'cover-the-ear' type with overlapping petals surrounding a textured sunflower center. This is one of several sets with the name sunflower (used as one word here, while some are "sun flower"). Matching pin on page 66. A; $10-25. *Fashion Round* earring (one single) is an open textured loop surrounding a silvertone ball center. Many customers purchased a single earring to wear as a pendant with a pair of earrings. Also, in earlier years, FSDs received only one earring in their display kit. Matching pin on page 70. A; $8-15 (pair). **Bottom row, left to right:** *Summer Festival* earrings were part of an ensemble with a necklace and bracelet that was "designed for the lovely Festival Queen who will travel all over the United States wearing her Sarah Coventry jewelry wardrobe. Its simplicity of design, coupled with its use of gleaming silver and enameled snow, makes it an ensemble you'll want to wear with everything you own from one season to the next." There was also a goldentone set. This set was found on the pre 66 cards. A; $10-25. *Woodland Flight* earrings show the "grace of the deer in flight captured in this design of classic beauty. Its clean, simple lines combined with its antique SarahSheen luster make it a once in a lifetime set." Matching pin on page 70 A; $10-25.

Top: *Evening Splendor* earrings are "the look of a million rhinestones achieved through this fine design and a high luster finish and boasts a large hand polished Austrian rhinestone." Matching pin on page 69. A; $15-35. **Center row, left to right:** *Camelot* earrings are "links of silvertone fashion created for the town and country set" that are "perfect for those tailored moments when only the simplicity of hi-fashion will do." Matching bracelet on page 79. B; $10-25. *Mountain Flower* earrings have light green Austrian crystals clustered for the center of the flower and tiny clear rhinestones paving the surrounding petals. This is a superb set by Sarah's designers. Matching pin on page 70. B; $15-35. **Bottom:** *Black Diamond* (Imitation) earrings are "exquisite rhodium blossoms with a unique and sparkling tiffany cut stone of deep and lasting beauty." The earrings and pin were from the late 1950s and early '60s but were continued through the late 1960s and into the '70s as hostess credit items. This set is very different and striking. Matching pin on page 70. A; $10-25.

Top row, left to right: *Dancing Magic* earrings are half circles formed from medium-sized chaton cut iridescent rhinestones surrounded by golden rope mounting. These earrings and a matching necklace were created in the late 1950s and early '60s, but were carried over as hostess credit throughout the 1960s and early '70s. Matching pendant necklace on page 46. B; $15-30. *Temple-Lites* earrings are created from an antiqued goldentone diamond shape accented with three colored rhinestones and six teardrop shaped beads dangling from the bottom point and two sides. Matching pin on page 67. B; $15-35. **Center:** *Mystic Blue* earrings feature an amazing goldentone reverse application of flower petals encircling a large Austrian iridescent blue crystal set in prongs. Matching pin on page 67, matching ring on page 81. C; $15-35. **Bottom row, left to right:** *Color Frame* earrings in two different sizes were very versatile in that the sets are removable and reversible. One FSD commented that fabric could be used around the center set, thereby matching clothing. Through the party plan, many such ideas were shared with customers. These earrings were very inexpensive, yet very attractive. A; $8-20.

Top row, left to right: *Black Beauty* earrings are five petal silvertone flowers with a black chaton cut jet set. There are several Black Beauty sets. The matching pin for this one is on page 29. A; $10-25. *Enchantress* earring (single) is "After-5 sparkle and glitter designed to make the night more exciting. Sparkling Austrian Crystals in exclusive designs to make a more glamorous you." This single earring could have been given to an FSD singly, especially if the employee didn't have pierced ears and wouldn't be able to wear the set. There was a totally different set from 1971 also called Enchantress. Matching necklace on page 83, matching bracelet on page 83. B; $15-35 (for pair). *Silvery Cascade* earrings were created in the 1950s and continued through to the '70s. These earrings were sold singly to be worn as a pendant on the matching necklace chains—versatility was very important to Sarah's designers. Matching necklace on page 113. A; $10-25. The description for *Heirloom Treasure* pierced earrings noted that "the new look in fashion is the 'old look.' The 1968 fashion leader is the antique look." Matching necklace on page 76. B; $15-30. **Bottom row, left to right:** *Pearl Swirl* earrings have one simulated pearl in a swirl of goldentone wire in a pierced look fashion. Same earrings on page 42, matching necklace on page 78, matching bracelet on page 80. A; $8-20. *Hi-Swinger* earrings: "Milady's ears have never been so exciting or so important. Swingers for every occasion for that up-to-the-minute fashion feeling." B; $8-20.

Top row, left to right: *Harvest Wheat* earrings (this name is from *Fifty Years of Collectible Fashion Jewelry 1925-1975* by Lillian Baker, pages 44-45) are not totally documented, but for now we'll use this name. Matching bracelet on page 51. $15-30. *Unidentified* earrings are highly unusual with their enamel puzzle effect. Again, a name has not been forthcoming and they haven't appeared in any of the catalog materials I have located. $10-25. **Center row, left to right:** *Unidentified* earrings have aurora glass stones nestled among tiny goldentone leaves that make these very exquisite and expensive looking. Matching pin on page 70. $15-30. *Filigree Clover* are open-weave goldentone four leaf clovers. Matching pin on page 70. A; $10-25. **Bottom row, left to right:** On *Sun Flower* earrings, "the swirl of goldentone leaves and rays extend from a golden ball center producing this stunning motif of the sun flower." This is one of the several sets with the sun flower or sunflower name. Matching pin on page 70. B; $10-25. *Golden Trillium* earrings were found in only one of the 1969 catalogs. These large goldentone leaves are similar to lily leaves and the group of three is also reflective of the name. Matching pin on page 70. B; $10-25.

Necklaces

Top to bottom: *Golden Embers* necklace is "a goldentone chanel type chain with the fashion accent of synthetic Topaz Glass stones." Matching ring on page 82, matching earrings on page 74. C; $15-30. *Wild Honey Pendant* necklace has a large emerald cut amber colored stone prong set in goldentone with a supporting criss-cross design with smaller amber colored stones. All are securely stationed to the double linked chain. Matching ring on page 132. B; $20-45. *Tortoise Fashions* necklace: "versatile lariats and chains lead the fashion parade any season of the year." This amber/orange bead and chain combination is very striking. Matching bracelet on page 80. B; $15-35. *Jet Elegance* pendant hangs from a delicate goldentone chain. The oval shaped pendant is a highly polished jet stone encased in a goldentone locket-like mounting. Matching ring on page 81. A; $10-30. Description for *Heirloom Treasure* necklace notes "the new look in fashion is the 'old look.' The 1968 fashion leader is the antique look." Matching earrings on page 75. A; $10-25.

Left to right: *Fashionette* necklace: "lovely and light is this new fashion lariat with its triple chain, decorative tassels. As versatile as your imagination and fashion-right for any season." Also came in goldentone. B; $10-25. *Fashion Parade* pendant is attached here to a close linked chain double necklace. The pendant could be worn with any kind of chain, pearls, or beads. Similar necklace on page 45. A; $8-20. *Carousel Fashion* necklace is "vivid fashion colors combined in a light lariat…The perfect companion for spring and summer fashions." This one is in the citrus shades. Other colors of necklace on page 77, matching earrings on page 73. B; $10-25. *Fashion Parade* necklace is this chain that was coupled with the original pearl lariat. "Wear the golden chain separately, or combine the two in a parade of different fashions." The pendant is removable. This whole set was very popular when first offered in the late 1950s as it continued through the mid-70s. Matching necklace on page 45, matching stick pin on page 67, matching earrings on page 35, matching ring on page 82. B; $8-20.

Left to right: *Multi-Fashion* necklace lent itself to "many different fashion changes. The ropes of turquoise and silver color beads can be worn separately or in combination. Wear any length—as a choker, matinee length or as a rope of color." SarahGlo silvertone. B; $15-30. *Fashion Flirt* necklace is a versatile chain and baroque pearls (simulated) that could be worn as a 36" rope necklace, lariat, or belt. Matching earrings on page 71. B; $10-25. *Rose Cameo* necklace is "this representation of the century cameo adding a touch of yesteryear to any wardrobe. The SarahGlo goldentone is famous for its tradition and beauty." Matching ring on page 82. B; $15-30. *Carousel* necklaces: "these vivid fashion colors are combined in a light lariat to be worn with spring and summer fashions." These two colors complete the full complement of this fashion design. Other colors on page 76, matching earrings on page 73. B; $10-25. *Fashion Loops* pendant is "a loop of golden fashion swinging within a larger loop as SarahGlo goldentone to give any costume that look of up-to-the-minute fashion." Matching earrings on page 71. B; $10-25.

Contessa was described as "The newest idea in a high fashion pearl (simulated) necklace. Wear it as a five strand matinee-length necklace or for costumes that require a lesser number of strands, 'Contessa' converts to a two or three strand necklace." B; $20-45. *Courtesy of Otheda Smith.*

Left to right: *Goddess of Fashion* was described as "the new, the unusual, the eye catching 'Sautoir' necklace. Notice the new flat chain and there is a detachable bracelet section. Even without the stunning pendant dangle it is a necklace of unusual charm and beauty." This set was a part of the cardex in the early 1960s. Matching earrings on page 71. B; $20-45. *Chain-o-lites* necklace is a double strand of silvertone chain interspersed with sparkling balls of Austrian crystals. Found in the 1969 catalog, this is a part of Sarah's "After-5 jewelry with a touch of evening elegance." Matching earrings on page 72. C; $20-45. *Swingalong* necklace is composed of bracelet, pin, and 20" chain necklace that can be worn separately or as one piece. The three strand dangle is actually a bracelet; the goldentone solid circle is a pin attached to the chain. This was found in the early '70s catalog. D; $20-45. *On Stage* necklace is a combination of pearl strand and a silvertone chain strand with a baroque (simulated) pearl suspended by a silvertone cap from each end of the chain. Matching earrings on page 72, matching pendants on page 98. B; $20-45. *Courtesy of Dawn Michael.*

Left to right: ***Versatility*** is a "beautifully woven chain every woman needs for a complete jewelry wardrobe. Sarah's chains are graceful, yet sturdy and designed for lockets, pins, brooches, watches or chatelaines. The uses are endless. This new 18" chain has adjustable ends that allow it to expand to 21"." This was matched and mixed with the tailored swirl pin and earrings and heritage bracelet. It also came in silvertone starting in the early years and continuing through the mid-70s. A; $8-15. ***Pearl Swirl*** necklace has "lustrous simulated pearls encased in golden cages, making a necklace of unusual beauty." Matching bracelet on page 80. B; $10-25. ***Ming Garden*** necklace, found in the early 1970s catalogs, has a green plastic Chinese emblem secured in an oval goldentone setting. B; $15-30. ***Young and Gay*** necklace is one of the pieces produced in the early years and continued into the early '70s. "Small women and teenage daughters will enjoy wearing a delicate chain designed just for them. Young and Gay will hug your neck like a glove." I found several of these bracelets connected together to form a longer necklace; in addition, several bracelets could be attached to the regular necklace for a longer necklace. Same necklace on page 46. A; $10-25. ***Serene*** necklace is a "dainty pendant in Pearl (simulated)." The dainty chain complements the look of this petite goldentone pendant. Matching earrings on pages 37. A; $10-25.

Left to right: ***Colleen*** necklace features a heart shape of silvertone with clear Austrian rhinestones channeled around the heart edge. Three chaton cut emerald green stones are secured within the center of the heart shape. This was from the late 1950s and early '60s. A; $15-30. ***Antique Lady*** pendant from 1975 is attached to a 25" silvertone chain. The oval silvertone shape with its wrapped effect has a nautical appearance, while the attached chain tassel adds some drama. D; $15-30. ***Unidentified*** pendant has an oriental appearance, however I haven't been able to appropriately name it. Help me out here if you can. $15-30.

Bracelets

Left to right: **Heritage** bracelet in goldentone has "the look of antique beauty here in this lovely bangle bracelet with its delicate guard chain and beautiful floral engravings. The beauty of the past, combined with the workmanship of the present." B; $10-25. **Acapulco** bracelet is "the tailored look, simple in design, but with the look of goldentone elegance." Matching pin on page 68, matching earrings on page 72. B; $15-35. **Party Pastels** is "a bracelet so gay and colorful—you will want to wear it with all your party clothes. These lovely and colorful pastel stones will blend with your every costume anytime of year." B; $10-25. **Unidentified** bracelet is very similar to the one called Carousel, however, these stones are smaller. My guess is that it is from Great Britain or Canada as many of their pieces were similar but not quite the same. $20-45. **Golden Cuff** bracelet is a simple hinged bracelet with an arrow point closing, also made in silvertone. B; $10-25. *Courtesy of Dawn Michael.*

Left to right: **Heritage** bracelet in silvertone has "the look of antique beauty here in this lovely bangle bracelet with its delicate guard chain and beautiful floral engravings. The beauty of the past, combined with the workmanship of the present." B; $10-25 **Young Charmer** bracelet is a charm attached to a dainty bracelet chain. "The look of elegance at a piggy bank price. Textured Chain Bracelet with its filigree dangle. Right for any age." The charm could also be attached to any other bracelet or the whole bracelet could be coupled with other colorful or simple bracelets. A; $8-20. *Courtesy of Otheda Smith.*

Top to bottom: **Continental Silver** bracelet was found in the early 1960s. This silver band of mesh adds "sleek charm and distinction...around your arm." There was a golden Continental as well. A; $10-25. **Fashion Cuff** bracelet: "a wide golden band of fashion encircles your wrist when you wear Sarah's new high fashion cuff bracelet. A design unique and lovely, beautifully finished in a high luster goldentone finish. A fashion cuff to be worn single or on either wrist." B; $10-25. **Camelot** bracelet: "links of silvertone fashion created for the town and country set is Sarah's perfect accessory for those tailored moments when only the simplicity of hi-fashion will do." A; $10-25.

Left to right: *Crescent* bracelet has "the tailored simplicity of a beautiful design crafted in gleaming silvertone." The two half moon shapes with an open-weave effect are elegant. Matching earrings on page 72, matching pin on page 67. B; $10-25. **Moonlites** bracelet is made of slender goldentone set with multi-colored pastel chaton cut iridescent stones. This set is striking, however it was only available for a little over a year. I believe this was because the sets came out easily and replacements may have been difficult to locate. Matching earrings on page 106, matching pin on page 99. *Tortoise Fashions* bracelet is a dainty amber/orange beaded bracelet. The bracelet has the < > shape hanging tag and I was lucky to find the earrings attached, otherwise the earrings are not marked. Matching necklace on page 76. *Pearl Swirl* bracelet is a goldentone bracelet with simulated pearls swirled in goldentone wire. Matching earrings on page 75, matching necklace on page 78. A; $8-20. *Silvery Cascade* bracelet is created from many strands of "this aluminum feather light chain." Matching necklace on page 113, matching earrings on page 75. B; $8-20. **Multiple Strand** bracelet is another bracelet of many chains, this one of goldentone. These latter two bracelets provide good examples of the varied pieces Sarah Coventry designed to satisfy their many customers. A; $8-20.

Left to right: *Whispering Leaves* bracelet: "extravagant in everything but the price is this design by nature, duplicated in smart white enamel on metal. This new treatment of fashion jewelry has become increasingly popular because of the elegance of design and its clean cool look. Country bound or off to the city with equal ease is this leaf and grape design by Sarah's master craftsman." Made from SarahSheen silvertone. Matching earrings on page 38. B; $15-35. Potential purchasers of the **Pyramid Treasures** bracelet were advised to "notice its sharp, clear-line design artfully carried out in glistening silvertone…the design has the fascination of ancient Egypt." Matching earrings on page 74. B; $15-35. *Courtesy of Nancy Isgrigs*. **Circle Charm** bracelet was a way for customers to "start your charm bracelet with this sturdy gold filled chain with its unusually attractive SarahGlo dangle. The stones on the nature inspired charm are genuine Wyoming jade and cultured pearl." This bracelet was a part of the Lady Coventry collection, which used semi-precious stones and gold. C; $15-35. **Antique Garden** bracelet has rectangles of antiqued silvertone molded to replicate a garden of flowers, leaves, and stems in an open-weave effect. The set was continued as hostess credit into the early 1970s. Matching earrings on page 107. B; $15-35. *Courtesy of Nancy Isgrigs*.

Rings and Sets

This **South Seas** set was one of the most spectacular sets created by the Sarah Coventry designers. The pendant and earrings teardrop shapes are pearlized abalone shells with goldentone mountings. This set was located in only the 1968 catalogs but seemed to be a favorite of Fashion Show Directors. Pictured with the set is a stand used at parties to assist with the presentation given by the FSD. C; $20-35.

Left to right: **Parisienne Nights** ring: "all the glamour and romance of an evening in Paris when you wear Sarah's multi-rhinestone combination of diamond shape." This SarahSheen silvertone ring has the look of the "real" thing from the 1950s and early '60s. Matching bracelet on page 52, B; $15-35. **Sparkle Mountain** ring is from the early 1970s. "Sarah's Ring Fling. Wear them in multiples! Bold! Beautiful and eye catching!" C; $20-40. *Courtesy of Nancy Isgrigs.* **Mystic Blue** ring was found in the 1969 catalogs. It features a goldentone reverse application of flower petals encircling a large Austrian iridescent blue crystal set in prongs Matching pin on page 67, matching earrings on page 75. B; $10-25.

Top row, left to right: **Light of the East** ring is a striking colorfully painted oval stone of red, green, and blue with golden highlights in an open goldentone frame. Marking is "SARAH COV" engraved. Matching necklace on page 124, matching earrings on page 73, matching pin on page 67. A; $10-25. **Bewitching** is "a domed dinner ring of great sparkle and beauty. The combination of gleaming silvertone and multi-crystal aurora stones will bring many envious glances your way." B; $15-35. **Jet Elegance** ring is a jet black oval stone set in a goldentone mounting. Matching pendant on page 76. A; $10-25. **Bottom**: **Deep Burgundy** ring has "a colorful center of deep burgundy glass stones securely held by prongs." Matching pin on page 66, matching earrings on page 71. A; $10-25.

Top row, left to right: *Gala* is "sparkling and brilliant with a gala touch of bright green in the center. Oval shaped for finger flattery. Silvertone." B; $10-25. *Jonquil* has a goldentone mounting with orange, emerald, and amber rhinestones all in a striking oval shape. B; $15-30. *Golden Nugget* is a large goldentone nugget shape mounted on a SarahGlo goldentone adjustable ring. B; $10-25. *Vogue* "will be in vogue season after season and add just the right touch of glamour to your after-5 costumes. Silvertone." B; $15-30. *Twin Jades* "are gently but firmly protected with golden prongs in a daytime ring of great simplicity and beauty. Genuine Jade. Goldentone." B; $10-25. **Bottom row, left to right:** *Golden Embers* is "designed to match your lovely Chanel necklace or to wear alone. Adds a finishing look of fashion to your costume before or after 5. Goldentone." B; $15-30. *Trulove* ring is a rhinestone set in sterling silver mounting with two smaller sets to either side. Described as "rings of fashion for every occasion. A new man-made stone to sparkle." C; $15-30. *Fashion Parade* ring was designed "to match and harmonize with our versatile Lariat and Earring set. Sarah's designers have created a ring to enhance the beauty of any hand. A Baroque pearl (simulated) nestled in a Goldentone setting." Matching stick pin on page 67, matching necklace on page 45, matching earrings on page 35. A; $10-25. *Birthstone* ring is amethyst for February. "For centuries, birthstone rings have been a symbol of happiness and good fortune for the wearer. We present Sarah's sterling silver birthstone rings with imported glass stones." B; $10-25. *Rose Cameo* "has the same beauty and dignity you'll find in your pendant necklace. A ring for any hour or any season. Goldentone. The lady of the Cameo is an elegant representation of the 19th century cameos and will add a touch of yester-year to your wardrobe. The Cameo—famous for its tradition and beauty." B; $15-30. *All courtesy of Dawn Michael.*

Left to right: *Majorca* ring has "the beauty of a bright red imported glass stone combined with Antiqued goldentone." Matching earrings and pendant on page 117 of Lindbeck book. B; $10-25. *Symphony* ring is "after-5 jewelry giving you the touch of evening elegance." The Austrian clear rhinestones are prong set in a silvertone blossom setting. Matching earrings on page 74. B; $15-30.

Left to right: *Night N' Day*: "beautifully exotic is this unusual jet and crystal ring set in gleaming silvertone. Both of these many faceted stones are cut in the shape of a heart. A blend of high fashion and basic design is this striking ring which can be worn Night 'n' Day." This ring was found in the card files and continued through the late 1960s. A; $15-30. *New Bermuda Blue* ring has an "imported Bermuda Blue Crystal Aurora glass ball" set in silvertone prongs. A glamorous ring found in the 1970 catalog. B; $20-45. *Courtesy of Otheda Smith.*

Clockwise, from left: *Holiday Ice* is a large emerald green set surrounded by leaves paved with smaller crystal rhinestones. "After-5 jewelry gives you the touch of evening elegance." The larger piece is the pin, with the smaller pieces as earrings and pendant on the silvertone chain. This set was found in a 1968 catalog and continued for several years. D; $60-90 for the set. *Midnight Magic* is "a subtle beauty hiding secrets in its dark depths [that] will add a mysterious glamour to the most remembered evenings. Dainty smoky rose stones contrasting with the massive black, recall a moment supreme. This is Sarah's Prestige Piece, a once-in-a-lifetime luxury for the woman who dares to be ravishing. For majestic occasions…for You!." Acquiring this set of bracelet, pin and matching earrings from the 1950s is probably the ultimate goal for a Sarah collector. I found it before I really knew what I was looking for and because it wasn't labeled on the back of the earrings, I passed it up. The set was continued through the early '70s as hostess credit. D; $75-95 for the complete set, individual pieces lesser values appropriate to the region and quality of piece. On the *Evening Star* set "a cluster of rhinestones surround the elegance of a charcoal rhinestone. At the setting of the sun, you'll want EVENING STAR set to enhance your evening ensemble." This pin and earrings set was from 1967 and continued for several years. C; $35-55. *All courtesy of Helen Knapp.*

Top to bottom: The top pieces are two separate sets. They look very much alike and could easily be mistaken for each other. Be aware of these many similarities when obtaining your pieces, especially on these multi-rhinestone sets. *Leading Lady* set includes just the earrings and large pin at the top. These were identified in 1970 catalogs as "Sarah's sparkling After-5 jewelry gives you the touch of evening elegance." The matching bracelet for this set is designed similarly to the Enchantress bracelet. Be on the lookout for it. C; $25-40. *Crystal Snowflakes* necklace and bracelet (partially hidden) are also identified in a 1969 catalog as "Sarah's sparkling After-5 jewelry gives you the touch of evening elegance." The set is silvertone, paved with Austrian crystals. Matching pin and earrings shown below. D; $35-55. *Enchantress* bracelet and necklace: "Nothing makes a woman feel more feminine or glamorous than an exciting ensemble of after-five jewelry. For those very special evenings out when you want to look and feel more enchanting, Sarah Coventry has designed a 3 piece ensemble which is delicate in design and sparkling with imported Austrian Rhinestones. Destined to make its wearer feel like an enchantress." This is one of two sets with the name "enchantress," so look for both sets. Matching earrings on page 75. D; $40-65. *All courtesy of Helen Knapp.*

Counterclockwise, from top left: *Crystal Snowflakes* pin and earrings of Austrian rhinestones are sparkling six point snowflakes set in SarahSheen silvertone. Matching bracelet and necklace shown above. C; $30-45. *Aurora Blaze* pin and earrings set. "A blaze of multi-colored Aurora Crystal stones in a snowflake design for this set that will enhance any special occasion costume." Same pin on page 66, same earrings on page 72. D; $35-50. *Blue Lagoon*: "this vivid blue pin and earrings set is as romantic and colorful as the warm waters of a Lagoon in the Pacific. Navette shaped ocean blue aurora stones and sparkling sea foam rhinestones floating in a design as lovely as nature itself. Enchanting in its depth of color, Blue Lagoon adds a dash of fashion color to your costume." C; $35-50. Far right pieces: *Unidentified* necklace and bracelet set marked "GREAT BRITAIN" on the back. Notice how closely the design is to the earrings in the center of the necklace and bracelet. Each country created their own Sarah jewelry, however, there seems to be some similarities to those created in the United States. No original price is known. $35-50. *Hong Kong* earrings (in center of necklace and bracelet). Identified as "Continental Sparkle," these earrings are Austrian crystals set in SarahSheen silvertone in an oriental design. No other matching pieces. *All courtesy of Helen Knapp.*

Top: *World's Fair* set: "the New York City World's Fair with all its glamour, gaiety, international flavor and romance, inspired this exclusive rhinestone creation. You'll feel like a woman of mystery and glamour in this sparkling ensemble inspired by the city lights and its world famous World's Fair." Necklace also shown on page 46, bracelet also shown on page 51. D; $60-95. **Bottom row, left to right**: *Paris* earrings, from the "Continental Sparkle by Sarah Coventry" collection, have Austrian crystals set in SarahSheen silvertone imitating the Eiffel Tower. No other matching pieces. C; $20-45. *Leading Lady* pin is the same as that shown with matching earrings on page 83. B; $15-35. On *Kathleen*, "sparkling, fiery rhinestones paved in a sunburst design and centered around a brilliant emerald-type stone make a truly glamorous evening ensemble. These earrings and pin pick up the emerald color and sparkle, and bring a flattering glow to milady's costume." Same pin on page 27, matching ring on page 153. C; $35-50. *All courtesy of Helen Knapp.*

Vienna set of silvertone open circle and teardrop shapes is a part of the "Continental Sparkle by Sarah Coventry" collection. These imported Austrian rhinestones make an exquisite set. D; $35-55. *Courtesy of Alynda Kimbrough.*

Golden Avocado set was created in the early to mid-1960s and continued through to the early '70s as hostess credit. Avocado beads and tassel on the necklace and earrings are accented by the deep golden chain and earring mounting. C; $30-45. *Courtesy of Nancy Isgrigs.*

Mosaic set of pin and earrings is the same name as a set from the 1970s. However, I have discovered that using the same name in different decades was very common. This set was identified by a Fashion Show Director without actual documentation of its accuracy. One pin I found had cream colored pearls where the red beads are. They could have been changed in early years to better match a costume or, more recently, FSDs frequently changed stones for variety. *Courtesy of Otheda Smith.*

Lady Coventry

Lady Coventry was a unique collection of jewelry that, as far as I have been able to discern, started in 1967. Because these items were made of high quality materials, they did not qualify for some of the company's special pricing offers, such as the half price on third item special or the hostess half priced items. The brochure description read as follows:

For those very special occasions when an exquisite gift of quality jewelry is the only answer, Sarah Coventry presents her Lady and Lord Coventry line of classic jewelry designs. Each separate selection of jewelry is beautifully crafted in the finest materials, often hand polished or enhanced by the addition of genuine semi-precious stones or Austrian crystals.

Every item or set in this collection is artfully encased in a black and gold leather type case with soft white velour lining. We invite you to select gifts for others or for yourself from the exclusive designs…

These pages from the 1969 catalog show the deluxe Lord and Lady Coventry collection specifically designed with semi-precious stones or Austrian crystals. Both men's and women's jewelry were included; you will find some of the men's jewelry in Chapter Six. *Courtesy of Dawn Michael.*

To highlight the deluxe nature of Lady Coventry jewelry, descriptions of the various semi-precious stones used were included in the catalog. The descriptions below are from the April 1967 catalog, "Fine Fashion Jewelry by Sarah Coventry" (*Courtesy of Nona Wilson*). This deluxe collection of jewelry continued through the early 1980s.

Wyoming Jade • A warm, soft green stone found in Wyoming, Alaska, California and several foreign countries.

Rose Quart • Mottled, delicate rose in color and usually cut from larger stones found in Brazil, Madagascar, Bavaria, the Ural Mountains and occasionally in our own state of Maine.

Sodolite • A stone in the Lapis Lazuli family with a characteristic blue-grey color. It is found in Afghanistan, Siberia and Chile.

Cultured Pearl • Actually produced by oysters in the Far East with the skilled help of experts, but in the same manner as natural pearls.

Austrian Crystal, Navette, Dentelle, Rhinestone • All terms relating to various imitation clear stones produced by D. Swarovski of Tyrol, Austria. Austrian crystal and rhinestone are the names commonly given to round imitation stones with many individually polished facets. Dentelle is used only for those superior imitation round stones having extra polished facets for maximum brilliance. Navette is used to describe the imitation stone in the shape of a canoe which is made with many individually polished facets.

Gold Filled • A base metal to which has been soldered a layer of karat gold to produce superior beauty, luster and durability.

Sterling Silver • Ninety-two and one-half percent pure silver with copper added to give it the necessary hardness and durability.

Onyx • Translucent quartz found in many colors but we use the popular jet black.

SarahGlo • Is a high luster finish achieved by a process of covering metal with either an alloy of gold or rhodium.

These Lady Coventry pieces of jewelry are prized possessions because of the process with which they are made. Be on the lookout for these deluxe pieces.

Left to right: Both of these sets were introduced in the early 1970s. **Filigree Jet Onyx** set consisting of pendant on a 16-18" sterling chain and matching bracelet were listed as "The Silvery collection." Original price for the pendant was $17 and for the bracelet $21.50. Current value for set: $25-40. **Onyx Tears** non-pierced dangle earrings, pin, bracelet, and pendant are sterling silver with genuine black onyx stones. Many customers would buy two items at regular price and get the third at the half or special price (not quite half). Original prices were $15 for earrings, $30 for pin, $37 for bracelet, $13 for pendant. Current value for set: $40-70. *Courtesy of Alynda Kimbrough.*

Left to right: **Amethyst Oval** set of earrings, bracelet with charm, and pin was introduced in the early 1970s. The amethyst stones in each piece are genuine, set in goldentone mountings. Original prices were $27 for earrings, $26 for bracelet, and $25 for pin. Buying two gave one a chance to buy the third at a special price (usually $5-6 off the original). Current value for complete set: $50-75. **Aqua Treasure** pierced earrings and pendant are prong set in sterling silver mountings. The set originally included a ring. Original prices were for $20 for earrings, $16 for pendant. With the purchase of two items, these could be purchased at half price. Current value: $40-55 (because they were only shown in one catalog). **Opal Treasure** bracelet from 1974 was called Antique Treasure in 1975. This antiqued silvertone mounting sports two genuine opal sets surrounding a garnet set. Original price was $20. Current value: $25-40 (because it wasn't offered very long). *All courtesy of Alynda Kimbrough.*

Left to right: The Lady Coventry collection was rich in jade pieces, as exemplified by the variety in the following sets. **Jade Oval** set includes earrings, pin, bracelet, and pendant. These were among the first genuine jade pieces set in 12K gold filled mountings. Original prices were $17 for earrings, $30 for pin, $27 for bracelet, and $10 for pendant. Current value of set: $60-95. **Jade Rose** pin and earrings are genuine jade stones in a leaf or heart shape. The rose blossoms on the pin inspired the name for this glamorous goldentone set. Original prices were $24 for pin and $22 for earrings. Special discount was from one third to one half off original price on these Lady Coventry pieces. Current value: $25-45. **Jade 'n Pearl** set includes a pin and pendant featured in the mid-1970s. The pin and pendant are both genuine jade with a cultured pearl set in a goldentone setting. Pendant is on a 16-18" adjustable chain. Original prices were $25 for pendant and $24.50 for pin. The set also included a ring. Current value for set: $35-60. *All courtesy of Alynda Kimbrough.*

Left to right: In the late 1960s Lady Coventry pieces were focused on a variety of semi-precious and genuine stones. **Flowered Circle** pin and earrings were found in the 1967 catalogs. "The classic circle design is made more beautiful with the artistic use of semi-precious stones nestled among the leaves. This lovely set has the added beauty of genuine rose quartz (pink), Wyoming jade (green), sodolite (blue) and cultured pearl." The set was originally priced at $10. Current value: $35-60. **Semi-Precious Turtle** pin is created similarly, but was not a part of that set. The goldentone turtle shell is crafted from semi-precious stones, making it a highly collectible item as it wasn't continued very long. B; ; $20-45. **Genuine Jade** necklace and earrings were created in the late 1970s. The necklace has a 24" and 33" chain with stationed genuine jade beads. The pierced earrings are genuine jade balls on surgical steel posts. Original price of necklace was $26, earrings $11. Current value: $25-40. *All courtesy of Alynda Kimbrough.*

Left to right: **Genuine Tiger Eye Choker** is a 15" goldentone chain with stationed square shaped genuine tiger eye stones. This necklace was from the late '70s. Original price: $25. Current value: $15-30. **Tiger Eye Butterfly** pin is a goldentone flat open-weave butterfly shape with the body of genuine tiger eye. Original price: $17. Current value: $15-30. **Tiger Eye Cross** is a genuine tiger eye solid cross shape with chain through the top arm. Original price: $15. Current value: $15-30. **Genuine Tiger Eye** pierced earrings were designed to complement any of the genuine tiger eye pieces. Original price: $14. Current value: $10-25. **Genuine Sodalite** ring and earrings are set in sterling silver. The ring is adjustable and the earrings have surgical steel posts. These were found only in the late 1970s. Original price of ring was $12.50 and earrings $11. Current value: $20-35 (because they were not documented very long). **Carved Tiger Eye** pendant and one earring. The dainty pendant on an adjustable 16-18" goldentone chain matches the same rose carved shape in the genuine tiger eye stone. C; $20-45. *Courtesy of Alynda Kimbrough.*

Left to right: *Mother of Pearl Cameo* pierced earrings and pendant necklace are of sterling silver. The genuine mother of pearl was an exclusive part of the Lady Coventry "Deluxe Gift Collection." Original price for pendant was $13 and earrings $15, with half price option when purchasing two at regular price. Current value: $25-40. *Filigree Ivory* pendant is 12KT gold filled and bracelet is goldentone. Original price for pendant was $12 and bracelet $14. Current value: $25-40. **Center, top to bottom**: *Lovers Knot* earrings are goldentone rope knot with a simulated pearl center. B; $10-25. *Rejoice* ring is a 12KT gold filled ring with genuine ruby set in sterling. D; $10-25. *Diamond Classic* pin and earrings set is goldentone with a diamond chip in the center of the pin only. Original price: $35. Current value: $25-40. **Far right**: *Lady Coventry* earrings are from the late 1960s and are simulated pearls matching a set of simulated pearls. Original price: $5. Current value: $10-25. *Satin Drops* earrings are 12KT gold filled posts and chains utilizing a unique technique. The post and chain both went through the ear to attach to a satin drop on the other end. D; $15.50 *Courtesy of Alynda Kimbrough.*

Top row, left to right: *Horizons* sized ring is a genuine tiger eye ring identified as a hostess gift for 1700 points. $10-25. *Genuine Tiger Eye* adjustable ring is goldentone with the genuine tiger eye set. D; $15-30. *Genuine Opal* ring has an opal set in a goldentone mounting. Original price: $26.50. Current value: $15-30. *Initial* ring represents another set of initials from Sarah designers. E; $15-30. **Bottom row, left to right**: Sterling silver *Lord or Lady Coventry* ring could be purchased in sizes for him as well as her. The original price ranged from $21-24 in the late 1970s. Current value: $15-30. *Flower of the Month* designs in sterling silver were created in the late 1960s. The flowers for January through December were: carnation, violet, daffodil, daisy, lily of the valley, rose, lily, gladiolus, aster, calendula, poinsettia. Pictured here is the August pin with a gladiolus, priced at $10. Current value: $15-30. **Pendants, left to right**: *Diamond Accent* is a goldentone necklace with an adjustable 16-18" chain and a genuine diamond chip set in jet black. D; $15-30. *Lady Coventry Birthstone* pendant sports an imported Austrian glass stone set in sterling silver for the various colors of birth months. D; $15-30. *Silvery Moonstone* pendant, part of "The Silvery Collection," is created from a genuine moonstone surrounded by a sterling silver mounting on an adjustable 16-18" chain. C; $15-30. *Antiqued Amethyst* pendant has a 16-18" adjustable necklace. No original price known. Matching set on page 136. Current value: $15-30. Dark blue *Sodalite* pendant is set in sterling silver mountings. No original price known. Current value: $15-30. *All courtesy of Alynda Kimbrough.*

Top: *Mother's Pin (Family Tree)* pin in goldentone. "Custom set jewelry designed 'Especially for you.'" The birthdate stones were "designated by fine Swarovski Austrian Rhinestones." Such custom orders took up to 30 days for delivery. Originally priced at $20; special price was half. Current value: $25-40. **Center row, left to right**: *Children's Birthstone* ring is a delicate two stone goldentone ring highlighting two Austrian glass stones. A; $10-25. *Love Story* birthstone rings for March and February: "each romantic ring joins two beautiful Austrian rhinestone hearts together in an unusual silvertone leaf design." In the mid-1970s, the regular price was $5. These were very popular so will be easy to find. Other rings of this style are shown on pages 134 and 135. Current value: $10-25. *Sarah's Mother Ring* is "A family portrait for your finger…made of long wearing 24K gold plate and prong set with beautiful Austrian crystal rhinestones representing each member of your family." Prices ranged from $10 for one stone to $50 for nine stones, with increments of $5 for each stone in between. These could be purchased at half price as well and also obtained through hostess credit points. Current value: $20-45. **Bottom row**: *Miss Sarah Birthstone Pendants*: "The tiny and delicate pendant is worn by both the young and those who like small jewelry. This unusually attractive pendant boasts a well-cut glass stone in all the birthstone colors." SarahGlo silvertone mounting. B; $10-20 (on chain). *Sarah Coventry's Family Bouquet* ring: "this fashionable and unique ring is custom set with your personally selected birthstones, each representing someone close to you. Create your exclusive design with 7 stones from Sarah's elegant collection of synthetic birthstones. Your special bouquet will sparkle from the Goldentone setting which rests on a 14K gold filled shank." There was also a personalized service for replacing stones, available by sending $1.50 and the ring. The ring could also be sent for professional cleaning and reconditioning for a $1.50 fee. Regular price of the ring with seven sets was $50; it could be purchased at half price with multiple orders. Current value: $15-30. *All courtesy of Alynda Kimbrough.*

Lady Coventry was hooked on birthstone items. This advertisement (from a *Ladies Home Journal* magazine) shows **Sterling Silver Charms**, each designed like a bird cage with the birthstone nestled in the base. Another versatile item designed in the late 1960s, they were worn on chains as pendants, on link bracelets as charms, on earrings, watches, or on pins as dangles. D; $15-30.

Top to bottom: *Lady Coventry* bracelet in box is a sterling silver open link chain bracelet with a sterling silver charm waiting for an initial or name to be engraved. Sarah Coventry was very interested in giving each customer "a personal identity" through the use of initial options and birthstones. C; $15-30. **Cultured Pearls** are a 21" length of actual cultured pearls with a sterling silver clasp. Original price was $30, with a special discount of $7 when multiple purchases were made. Current value: $15-30. *Courtesy of Alynda Kimbrough.*

1969 Catalog

The following 1969 catalog is courtesy of Dawn Michael, who luckily had kept many of the original sales booklets. Enjoy viewing the original pieces and company information.

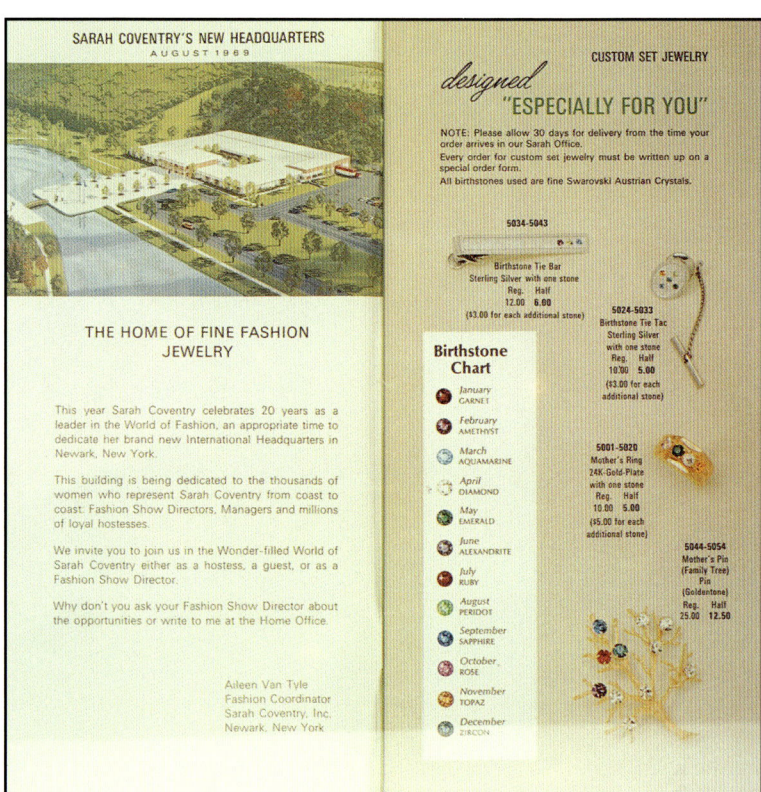

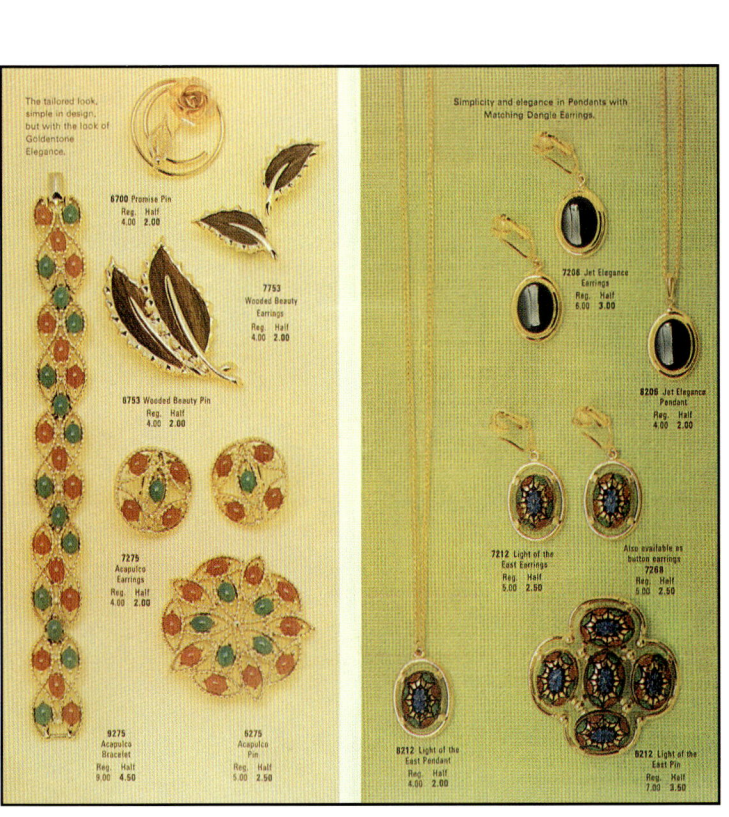

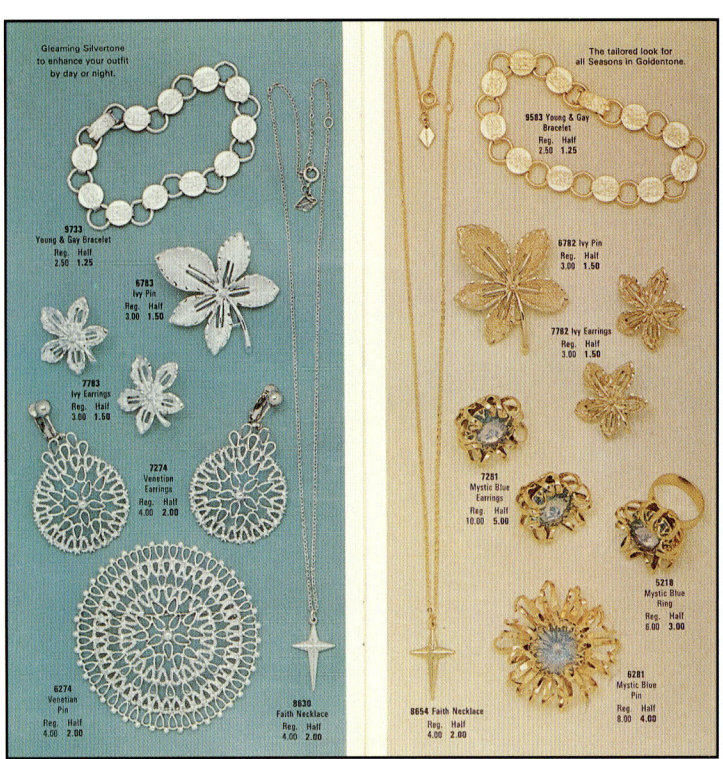

92

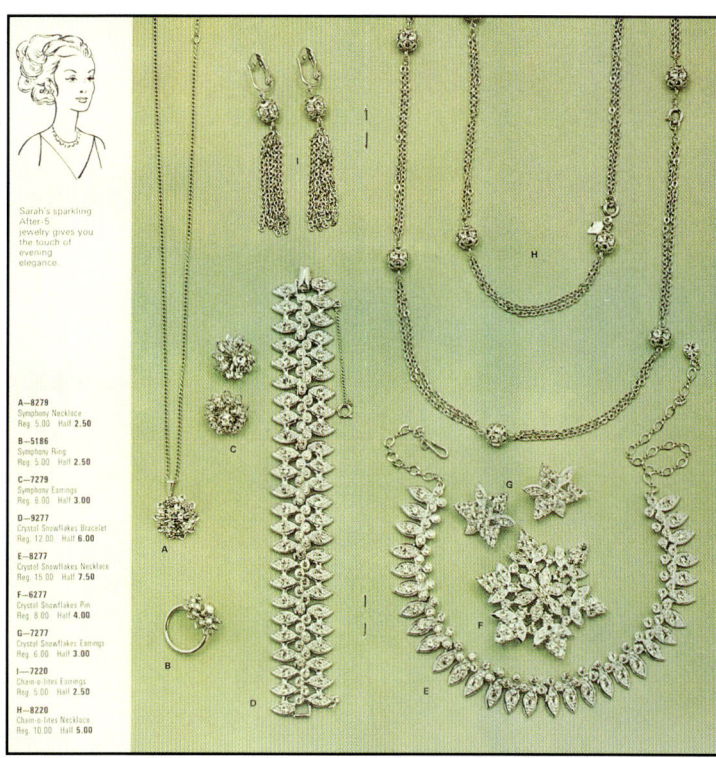

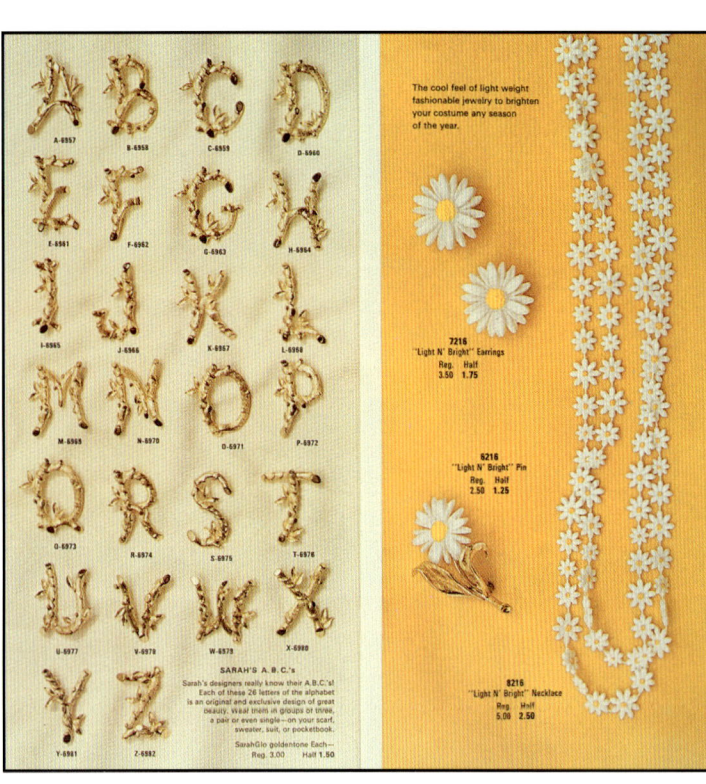

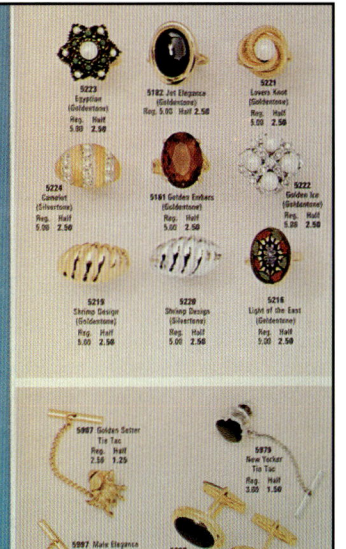

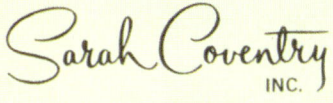

Sarah Coventry INC.

AS ADVERTISED IN

McCall's
TV Guide
Harper's Bazaar
Vogue
Glamour
Mademoiselle
Seventeen
Red Book
Cosmopolitan
Parents'
Ladies' Home Journal
Good Housekeeping
Family Circle
Woman's Day

For more information, contact me—your Fashion Show Director.

_____
Name

_____
Address

_____
City/State

_____
Telephone

NEWARK, NEW YORK
COPYRIGHT AUGUST 1969

PRINTED IN U.S.A.

Chapter Four

The 1970s

Alynda Kimbrough was one of the many Fashion Show Directors who continued up the ladder to Branch Manager. When visiting with Alynda, I met several of her daughters who were born during the time of her employment with Sarah Coventry: 1962 to 1980. Evidence of the "family" feeling toward Sarah Coventry as a company was voiced continually by the whole family. Their discussion and memories made my photography visit very special. Alynda was especially thankful for the job opportunity because it allowed her to be home with her children as much as she wanted to be. It also gave her the opportunity of owning and wearing "extremely gorgeous jewelry," particularly the Lady Coventry collection.

In the 1970s, costume jewelry was not exactly a must-have wardrobe addition. However, Sarah Coventry kept right on setting the kinds of fashion trends that kept customers coming back time and again. Some of these efforts came from two Limited Edition series—Christmas charms and crosses. These collectible items gave a new twist to the costume jewelry trends of working women, college students, and even the stay-at-home moms.

This charm bracelet shows Limited Edition Christmas charms from 1971 to 1977. The charms came in extraordinary boxes, such as the one pictured from 1972. Most of the employees I visited with had these charms. *Courtesy of Dawn Michael.*

Alynda Kimbrough began as a Sarah Coventry Fashion Show Director in 1962 and later became a Branch Manager. The ruby and diamond pendant she is wearing was one of the many awards she earned during her eighteen "wonderful" years with Sarah Coventry.

During my visit, Alynda mentioned Sarah Coventry's guarantee several times and how important customer satisfaction was to the company. She felt this gave Sarah Coventry jewelry the edge to "stay out there in front" while other costume jewelry companies were folding. Shown below are Sarah Coventry's Golden Guarantee and Additional Service Contract, both from the "Spirit of Summer '76 Jewelry Collection by Sarah Coventry®, INC" catalog (*Courtesy of Dawn Michael*).

SARAH COVENTRY'S GOLDEN GUARANTEE

Your Sarah Coventry jewelry is guaranteed for complete satisfaction. Any item not satisfactory to you may be replaced or you may request a refund of your purchase price.

To obtain either a refund or a replacement of your item, mail the item along with your Guest Receipt and a note instructing the Company as to whether you wish a refund or replacement. Mail insured to Sarah Coventry, Inc., Newark, New York, 14593. Your replacement or refund will be promptly handled upon receipt of item(s) at Sarah Coventry, Inc., Newark, New York, 14593.

ADDITIONAL SERVICE

If during the first ninety days after receiving your jewelry, it should become damaged due to normal use it will be replaced or repaired free of charge upon your returning the item with the Guest Receipt to the Company. After ninety days, it will be repaired or replaced upon return of the item with the Guest Receipt and $1.50 to the Company, providing the item is still carried in stock. Your request for repairs or replacements should be insured and mailed to Sarah Coventry, Inc., Newark, New York, 14593.

Please note that the item is to be returned directly to SARAH COVENTRY, INC., NEWARK, NEW YORK STATE, 14593 for replacing or refunding. The Fashion show Director is *not* authorized to accept returns.

Another factor contributing to Sarah Coventry's continued success throughout the '70s was the use of imported stones. Several employees with whom I spoke mentioned that additional stones were supplied to FSDs to take care of replacement problems. Some also interchanged stones in a bracelet in order to complement a costume, thus the total look of the piece was changed. The following information about the stones was found in the "Sarah Coventry Spring 1979 Jewelry Collection" catalog (*Courtesy of Dawn Michael*).

Sarah Knows How™. . . with Imported Stones

Sarah's 29 years of expertise in the creation of fashionable, fine quality jewelry has led to a close tie with the craftsmen of Tirol, Austria and the Bavarian craft shops of Kaufburen, Germany, where glass stones are made by hand using the art and skills passed from generation to generation in these family owned craft shops.

In appreciation of the artistry of these craftsmen, Sarah has developed a symbol to commemorate the glass stone making art around the world." [the following descriptions identify a few of the hand operations required to provide glass stones]

"**A. Beveling** Craft worker bevels stone edge on sandstone grinding wheel to final size and shape.
B. Glass Making Craft workers stretch molten glass to form glass rods. Different design effects require a wide variety of glass rods.
C. Stone Pressing Craft worker heats glass rod in open oven, then presses glass rod between steel tools to form basic stone shape.
D. Stone Pressing Craft worker separates group of stones from glass rod after pressing.
E. Painting Crafter worker hand paints a glass stone with various colors to obtain a mosaic design.
F. Shearing Craft worker removes excess glass from stone edge with hand shears.

. . . Please note not all stones in the catalog are from the Bavarian craft shops or Tirol craftsmen. Many beautiful stones come from Germany, the Orient and around the world.

Jewelry fashions of the 1970s ranged from delicate to large chunky pieces. Towards the end of the decade more feminine styles were created, with chains and colorful beads as attractive add-ons. The availability and affordability of real gold jewelry was creating the need for costume jewelry to imitate the "real gold" look. As you browse through the 1970s pictures, you will see how Sarah Coventry jewelry was able to survive the gradual downturn in costume jewelry—watch for more goldentone chains and tassels, more ornate metal work, fewer rhinestones, more painted sets, and genuine or semi-precious stones. You'll also notice that it was much easier for me to locate pieces from the '70s, suggesting how popular Sarah Coventry jewelry was during this decade.

Brooches

Top row, left to right: *Contessa* pin/pendant combination illustrates one of the ways Sarah made pieces of jewelry very versatile. It could be worn as a pin one day and then a chain or strand of pearls attached to the hook on the back the next day for a glamorous pendant. "Round the clock with Sarah." The signature on the back is just "COVENTRY." There is also a necklace with the same name, not a match. Found in 1976 catalogs. D; $20-45. *Black Charmer* pin/pendant generally appeared on a strand of black beads. D; $20-35 (without beads, value more if attached to the black beads). *Sunset Elegance* pin/pendant originally came on an 18" black cord. This striking flower gives the impression of a sunset. The piece I have was not marked on the back so I was lucky to discover it in a 1977 catalog. D; $20-35. **Bottom row, left to right**: *Emeraude Drop* was pictured with a variety of other drops and charms, with items identified "for young and young-at-heart." B; $10-25. *Polonaise* pendant has "rhinestones permanently set through new methods in Austria." Matching earrings on page 105, matching choker necklace under the name of New Polonaise in 1977 on page 136. D; $20-45. *Czarina* pendant has a beautiful turquoise stone embedded in an antiqued goldentone mounting. Smaller turquoise stones were embedded around the larger stone. These stones are often missing in pieces I've located. Matching ring on page 132. B; $10-25 (with chain, value without chain $8-20). *On Stage* necklace pendants are baroque (simulated) pearl beads in a silvertone cap necklace clasp. They were generally sold with a strand of pearls and a silvertone chain shown on page 77. C; $15-30 with strands (without strand and chain, $8-15 each).

Top row, left to right: *Ribbonette* pin in goldentone features a ribbon effect using both stippled texturing and gouged technique found in a 1971 catalog. Also came in silvertone. B; $10-25. *Fashion Splendor* pin is one of my early pieces. This striking goldentone pin is fun to wear and still gets lots of compliments. The contrasting opaque pink beads, pearls, and marquise shaped light green multi-faceted rhinestones makes it quite dynamic. Matching earrings on page 106. B; $20-45. *White Velvet* is a leaf of white enameled metal, another design from Sarah's nature theme. B; $10-25. **Bottom row, left to right**: *Springtime* silvertone pin uses a combination of four dynamically different colored rhinestones and a variety of shapes. There are several other pieces with the "springtime" name. C; $20-45. *Persian Princess* is a glamorous pin with one large and several smaller simulated pearls set within a silvertone, diamond shaped, open weave of rhinestone paved leaves. The first one I found had a pink pearl set in the middle. Someone had used fingernail polish to create a different look. BEWARE. Matching earrings on page 80 of Lindbeck book. C; $15-30. *Ceylon* pin is a beautiful goldentone pin with contrasting hot pink rhinestones and solid blue sets. Matching earrings on page105. B; $18-35.

Top row, left to right: *Remembrance Stick Pin* has an antiqued goldentone frame for a turquoise center stone surrounded by smaller simulated pearls. In 1971 stick pins were very popular items to wear with scarves as well as on jacket lapels, collars, coats, and cloth handbags. Matching regular pin follows, matching earrings on pages 72 and 104. B; $10-25. *Remembrance* pin has diamond shaped antiqued goldentone surrounding an oval turquoise cabochon with tear dropped turquoise sets and simulated pearls. Same pin on page 67, matching earrings on pages 72 and 104. B; $15-30. *Ember Flower* is a goldentone flower with stem and green enameled leaves. The center chaton cut, ember colored, Austrian prong set rhinestone makes this a dynamic pin to wear with almost any type of dress, suit, or coat. B; $20-35. **Bottom row, left to right**: *Delicious* is a striking peach colored, apple shaped stone created to portray this "delicious" apple. Matching earrings on page 105 of Lindbeck book. B; $10-25. *Sea Sprite* pins in goldentone and silvertone have a unique "U" shaped open effect. Marked on back "©SARAH COV" in raised lettering. Matching earrings on page 105. A; $8-25.

Top row, left to right: *Silent Spring* pin, pictured only in the 1970 catalog, is a stem of leaves in gleaming silvertone. A; $8-20. *Radiance* denotes these dazzling chaton cut, prong set rhinestones on a long curved, sleek stem nestled on a wider goldentone leaf. This pin and the matching earrings were originally from the pre 1966 cardex items but were continued through the early 1970s as hostess credit items. Matching earrings on page 39. A; $20-45. *Masterpiece Stick* pin has a stone picturing the Mona Lisa in "designs from the past recreated for today." Matching pin on page 100. B; $10-25.
Bottom row, left to right: *Multiple Choice* pins were another set of Sarah's ABC's. "Sarah's designers really know their A.B.C.'s. Each of these gleaming silvertone initials is an original design. The modern initials can be worn in groups of three, a pair or even a single, pinned to your scarf, sweater or pocketbook." Marked on back "SARAH" engraved. B; $8-20.
Moon-lites pin is a goldentone circle pin with multi-colored pastel chaton cut iridescent stones. They do give a moonlight effect in the sunlight. This set was striking, however, it can be found only in the 1970 catalog. I believe this was because the sets came out easily. Matching bracelet on page 80, matching earrings on page 106. *Silvery Swirl* achieves a swirling effect by alternating shiny with textured silvertone. A; $8-20.

Top row, left to right: *Jet Set Versatile* pendant/pin combination is a silvertone geometric circle design with a jet black center set. Matching earrings on page 105, matching bracelet on page 129, matching ring on page 131. C; $10-25. *Silvery Mist* pin is a simple circle pin created from silvertone swirls. Matching earrings on page 105. A; $8-20. *Peace* pin features a dove shape with various silvertone techniques. A; $10-25. **Bottom row, left to right**: *Carousel* pin is another silvertone circle pin that demonstrates the variety of techniques used to create a uniquely different piece of Sarah jewelry. This piece is from the late 1970s and is not like any of the other pieces with this same name. B; $10-25. *Flair* is a slim-lined striking silvertone pin giving a "flair" to any costume. Earrings similar to this pin on page 105. A; $8-20. *Slick Chick* is a goldentone bird shape from "Nature's friends for a whimsical touch of fashion." Marked "©COVENTRY" in raised letters. B; $8-20.

Top row, right to left: *Touch of Elegance* pin is created from oval multi-faceted Austrian stones capped with mesh goldentone stems. Matching earrings on page 105. C; $15-30. *Royal Velvet* is an appropriate name for this glamorous purple chaton cut rhinestone surrounded by a silvertone ridge entrenched with small clear rhinestones. Marked on back "©SARAH" in raised letters. Matching earrings on page 106. D; $20-45. *Americana* is a patriotic red, white, and blue starburst goldentone pin created in anticipation of the Bicentennial celebration in 1976. Bring it out to be worn any time you're celebrating our freedom. Matching earrings on page 104. B; $15-30. **Bottom row, left to right**: *Saucy* pins in silvertone and goldentone are open circle/apple shapes with textured leaves and stem completing the design. There are several pieces with the name "Saucy." Marked on gold with "©SARAH" raised, on silvertone as "©SARAH COV" raised. A; $8-20. *Masterpiece* pin has an antiqued goldentone oval mounting supporting the Mona Lisa. The final touch are the miniature simulated pearls accenting the edges. "Designs from the past recreated for Today." Matching stick pin on page 99. C; $20-45.

Top row, left to right: *Criss-Cross* pin is exactly as its name says, a criss-cross effect in silvertone. Same pin shown on page 101. B; $10-25. *Serenade* pin is a striking goldentone circle with a starburst shape within. Brilliant red cabochon sets create an exquisite contrast. There is a necklace with the same name but it is totally different. Matching earrings on page 105, matching bracelet on page 128. B; $20-45. *Mr. Sea Gull* is a sleek silvertone flying seagull, showing again how Sarah's designers had an eye for how designs from nature would make unique pieces of jewelry. B; $10-25. **Bottom row, left to right**: *Venetian* pin is a unique open-weave silvertone circle. "Gleaming silvertone to enhance your outfit by day or night." The identifying mark is very difficult to see on the back of this pin so look closely. Matching earrings on page 106. B; $10-25. *Westminster* is a stately sized yet proper and richly designed pin with a hint of a crown on the red button set. Marked "©SARAH" in raised lettering. Matching earrings on page 106. C; $10-25. *Granada* pin can also be attached to black pearls and worn choker fashion. The gray cabochon bead is surrounded by textured silvertone giving the appearance of a million rhinestones. There are no matching pieces to this pin, however there are other pieces with this same name. B; $15-30.

Top row, left to right: *Jubilee* pin is a true replica of silvertone open-weave cherries artfully dangling from their stem and leaves. Marked "SARAH" raised. B; $8-20. *Silvery Sunburst* pin has textured and shiny swirls in a sunburst effect, plus a large simulated pearl in the center. This pin became a very popular piece and will be easy to find. Some have even received a paint job. B; $10-25. *Suzette* is a goldentone poodle pin created in 1971. The open-weave and red-eye rhinestone made this pin a delight for any age wearer. A; $10-25. *Sparkle Lites* pin is a fantastic blossom of crystal rhinestones set in a shimmering silvertone setting. Matching earrings on page 106. B; $15-35. **Bottom row, left to right**: *Hooter* appropriately names this glamorous owl of goldentone. Yellow iridescent rhinestone eyes give the impression they are really looking at you. Be sure to find one of these pins. A; $10-25. *Fleurette* pins in silvertone and goldentone were identified as "Sarah's Classics." Marked "©SARAH" in raised lettering. B; $10-25. *Professor* pin is a cute little owl with moveable glasses and red rhinestone eyes, an eye-catching small-sized pin for any age wearer. It's another indication of the creativity and uniqueness of the Sarah designers. Marked "©COVENTRY" in raised letters. B; $15-30.

Top: *Peking* is an open-weave goldentone pin with cabochon bead center and tassel—an oriental looking piece. Matching earrings on page 106. C; $15-30. **Center**: *Burgundy* pin is a luscious burgundy colored clear apple set in goldentone. Matching earrings on page 106. A; $10-25. **Bottom row, left to right**: *Orbit* is the unique name given to this goldentone shiny and textured piece bringing to mind a satellite path. The center cabochon bead of dark orange/red provides a colorful accent and no doubt symbolizes the space events happening in the late 1960s and early '70s. Silvertone pin and earrings on page 111 of Lindbeck book. B; $10-25. *Madame Butterfly* pin in goldentone is a replica of a butterfly in artfully detailed fashion. Also came in silvertone. These butterflies continued all through the 1970s. A; $10-25. *Fashion Twist Stick* is a stick pin of silvertone with a very simplistic swirl or twist design. Marked "©SC" in raised letters. B; $10-25.

Top row, left to right: *Golden Tulip* pin is "delicate golden jewelry for the precious look." This circle pin is designed with tulip blossoms and leaves. Matching necklace/pendant on page 124, matching earrings on page 108. C; $20-35. *Magic Moods* is a large oval turquoise cabochon surrounded by simulated pearls embraced in scallops around the outer edge. This pin can also be worn as a pendant and originally came with two chains: one fine, the second a larger link. A tassel of goldentone was also attached to the pin and of course could be removed. Again, an example of versatility. C; $20-35. *Tracery* pin is bold, textured goldentone with intertwining "e" shapes. Marked on back "©COVENTRY" in raised letters. B; $15-30. **Bottom row, left to right**: *Antique Rose* is a circular antiqued silvertone pin formed by alternating rose buds with leaves. Simple, but dynamic. Matching earrings on page 104, matching bracelet on page 129. A; $8-20. *Moonlight* pin has "gleaming pearls and sparkling rhinestones for that special occasion look." C; $20-45. *Strawflower* pin is a circle shaped pin with tiny strawflowers among goldentone leaves. Matching bracelet on page 129. B; $10-25.

Top row, left to right: *White Petals* pin is a simple combination of silvertone and white enameled petals creating a 3-D effect. This pin was designed to be coupled with the Pastel Parfait beads in 1972 catalogs. Matching earrings on page 104, matching beads on page 115. B; $15-30. *Festival* pin has multi-colored cabochon beads entwined with a rope-like goldentone mounting. C; $20-35. **Bottom**: *Criss-Cross* pin is exactly what it sounds like—a silvertone square shape with a criss-cross effect in the center. This was a fairly popular pin, however, it was only found in one year's catalogs (1971). Same pin shown on page 100. B; $8-20. *Courtesy of Otheda Smith.*

Top row, left to right: ***Split-Trick*** is a silvertone antiqued pin with a versatile use. The raised front opening allowed it to be used with scarves or chains or worn solely as a pin. Another innovative trick of Sarah's designers. B; $10-25. ***Silvery Nectar*** appropriately describes this textured silvertone peach, another design from nature. B; $10-25. ***Shangri-la*** makes glamorous use of turquoise beads and clear and amethyst rhinestones in a wavy replica of a scarf or rug. Matching necklace on page 123, matching earrings on page 109, matching ring on page 131. matching bracelet on page 128. D; $25-40. ***Sabu*** is a unique small elephant in goldentone, an action oriented replica of one of our friends from nature. A; $8-20. **Bottom row, left to right:** ***Unidentified*** is a 3-D crescent moon shaped pin. A similar pin is called "crescent," but this one is uniquely different. $10-25. ***Blue Snowflake*** is a simple yet elegant silvertone snowflake with a dark blue rhinestone surrounded by smaller light blue and dark blue rhinestones. C; $20-45. ***Flirtation*** was from the early 1960s so obscure it being in this grouping of '70s pins. This sparkling, glistening, flirtatious SarahSheen silvertone pin is shaped like a lily pad with a fluted edge. A; $10-25.

Left to right: ***Feather Bright*** pin is a three-leaf flower on stem of goldentone. This pin was found in only one of the catalogs from 1973. A; $10-25. ***Unidentified*** is a curved goldentone leaf with two simulated pearls in the curve. It is interesting that this pin is similar to one named Feather-Brite, which is without the pearls. Help me document this one. B; $10-25.

Top row, left to right: ***Azure Skies*** pin is an exquisite yet simple circular pin with turquoise center and teardrop shapes on goldentone textured swirls culminating in tiny rhinestones. Marked "©SARAH" in raised letters. Matching necklace on page 112, matching ring on page 131. C; $15-30. ***Inca*** pin has a turquoise and silver cross shape pin inspired by America's own native lore. Matching earrings on page 107. B; $15-30.
Bottom row, left to right: ***Golden Acorn*** is a goldentone acorn shaped pin with open weave. Marked "©SARAH" in raised lettering. A; $10-25. ***Fire'n Ice*** pin in goldentone has a circular flame-like shape and is overlaid with an icy effect of silvertone. Marked "©SARAH" in raised lettering. B; $15-30.
Candy Land pin features a leaf design on stem with plastic cabochons in pastel pink, yellow, teal, and tangerine for the leaf positions. Marked "©SARAH" in raised letters. Matching earrings on page 104. B; $10-25.

Top row, left to right: *Wings of Fashion* pin was described as "ecology and…the look of today." This butterfly was created in goldentone with dark green and coral beads and a clear light green rhinestone as the head. One coral bead is missing. This pin was found in only one catalog for 1974. B; $10-25. *Coraline* pin is also a pendant with the hook. The oval shaped coral set in goldentone is striking yet simple. C; $15-30. *Circlet* pin is created from two circles within each other, both of shiny silvertone, held together by textured silvertone and a shiny hook connecting all three at the top. Matching earrings on page 108, B; $10-25. **Bottom row, left to right**: *Space Age* is a skewed shiny goldentone shape open in the center with a large simulated pearl on the rim. This was created in 1970, no doubt coinciding with the space exploration being done at the time. Matching ring on page 132. B; $10-25. *Imperial* pin, also a pendant, is created of antiqued silvertone shaped like a royal motif with a turquoise teardrop shaped cabochon, simulated pearls, and amethyst colored rhinestones. Matching ring on page 135. C; $15-35. *Sign of Spring* is a very small goldentone pin featuring a bird with a faux jewel eye sitting on a branch, along with a nest with three tiny simulated egg pearls. B; $10-25. *Trellis* pin was identified as "tailored silvertone in classic designs." This is a circular shaped open trellis silvertone pin. Matching earrings on page 108. B; $10-25.

Top row, left to right: *Autumn Splendor* pin has salmon colored inlay on a goldentone leaf pattern. C; $15-30. *Ember Light* (this pin is exactly like a necklace of this name found in catalogs of 1967, so I am giving it the same name even though it is a pin) features a "beautifully faceted golden colored stone imported from Austria and handsomely encased in a high polish oval frame. Feminine and delicate and fashion right for any age." A; $10-25. **Far right:** *Jonquil* is a starburst shaped pin of goldentone with gold, orange, and light green small rhinestones. Matching ring on page 82. B; $15-30. **Bottom row, left to right**: *Austrian Lites* is one of my favorite pieces. It has imported Austrian stones of light green, light pink, and dark burgundy in a square shaped goldentone antique frame and "…could be worn with sweaters, dresses, casual or romantic wear." Matching earrings on page 104, matching bracelet on page 128, matching ring on page 131. C; $20-45. *Tangerine* pin is open-weave goldentone with the look of threaded orange beads. Matching earrings on page 110. B; $10-25.

Earrings

Top row, left to right: *Antique Rose* earrings have a small rose and two leaves carved from antiqued silvertone. Matching pin on page 101, matching bracelet on page 129. A; $8-20. *White Petals* earrings are multi-leveled enamel and silvertone leaves with a center silver ball. Can be worn alone or coupled with the Pastel Parfait, various pastel colors, or white. Matching pin on page 101, matching Pastel Parfait necklaces on page 115. B; $10-25. *Aloha* earrings are bronzed goldentone dangles with a leaf and bead motif. Matching necklace on page 119. B; $15-30 **Bottom row, left to right**: *Austrian Lites* earrings are imported Austrian rhinestones of light pink and light green surrounding a large light green rhinestone in goldentone. A favorite of many, so easy to find. Matching pin on page 103, matching ring on page 131, matching bracelet on page 128. B; $15-30. *Candy Land* earrings are pastel plastic cabochons creating a three leaf design on a stem of goldentone. Matching pin on page 102. B; $10-25.

Top row, left to right: *Taste of Honey* pierced earrings from the mid-1970s have a plastic golden colored disk centered in a goldentone wire cage. Identified as "multiple embertones." Matching necklace on page 115. B; $10-25. *Aquarius* earrings are clip-on buttons created from solid turquoise beads and clear rhinestones. They are from the late 1960s and early '70s. Matching pin on page 65 of Lindbeck book. B; $15-30. *Sea Star* earrings are from the Ecology Collection. "The eternal mystery of the sea, the graceful starfish. Finely crafted, exquisite in every detail, your starfish earrings are distinctively modern yet classically sophisticated, shimmering and warm, with the subtlety of the sea itself. *A donation has been made by Sarah Coventry to the Cousteau Society for the preservation of the Society for the preservation of the environment.*" Matching bracelet on page 127, matching ring on page 132. C; $15-30. **Bottom row, left to right**: *Nocturne* pierced earrings are miniature owls with amethyst rhinestone eyes. The larger owl on matching bracelet is on page 129. B; $8-20. *Remembrance* earrings came in two styles. This style is a smaller pierced version with surgical steel posts. The center turquoise stone matches the stones in the larger matching earrings on page 72, matching pin on page 67, and matching stick pin on page 99. *Diamonice* earrings are pierced simulated diamonds with 14K gold posts. B; $10-25. *Americana* earrings are pierced red, white, and blue cabochon beads mounted in textured goldentone. Even though they are pierced, they are marked "©SARAH COV" engraved. Matching pin on page 100. B; $10-25. *All courtesy of Alynda Kimbrough.*

Top row, left to right: *Charisma* earrings have a silvertone open-weave curve design with three spoke dangles. These are "chicken" type earrings. Pierced were listed at a slightly higher price. Matching necklace on page 113. B; $10-25. *Golden Petals* are dangles of goldentone identified as "Golden classics for any age." Matching necklace on page 114. B; $10-25. *Hi-Lo Elegance* truly describes these goldentone diamond shaped earrings with a tassel dangle. Matching necklace on page 112. B; $10-25. **Bottom row, left to right:** *Silvery Mist* are circle shaped earrings with a silvery curve misty effect. Matching pin on page 99. A; $10-25. *Unidentified* earrings are similar to a pin called "Flair." These have extra hatchwork of silvertone on top that the pin does not have. $10-25. *Fashion-rite* is the rather plain name given these intricately designed seed-like earrings. A; $10-25.

Top row, left to right: *Jet Set* earrings have a jet black cabochon set surrounded by a narrow geometric open-weave band. Matching ring on page 131, matching bracelet on page 129. B; $10-25. *Ceylon* earrings are richly colored opaque turquoise beads and dark red rhinestones on goldentone wire circles. Matching pin on page 98. B; $15-30. *Polonaise* earrings (only one shown here) came in both pierced look and pierced with the dangle removable. "Polonaise—rhinestones permanently set through new methods in Austria." Matching pendant on page 98. C; $15-30 (pair). **Bottom row, left to right:** *Serenade* earrings are very striking with red beads and rhinestones set in goldentone. There is a necklace with this same name that is not a match. Matching pin on page 100, matching bracelet on page 128. B; $15-30. *Sabrina* pierced earrings have a delicate goldentone dangle design with simulated pearl attached. There is a very delicate chain necklace that has sections of pearls alternating with chain and sections of this same goldentone dangle design. Look for it, the set is very wearable today. Same earrings on page 109. B; $10-25. *Pyramid Treasure* is a single earring with two dangle disks of silvertone. Very lightweight and petite. Matching necklace/bib on page 121. B; $8-20 (pair).

Top row, left to right: *Touch of Elegance* earrings have a large multi-faceted green stone capped with an open-mesh goldentone case. A smaller green rhinestone accents the ear at the post. Matching pin on page 100. B; $15-30. *Fancy Free* earrings are textured and shiny circle silvertone dangle pierced hoop earrings. There are several non-matching sets with the same name. Matching bracelet on page 126. B; $8-20. *Ming Garden* earrings are green plastic oriental designs encased in a goldentone scalloped design. The designs are removable and can be attached to a hook or a post. Matching pendant/necklace on page 78. B; $10-25. **Bottom row, left to right:** *Mosaic* earrings are goldentone buttons with diamond shapes engraved in the top, each colored green, orange, yellow, or red. Matching necklace on page 113, men's set on page 166. B; $8-15. *Sea Sprite* earrings in goldentone and silvertone resemble a sea creature with their open "U" shaped design. Matching pin on page 99. A; $8-20.

Top row, left to right: *Button Pearl* earrings are small simulated pearls mounted on silvertone clip backs. Very classic and yet very inexpensive even in 1970. A; $10-25. *Tudor* earrings have dark blue multi-faceted square opaque stones surrounded by a frame of antiqued silvertone. Reverse side is antiqued scrolled silvertone. Matching cross necklace on page 139, matching pendant called Roman Holiday on page 116. B; $10-25. *Burgundy* earrings have clear, burgundy colored stones replicating apples on goldentone. Matching pin on page 101. B; $10-25. **Bottom row, left to right:** *Catherine* earrings are iridescent oval fuchsia colored cabochons surrounded by antiqued silvertone mounting with accents of four small simulated pearls. Matching pendant on page 47 of Lindbeck book, matching ring on page 135. B; $10-25. *Westminster* earrings feature a simulated crown shape of goldentone, a large red flat bead accented with a center simulated bead, and a bead dangle. Matching pin on page 100. B; $15-30. *Fashion Splendor* earrings are some of my favorites with their attractive contrast of light green rhinestone, pink bead, and simulated pearl on goldentone. Matching pin on page 98. B; $15-30.

Top row, left to right: *Wayside* earrings are oval goldentone clips with a simple engraved leaf design. Marked on clip "©SARAH." B; $8-20. *Goldenrod* earrings have an intricate goldentone design of leaves and tiny gold balls as the flower center. B; $10-25. *Moon-lites* earrings have goldentone ropes encircling pastel iridescent rhinestones of variegated colors. Matching bracelet on page 80, matching pin on page 99. B; $10-25. *Royal Velvet* earrings are strikingly attractive round purple multi-faceted rhinestones surrounded by a channel of smaller clear rhinestones, all set in silvertone mountings. Matching pin on page 100. C; $15-30. **Bottom row, left to right:** *Peking* earring (single) features a dark green cabochon bead centered in an oriental goldentone design with chain tassels. Matching pin/pendant on page 101. B; $10-25 (pair). *Hidden Rose* pierced earrings are handmade glass stones with a hidden rose encased in the stone. Matching ring on page 132, matching necklace on page 114. C; $10-25. *Golden Lace* earrings are pierced open-weave lace hoops, very simple yet elegant. All earrings had either surgical steel posts or surgical steel wires. Marked with "SARAH" engraved inside. Matching ring on page 135. B; $10-25.

Top row, left to right: *Venetian* earrings are kaleidoscope circles intertwined in silvertone to "enhance your outfit by day or night." Matching pin on page 100. A; $10-25. *New Mode* earrings are large simulated pearls dangling from a goldentone cap extending from pierced-look hooks. Matching necklace on page 117. B; $10-25. *Two-Timer* earrings are saddle-bag shaped, textured, and cut-out design goldentone earrings that can be removed from hoop earrings. Can be worn singly or together. Also came in silvertone. B; $10-25. **Bottom row, left to right:** *Times Square* earrings are square shaped goldentone metal with either pierced or clip backs. B; $10-25. *Sparkle Lites* earrings are "Sarah's sparkling After-5 jewelry giving you the touch of evening elegance." Matching pin on page 100. A; $10-25. *Golden Tassel* earrings have multi-chain goldentone tassels dangling from the front and back of the earring clip. B; $10-25.

Top row, left to right: *Chain-Ability* goldentone earrings have medium-sized pearlized beads encased in goldentone casing, hanging from a single chain. Matching necklace/belt on page 115. B; $10-25. *Antique Garden* earrings are large rectangles with antiqued silvertone design of flowers, leaves, and buds portraying a garden. Along with the matching bracelet, this set was continued as a hostess credit item for many years. Matching bracelet on page 80. B; $10-25. *Night Garden* earrings have iridescent dark bluish/green beads dangling from a goldentone chain. Matching necklace on page 118. C; $10-25. **Bottom row, left to right**: *Chain-Ability* silvertone earrings have medium-sized pearlized beads encased in silvertone casing, hanging from a single chain. Matching necklace/belt on page 115. B; $10-25. *Golden Lanterns* are amber colored cylinders encased in goldentone caps dangling from chains. B; $10-25. *Free Fall* earrings are comprised of four fine goldentone chains dangling freely from pierced posts. These were found in a 1978 catalog and continued into the 1980s. No identifying mark. B; $10-25.

Top row, left to right: *Carameltone* earrings are caramel colored variegated oval stones in a goldentone off-set frame. Matching necklace/pendant on page 119. B; $15-30. *Talisman of Love* earrings have a silvertone crab design dangling from an open circle of a smiling face. Matching necklace/pendant on page 119. B; $10-25. *Textured Links* are goldentone rectangles dangling from the clip-on hook. Matching bracelet on page 127, matching necklace on page 119. B; $10-25 **Bottom row, left to right**: *Jet Ice* earrings have large clear, grooved beads attached to a black cylinder bead dangling from a silvertone pierced-look earring clip. B; $10-25. *Inca* earrings are simple turquoise and silver arrow shaped earrings inspired by America's own native lore. Matching pin on page 102. B; $10-25. *Aura* earrings are two-tone, combining a goldentone open-weave teardrop shape with silvertone texture on the outer edge. Matching pendant on page 120. B; $10-25.

Top row, left to right: *Mandarin Magic* earrings are open-weave goldentone diamond shapes with three diamond shaped dangles. "A magical look of fashion." Matching necklace on page 123. B; $10-20. *Venetian Treasure* earrings are painted red beads suspended from a goldentone cylinder and wire hoops. Matching necklace on page 124. B; $10-20. *Three Cheers* white earrings are silvertone bowling pin shapes with a large white ball suspended in the center on a pierced hook. Also came in red. Matching pendant on page 52 of Lindbeck book. B; $8-15. **Bottom row, left to right**: *Watusi* earrings are wide-shaped hoops with relief texturing of embossed flowers and leaves on goldentone. Dynamic yet simple and styled so they can be worn even now. B; $10-25. *Mood Magic* earrings are three gray beads of light, medium, and dark hue dangling from goldentone pierced posts. Matching necklace on page 119. B; $10-25 *Three Cheers* blue earrings are the same as above and came in pierced or "chicken" look. B; $10-25

Top row, left to right: *Trellis* earrings are triangle shaped open-weave silvertone. Matching pin on page 103. B; $10-20. *Umber Tones* were created from two beads—a dark gray and a brown umber—suspended from goldentone "chicken" clip backs. B; $8-15. *Lotus Blossom* earrings are appropriately named as you can see a lotus blossom in their silvertone wire shapes. This is the second set of jewelry with this same name. Matching necklace on page 123. B; $10-25. **Bottom row, left to right**: *Circulet* earrings are two circles—one gleaming satin and one textured—attached together at the top. Matching pin on page 103. B; $10-25. *Soft Swirl* earrings have two goldentone, highly textured, concentric oval shapes with two beads in the center. Matching bracelet on page 129, matching ring on page 134. A; $10-25.

Top row, left to right: *Golden Tulip* shapes suspended in open wire hoops. Matching pin on page 101, matching necklace on page 124. B; $10-20. *Polka* earrings are brown plastic barrels with bands of intricate detail. Matching necklace on page 124. B; $10-25. *Sassy* earrings are silvertone geometric convex curves with seven dangling strands of chain tassels. Matching necklace on page 119. B; $10-20. **Bottom row, left to right**: *Starburst* earrings are highly textured goldentone oval shapes with a diamond opening holding an imported Austrian amber crystal. Marked "©SARAH" on back of clip. Matching pendant necklace on page 119. B; $15-30. *Embassy* earrings are small open-weave four-leaf clover goldentone heart shapes. B; $10-20.

Top row, left to right: ***Golden Sunset*** earrings are solid stippled goldentone hoops with clip backs. Marked on back "©COVENTRY" engraved. B; $15-30. ***Mirage*** earrings have delicate crystal clear beads dangling from a goldentone chain from pierced posts. B; $10-25. ***Minuet*** earrings are delicate plaques with tiny pearls and rhinestones with an attached goldentone rhinestone dangle. Matching bracelet on page 127. B; $10-25. **Bottom row, left to right:** ***Golden Coin*** dangle earrings are created from a goldentone coin suspended from a pierced hook. B; $10-25. ***Sabrina*** earrings are delicate goldentone plaques encrusted with tiny pearls and rhinestones with a pearl dangle. Same earrings shown on page 105. B; $10-25.

Top row, left to right: ***Showtime*** earrings are from 1977 catalogs and are goldentone hoops that are wider in the center tapering to narrower at the ends. B; $10-25. ***Matchmaker*** earrings are silvertone 1/2" wide concave bands with ribbed texture on the clip closing. They also came in goldentone and were continued through the early 1980s. B; $10-25. ***Shangri-la*** earrings from the early 1970s have tiny turquoise beads along with clear and amethyst rhinestones. One of my favorites. Matching bracelet on page 128, matching ring on page 131, matching pendant on page 123, matching pin on page 102. D; $15-30. **Bottom row, left to right:** ***Wisteria*** is another name used twice for different sets. These earrings from 1973 have simple multi-faceted iridescent glass drops of light purple dangling from a silvertone mounting. Matching necklace pendant on page 114. B; $10-25. ***Golden Tassel*** earrings are chains dangling from shiny goldentone caps. B; $10-20. ***Ember Tears***, another dangle type earring, features clear amber, tear shaped drops hanging from a goldentone tube-like link. Matching necklace on page 115. B; $10-25.

Top row, left to right: *Eleganté* earrings are open framed triangle shapes of silvertone with prong set rhinestones dangling freely. Identified as part of the "holiday collection" in the fall and winter 1972 catalog. Matching necklace on page 136. B; $15-30. *Candelite* earrings are diamond shapes of goldentone with clear rhinestones dangling from "chicken" clip-on clasps. Matching necklace on page 119. B; $10-25. *Tangerine* earrings have an open-weave bell shape with a "V" of orange beads. Matching pin on page 103. B; $10-25. **Center row, left to right**: *Northern Lights* button earrings are designed to give off an iridescent effect similar to the northern lights phenomena. The textured stone is surrounded by a rope-frame of SarahSheen silvertone. Matching bracelet on page 127, matching ring on page 132. B; $10-25. *Romanesque* earrings are from the late 1960s and 1970s. Silvertone coins are attached to clip-on clasps. Matching pendant on page 122. B; $8-20. *Oriental* earrings from 1972 have a two-tone oriental design. Combining goldentone and silvertone has been a favorite fashion trick of mine for many years so I find these very striking. B; $10-25. **Bottom row, left to right**: *Autumn Splendor* earrings are salmon colored inlay on a goldentone leaf pattern. Matching pin on page 103. C; $15-30. *Fanfare* earrings have silvertone shell designs with full chain tassels. There is another pair of earrings with the same name: Fan Fare. Marked on clip back of one earring "©COVENTRY," on the other earring clip "©SARAH" engraved, and on the actual back of the earring "©COVENTRY" in raised letters. Matching necklace on page 119. B; $10-25. *Golden Ice* earrings are crystal clear balls dangling from goldentone chains. There is another set also with this same name. Matching necklace on page 114. B; $10-25. *All courtesy of Dawn Michael*

Princess earrings are attractive "gleaming silvertone combined with pearls (simulated) and sparkling rhinestones." Marked on clasp back is "©SARAH" engraved, as well as "©SARAH" in raised lettering on the back of the earring itself. Matching pendant on page 122. B; $15-30. *Courtesy of Otheda Smith.*

Silvery Nile earrings: "All the romance and splendor of ancient Egypt with its Pyramids and Kings are reflected in this unusual design by Sarah. The heavy look of fashion and yet feather light to wear." This whole set was in the card files and was continued through the early 1970s as hostess credit items. Matching pin on page 33, matching bracelet on page 114 of Lindbeck book. B; $15-30.

Necklaces

Four Dimensions necklaces of goldentone and silvertone plus silvertone bracelet are versatile. The goldentone necklace is shown with the bracelet attached for added length of 33" while the silvertone has been left separate. The necklace is created from four strands of chain created from two different textures and shapes. D; $15-30 (each set, less for individual pieces). *Courtesy of Alynda Kimbrough.*

Left to right: *New Seasons* necklace is approximately 24" with goldentone leaves stationed every three links the full length of the necklace. It was shown in 1978 worn with another locket necklace. C; $10-25. *Floral Locket* dangling from a length of chain attached to another chain is 27-1/2" long. The chain could also be worn with other chains. D; $15-30. *Christina Locket* is an attractive reverse colored black locket with basket. The chain is 32" and was from the late 1970s, though carried over into the 1980s as were most of the late '70s necklaces. D; $15-30. *All courtesy of Alynda Kimbrough.*

Left to right: *Holiday Garden* came in 33" and 36" lengths of this tortoise-tone as well as in black and white, aqua, and the last set pictured here, melon, in the mid-1970s. D; $15-30. *Satin Beauty Choker* is "Natural Beauty" adjustable 15-16". C; $10-25. *Golden Teardrop* actually came on a hoop but is shown here on a chain from 1976. "Stylish Sarah." B; $15-30. *Bittersweet* necklace is one of two sections of chain with this set. C; $10-25. *Melon Holiday Garden* necklace is just one section of the set. The rest of the set was a chain with sections of this design stationed throughout, like the first necklace in this grouping. C; $8-20.

Left to right: *Coventry Square Choker* from 1977 is an adjustable 15-17" chain with a 2" piece of chain separated from the rest of the chain by an "o" ring. "Fashion begins with basic black." C; $8-20. *Papillion* is a simple butterfly design on an adjustable 16-18" chain. Matching ring on page 133. B; $5-15. *Counterpoint Choker* is a unique chain necklace 16" long. Matching bracelet on page 128. *Caravan* chain is a goldentone 33" rope-like necklace. C; $10-25. *Timeless Beauty* necklace has a removable drop on a 22" chain. It was originally from 1977 and came with a 30" chain with wide links. C; $10-25. *Thea Pendant* from 1976 is "Intaglio Cameo of imported glass stone from Bavaria, Germany" and has a 16-18" adjustable chain. D; $15-30. *Victoria Blue* necklace is a 44" chain with blue beads stationed on the chain. Matching ring on page 134, matching cross pendant on page 116, matching earrings on page 75 of Lindbeck book. D; $10-25.

Left to right: *Emberwood* necklace is comprised of two chains, 20" and 32". "So Versatile, So Sarah." I found it only in 1977 catalogs. D; $15-30. *Oriental Lanterns* is a 33-1/2" necklace of goldentone and dark green barrel shaped beads. Same necklace in brown on page 125. C; $15-30. *Empress* is a glamorous 18" adjustable necklace created in 1972. "Designs from the Past Recreated for Today." Matching bracelet on page 128. C; $15-30.

Left to right: *Mosaic* pendant on a 22" length chain was created in 1972. It has multi-colored diamond shapes carved into the button-like removable pendant. Matching earrings on page 105, matching men's set on page 166. B; $10-25. *Hi-Lo Elegance* necklace is a goldentone diamond shaped pendant with tassel. The original necklace had a larger pendant with three tassels. Matching earrings on page 105. B; $8-20. *The Big Apple* pendant is a wire-frame apple attached to a 16-18" adjustable chain. Also came in a goldentone. B; $8-20. *Fire-Lite* is an "Austrian Glass Stone" pendant on a 14-16" adjustable chain. This choker has "The uptight look of chokers worn close to the neck fashionable and new." C; $10-25. *Azure Skies* is a very small pendant created from a cabochon variegated turquoise bead surrounded by tiny pearls. Matching pin on page 102. B; $10-25. *Rose-Marie* is a delicately designed pendant. "The Antique look you'll treasure," found in late 1970s. The chain is adjustable from 20-24". C; $15-30.

Left to right: *Golden Cascade* is a necklace created from multiple lightweight strands of goldentone. *Silvery Cascade* is the same necklace created from multiple lightweight strands of silvertone in 16-18" lengths. The silvertone one on the left is identified on its hang tag as "Celebrity," while the one on the right says "©SARAH COV." These cascade necklaces were some of the early 1950s and '60s necklaces and were continued right through to the 1970s. They were very popular and inexpensive, making them easy to locate today. They were worn in a variety of ways and are often still in excellent condition. Matching earrings on page 75. A; $8-20. *Carefree Choker* is a simple 16" chain of silvertone. C; $10-25. *Rock Trio* pendant was originally on a hoop necklace choker with two other interchangeable pieces—one round and the other star shape with a turquoise center. This was identified for the younger set. B; $8-20. *Golden Nugget* choker is a 16-1/2" unique chunky chain found in a 1977 catalog. C; $15-30.

Left to right: *Perfection* necklace is 31" long and was described as "White 'n Bright." My necklace had no tag so there may be no way of identifying others. I was lucky and found it in a 1978 catalog before discarding it. D; $20-35. *Chiffon-Bib* is 19-1/2" long with ten strands of silvertone chains and this unique clasp. Also came in goldentone. Marking on back of clasp is "SARAH" engraved. Matching bracelet on page 128. D; $10-25. *Stone Age* choker is created from variegated dark blue flattened circles and circle beads. It was identified for "the little Sarah and her teen years." B; $8-20. *Grecian* pendant was identified as "Heirlooms." This eye-catching silvertone pendant has the appearance of Greek costuming. The pendant is also holding the matching bracelet, which has its own clasp when detached from the pendant. A uniquely made and versatile item. D; $10-25.

Left to right: *Charisma* necklace from the mid-1970s is a bib-type silvertone necklace very appropriately named. Matching earrings on page 105. D; $15-30. *Autumn Mist* choker is a 15-17" adjustable length found in a 1978 catalog as Sarah's Special Hostess Choice for 1150 points. "Goldentone Classics—for Sarah's Special Hostesses." $10-25. *Sparkle by the Yard* necklace is 49" long in clear sets called "ice." "Look into Sarah's crystal." D; $8-20. *Charisma* necklace also came in goldentone. These were shown worn with turtleneck sweaters for very fashionable looks in the mid-1970s. D; $15-30.

Top row, on rocks: *Moon Beam* pendant is an imported Austrian glass stone on an adjustable 16-18" chain. Matching ring on page 135. B; $8-15. *Hidden Rose* pendant has a delicate "Exclusive Handmade German Glass Stone" on a 16-18" adjustable chain. Matching earrings on page 106, matching ring on page 132. C; $10-25. *Legend* is an artfully inscribed pendant that originally came with two chains: 22" and 30" (shown here with only one chain). There were also pierced earrings. C; $15-30. **Center**: *Wisteria* is the name given to this silvertone and lilac pendant. Wisteria is also the name of a very early 1950s and 1960s set. Matching earrings on page 109. D; $20-45. **Bottom**: *Lilac Time* necklace is a 50" chain with a removable 16" choker created from small lilac and pink glass beads stationed on a silvertone chain. At first it was thought that wisteria was the pendant for this necklace. They could have been used in combination, but are two completely different sets. D; $10-25.

Left to right: *Zodiac* pendants on chains came about in 1971. "This is the year of the Zodiac and women love to wear their very own sign. Sarah predicts a beautiful future for Zodiac accessories, especially in goldentone." Some of these pendants were also designed for the male customers. Matching necklace on page 168. B; $8-20. *Golden Ice* is a three strand necklace made from two clear bead strands on goldentone wire and one goldentone chain. "So Versatile—So Sarah." D; $20-45. *Calvary Cross* was "For that delicate look" with its three overlaid goldentone crosses. The chain is 16-18" adjustable. B; $10-25. *Golden Petals* pendant is "golden classics for any age." Matching earrings on page 105. B; $10-25.

Left to right: *Limbo* pendant, from the late 1970s, is a removable drop from a 30" chain. D; $10-25. *Timely* is a 36" long silvertone chain with cylinders spaced throughout the length of the chain. It was one of many created in the mid-70s for the new fashion of chains. C; $8-20. *Ultra-Versatile* necklace is a 24" chain advertised as "twenty-four different looks achieved with this ultra-versatile ensemble which includes earrings with interchangeable sections as shown." Drops also came in red, white, and blue. D; $10-25. *Pandora* is a delicate 3-D effect butterfly on a 15-17" adjustable chain. C; $8-15.

Left to right: *Pastel Parfait* (white) is a 37" length of beads that originally came with an attached silvertone chain. It also came with lilac, pink, yellow, avocado, pink and lilac beads, and yellow and avocado beads. Other necklaces on page 125, matching earrings on page 19. B; $8-15. *Fashion Wrap* 43" long necklace is also a belt (for skinny waists) from the mid 1970s. Also came in silvertone. It was shown in a catalog looped in the center for a necklace or on the end for a belt. C; $10-25. *Chain-Ability* came in both silvertone and goldentone and is 41" long with a caged simulated pearl at each chain end. Again, this was shown in various lengths for a necklace and looped at the end as a belt in the early '70s. Matching earrings on page 107. C; $10-25. *Exquisite Lady* is a 36" necklace of simulated pearls from the mid-1970s. C; $10-25.

Top to bottom on left: *Tiger Fish* from the mid-1970s is a very attractive tiger-eye stone in goldentone with a simulated pearl eye attached to a 24" chain. D; $15-25. *Applause* necklace originally came with two chains (28" and 35"), creating 63" in overall length. Another necklace of different color shown on page 117. D; $10-25. *Safari* necklace here is created from two chains with attached wooden beads. The detachable pendant with matching cabochon center could be attached to these chains or coupled with a total brown bead of 37 1/4" length. C; $15-30 (more if with brown beads). *Taste of Honey* necklace has 37" and 40" chains. "So Versatile. So Sarah." This necklace was carried through much of the 1970s. Matching earrings on page 104. D; $15-30. **Top center**: *Cameo Fashions* necklace originally had two chains: 24" and 30". D; $15-30. **Far right**: *Ember Tears* choker is 16" long and has "The uptight look of chokers worn close to the neck – fashionable and new." Also described as "The understated Look for Evening." Matching earrings on page 109. C; $10-25.

Top row, left to right: *Danish Mood* (on its original card) is a 24" silvertone chain directly attached to a silvertone pendant with dark blue center. C; $15-30. *Exclusive* necklace (on original card) has an "Imported Stone from Germany" and was identified as "Around the Clock with Sarah." In the late 1970s it was listed as a Hostess Bonus item for 1150 points. C; $15-30. *Cupid's Touch* is a very delicate pendant on a 15-16" adjustable chain. The jet heart with an "Imported Austrian Crystal Stone" is "Sophisticated Sarah...after 5." Marked with "SARAH" engraved on back of heart. C; $10-25. **Center**: *Swan Lake* necklace pendant on original card from the early 1970s. The first pendant I found was not on chain and had no identifying mark on the back. I nearly missed it. Matching earrings on page 82 of Lindbeck book. C; $15-30.

Left to right: **Casual Classic** pendant is half golden beads on a wooden base from the early 1970s. Matching earrings on page 43. B; $10-25. **Nite-Owl** pendant has a mobile-like body and tail feathers. "Nature's Friends created in gleaming goldentone." C; $10-25. **Victoria Blue** pendant of textured goldentone is a cross shape with dark blue cabochon beads on a 23" chain. Matching ring on page 134, matching necklace on page 112, matching earrings on page 75 of Lindbeck book. C; $15-30. **Encounter** pendant is a black and goldentone arrow shape on a wider link 21" chain. C; $15-30. **Athena** necklace has textured metal suspended between an adjustable 16-18" length of beads. These were the "Newest Fashion Trends from Sarah" in the late '70s. C; $15-30.

Left to right: **Omega** pendant of textured goldentone encircles an "Imported Austrian Glass Stone." C; $15-30. **Interlude** is a removable pendant of plastic resin design on a 28" chain. D; $10-25. **Roman Holiday** is a variegated blue imported stone surrounded by antiqued silvertone frame. The removable pendant could be attached to other chains and bracelet or combined with other necklaces. "Heirloom." Matching pieces under Tudor name on pages 106 and 139. D; $15-30. **Fashion Flair** pendant on strand of green beads is also coupled with a strand of red beads and a gold chain. The lengths are 17", 24", and 30" for the very fashionable look. D; $20-45. **Continental** necklace is a unique pendant of dark red flat sets on a silvertone background stationed on a 16-18" adjustable chain of cylinder links. Identified "Sophisticated Sarah." Bracelet with this name is not a match. Matching ring on page 134. D; $20-45. **Broadway** pendant is a goldentone oval surrounding a dark set. A 24" length of brown cording replaced the usual chain for this simple pendant drop from the late 1970s. C; $10-25.

Left to right: **Allure** choker in goldentone is from the mid-1970s and fashioned from curved pieces linked together to approximately 15-1/2" in length. B; $10-25. **Chinatown** necklace of 19" is very unique and could easily be taken apart. The tassel can be removed for one look, the curved attachment can be taken off and the tassel placed directly on the linked choker, or the choker can be worn alone. D; $20-45. **Sea Star Hoop** is a 14-1/2" to 17" adjustable necklace hoop that was part of the Ecology Collection. "The eternal mystery of the sea, the graceful starfish. Finely crafted, exquisite in every detail, your starfish necklace is distinctively modern yet classically sophisticated, shimmering and warm, with the subtlety of the sea itself. *A donation has been made by Sarah Coventry to the Cousteau Society for the preservation of the Society for the preservation of the environment.*" Matching bracelet on page 127, matching ring on page 132, matching earrings on page 104. C; $15-30.

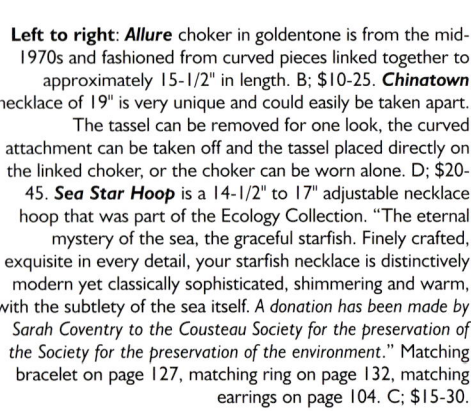

Bottom left to top right: *Applause* is a red, white, and blue silvertone necklace that originally came with two chains (28" and 35"), forming 63" in overall length. Only one chain shown here. Matching necklace of different color on page 115. C; $10-25. *Inca Fire* pendant necklace is 20-22" adjustable with two versatile drops on the chain. Identified as "Heirlooms." Matching pin/pendant on page 19. D; $20-45. *Tricia* chokers in silvertone and goldentone were in 1971 catalogs and are very similar to bracelets with other names. Mark on the hand mirror tag inscribed with "SC." B; $10-25. *Blaze* pendant is a 16-18" adjustable chain with an "Antique look you'll treasure." It has a dark stone encircled with goldentone in a flame effect. C; $15-30. *Golden Sunset* pendant is a highly textured detachable pendant on a 21" chain. Matching earrings on page 109, matching bracelet on page 128. C; $10-25. *Fancy Free* pendant is a very dainty butterfly design different from any of the others and attached to a 16-18" adjustable chain. It was found in the mid to late 1970s catalogs. Another set with the same name is very different. The butterfly motif was very popular. B; $10-25.

Left to right: *Holiday Chain* is a 36" necklace that also came in silvertone. This chain was also used with the holiday beads on page 125. B; $8-15. *Phoenix* pendant is on a 16-18" adjustable chain. Identified as "For Him." C; $10-25. *Jet Streamer* choker is attached to a 15-17" adjustable chain. "Sarah Shines On" in 1978. D; $10-25. *Heirloom* is a goldentone locket-like pendant with a scroll of SC on the front. This locket doesn't have any identifying marks on the back, only on the necklace chain. My first encounter was after I had seen it in one of the catalogs, whetting my appetite for doing more research. C; $10-25. *Tradewinds* necklace is a goldentone pendant on a solid cord-like golden chain. It could also be worn with a ribbon or cloth cord for a very low-key look. C; $10-25. *Mademoiselle* choker: "Imported Austrian Glass Stones…Sophisticated Sarah…after 5" pendant attached to a 16-18" adjustable delicate chain. C; $15-30. *New Mode* necklace is a choker hoop with a pearl drop attached. It was from the early 1970s, held over from late '60s. Matching earrings on page 106. B; $10-25

Left to right: *Twisted Rope* chain is one of many chains brought into fashion during the late 1970s. Other chains on page 150, matching bracelet on page 152. D; $10-25. *Classic Partners* chain with a shell pendant came about in the late 1970s along with both dainty and bold chains. This chain is 16-1/2" of goldentone. B; $8-15. *Secrets Locket* is one of many dainty pendants and chains designed in the mid-1970s. The chain is an adjustable 16-18" in goldentone. B; $8-15. *Golden Dove* pendant on a 21" chain was described as "Nature's friends created in gleaming goldentone" in 1976. A blue rhinestone accenting the dove's eye makes this a "must" for any collection. B; $10-25. *LaBelle* necklace is a cluster of imported Austrian glass stones embraced by a goldentone bar attached to a 15-16" adjustable chain. "Sarah after sundown." Matching ring on page 133. C; $15-30. *Flutter Byes* necklaces of goldentone and silvertone are chains containing tiny solid butterflies stationed along the links. C; $10-25.

Left to right: *Folklore* necklace strikingly combines a turquoise and silver pendant with a silver chain. One of two necklaces with the name, it was created in the early 1970s. B; $15-30. *Love Story Birthstone* pendant is golden topaz for November and uses "Imported Austrian Glass Stones" on a 22" chain. Matching rings on page 135. C; $10-25. *Spanish Moss* 22" chain and pendant of antiqued goldentone comes also in silvertone. C; $10-25. *Patrician* necklace is a 36" chain interspersed with "Timeless beauty simulated pearls." C; $10-25. *Serenade* necklace of silvertone has "Imported German Glass Stones." The original set included 32-1/2" and 20-3/4" chains. Just one chain is shown here. There were also pierced earrings, which are not marked. Another set of jewelry with this same name was also made. C; $10-25.

Left to right: *Night Garden* necklace from the late 1960s and early '70s has dark blue beads attached to a goldentone 15-17" adjustable chain. "The look belongs to Sarah." Matching earrings on page 107. C; $10-25. *Jamie Choker* is a 16-1/2" chain with silvertone crystals and metal beads stationed throughout. "Sarah's Sweet Hearts." B; $8-20. *Summer Flirt* is made from two silvertone chains (22" and 29") containing circular and oval white carved beads. D; $15-30. *Over The Rainbow* necklace from the early 1970s is an iridescent imported rhinestone prong set in a dainty silvertone mounting. The only marking for this pendant will be on the necklace hang tag. B; $10-25. *Candlelite* necklace is a combination of goldentone and imported rhinestones attached to a 19" adjustable chain. There are other pieces with "candlelight" spelling. Matching earrings on page 110. *Dream Boat Locket* is a very dainty silvertone circle with pearl center on a 16-18" adjustable chain. B; $8-20. *Double Choice* pendant includes interchangeable rose and eggshell drops on a 24" chain, giving a very versatile necklace. B; $10-25.

Left to right: *Holiday Chain* in goldentone is 36" long. Matching necklaces on pages 117 and 125. B; $10-25. *Delicate Twist* goldentone and silvertone chains are 36" in length. "Sarah's Basics in Goldentone and Silvertone." C; $10-25. *Holiday Chain* in silvertone is 36" long. Matching necklaces on pages 120 and 125. B; $10-25. *First Love* is a 54" chain with flat-twist metal sections and pearl-like beads stationed through the entire length. C; $10-25. *Fantastic* silvertone chain is a combination of plain chain and twisted chain creating a fantastic looking piece of jewelry. B; $10-25.

Left to right: *Fashion Zodiac* pendant is on a 36" chain that could also be used as a belt. This pendant is Gemini for May-June. B; $15-30. *Fashion Melody* chain necklace is two chains of 18" and 40" with overall length of 58". This goldentone double chain has amber tone spiraled cylinder beads stationed 7-9" apart. The short 18" chain has one bead on it. D; $15-30. *Mood Magic* silvertone necklace is 44" in length with three shades of gray beads intermittently spaced. Matching bracelet on page 130, matching earrings on page 107. C; $15-30. *Vogue* necklace is a goldentone chain interspersed with colored cylinder beads of black, clear, red, and green. The addition of a bracelet makes this necklace 43" long. There is a Vogue ring that is not a match to this set. Matching bracelet on page 130. D; $15-30.

Left to right: *Textured Links* pendant is glamorous with goldentone rectangular links in decreasing sizes. Matching earrings on page 107, matching bracelet on page 127. C; $15-30. *Carameltone* pendant is a large tiger-eye like oval stone encased in a textured frame of goldentone on a 25" chain. "Golden Looks for Golden Moments." Matching earrings on page 107. C; $15-30. *Fanfare* pendant is an artfully designed fan with tassels of textured silvertone on a 23" chain. This set was presented in 1974: "1974 Represents 26 years of exciting jewelry fashions by Sarah Coventry." There are other non-matching pieces and sets with the same name. Matching earrings on page 110. D; $15-30. *Starburst* pendant has "Multi-color stones for a multi-fashion look." The stones are imported Austrian crystals in amber and muted yellow. This necklace is easily found so must have been very popular. The name has also been given to several other sets through the years. Matching earrings on page 108. D; $15-35. *Talisman of Love* is a silvertone circle pendant with alternating sections of face and crab-like shapes. Matching earrings on page 107, matching bracelet on page 127. C; $10-25.

Left to right: *Aloha* pendant, commonly called the pineapple pendant, is in antiqued goldentone presented on a 22" chain. Matching earrings on page 104. D; $15-30. *Desert Flower* pendant is open goldentone with embertone stone and an oval cream colored cabochon. Matching ring on page 134. C; $10-25. *Safari* pendant is a 22" unique chain with an equally unique pendant. This was designed for 1975. It is not a match to another set with the same name. C; $10-25. *Sassy* pendant is a geometric convex curve with seven strands of chain as dangling tassels. The necklace is 18-20" adjustable. Matching earrings on page 108. B; $10-25. *Turn-a-bout* pendant is 22" and reversible. One side is a patchwork of highly colorful design, the second side is shown here. There are other pieces with this same name, but none match this pendant. D; $10-25.

Left to right: ***Golden Nile*** pendant is a goldentone design on a 24" chain. B; $10-25. ***Designer Links*** necklace is a chain designed with metal casings. The length of this chain allows for double stranding and attaching of other pendants or earrings to create a totally different look. D; $15-30. ***Contempo*** pendant is a 22" chain with this goldentone circle attached. Originally, there was a ring attached to the underside hook for attaching a tassel. In 1975, this necklace was modeled by Dianne Lennon, one of the singing Lennon sisters. D; $10-25 (more if tassel is attached). ***Flight*** is a silvertone, heart shaped pendant hinged to ever increasing wings, giving the impression of flight. It is amazing how the names and design become one. C; $10-25. ***Twilight*** pendant is a goldentone diamond shape of textured open-weave with clear rhinestones surrounding a large rectangular Austrian crystal of amethyst color set in prongs. This necklace was not marked on the back of the pendant but on the chain with the mirror hang tag is "SC" on one side and "©SARAH COV" on the other. Matching bracelet on page 129, same set shown on page 137. D; $20-45. *Courtesy of Nancy Isgrigs*. ***Aura*** pendant is a goldentone textured open-weave teardrop shape with silvertone texture on the outer edge of the teardrop. Matching earrings on page 107. C; $15-30.

Left to right: ***Holiday Chain*** is a very popular 36" chain to be coupled with beads and other chains. Other chains and matching beads on page 125. B; $10-25. ***Sparkle Chain*** in silvertone truly sparkles in the light. A; $8-15. ***Golden Chain*** and ***Golden Chain*** have the same name, but are different chains in size and length of links. Various chains were designed to wear together, with charms, or other pieces of jewelry. Also many customers removed pendants from some of these chains, so knowing if these chains were originally paired with a pendant may be hard to determine. B; $8-15 each.

Left to right: ***Gold Chain*** is a 16-18" adjustable chain for any kind of small pendant or to be worn plain. A; $8-15. ***Serpentine Chain*** is 24" and from the late 1970s to early '80s. D; $10-25. ***Holiday Chain*** is another of these very popular chains that could be worn separately, with any kind of pendant/pin, or with the matching beads on page 125. B; $10-25. ***Swingalong*** necklace is a 20" chain from the early 1970s. B; $10-25. ***Sparkle Chain*** is another common chain that is 25" long and from the early 1970s. A; $8-15. ***Pixie Pets*** necklace is a 14" chain without a pendant created for the younger set of customers. A; $8-15.

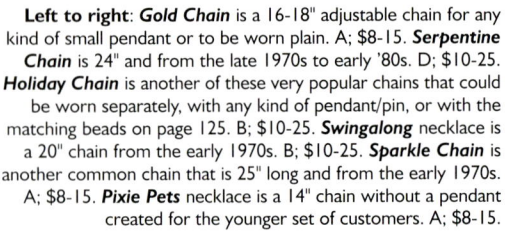

Left to right: *Evergreen* pendant is an "Imported German Glass Stone" on a 24" chain. The pendant is reversible and also removable. C; $15-30. *Nature's Treasures* necklace is a simple bead pendant on a 19" chain. B; $10-25. *Fashion Duet* is a glamorous shiny goldentone tassel dangling from a matching chain. C; $15-30. *Navajo Pendant* is on a 16-18" adjustable silvertone chain. Matching ring on page 134. B; $15-30.

Left to right: *Fashion* consists of simulated pearls in a 60" necklace to be worn in multiple strands around the neck or with pins attached to the side on the collar or lapel. Very popular in 1971. B; $15-30. *Pompeii* necklace is a 20" simulated pearl strand with a very attractive removable drop created from a large simulated pearl with large goldentone loop. C; $15-30.

Top row, left to right: *Rajah Pendant* is a 25" length of hand strung embertone beads imported from Germany with a removable drop of a small goldentone elephant. D; $20-35. *Unidentified* silvertone and jet black pendant has a shape that is similar to others, but not exactly right. $10-25. Another *Unidentified* is this dainty pendant. Again, there are many that are similar but not exactly like this one. Help me identify it if you can. $10-25. **Bottom**: *Pyramid Treasure* necklace is a silvertone bib-like necklace, very simple and yet elegant especially on a dark colored costume. There is an earlier set called Pyramid Treasures that is very different from this set. Matching earrings on page 105. C; $15-30.

Left to right: "Chains, Chains, Chains is the newest look in fashion." Many of these chains are complementary pieces to the myriad of goldentone chains that were produced and provide opportunities for creating different chain fashions, such as adding a pendant/pin or even earrings. Their names are ***Silver Chain, Roman Holiday Necklace, Antiqued Chains***. **Center**: ***Romanesque*** necklace features a silvertone pendant on a flat-link chain. Matching earrings on page 110. B; $10-25. **Far right**: ***Silver Chain***. Most of these chains were originally priced at less than $8. Value now: $8-15.

Left to right: ***Unidentified*** locket with inscription of intricate detail is similar to many in the catalogs, but not exactly the same. Help me out. $15-30. ***Scarlet Tears*** pendant on a 25" goldentone chain combines scarlet red and goldentone in a teardrop shape. C; $15-30. ***Princess*** pendant is a dainty diamond shape of pearls and rhinestones set in silvertone on a 16-18" adjustable chain. Marked on back of pendant with "©SARAH" in raised letters. B; $15-30. ***Pastel Glo*** necklace is a silver chain containing pastel pink and lavender spherical beads. C; $15-30. *All courtesy of Otheda Smith.*

Top to bottom: ***Spinner Choker*** necklace is a silvertone chain with an attached pendant of a spinner and adjacent beads. B; $10-25. ***Trapeze*** necklace is a 16-18" adjustable chain with attached embertone and gold beads. B; $10-25. ***Frosted Ice*** necklace is a 30" chain with a 35" stationed chain with frosted ice plastic beads. D; $15-30. ***Granada*** necklace is comprised of one strand of beads 37-1/4" in length and one with stationed matching blue beads and silvertone designs on a 29-1/2" chain. These were from the late 1970s into the early '80s. D; $15-30. *All courtesy of Otheda Smith.*

Left to right: *Filigree Lady* is a silvertone chain with stationed lace beads and pearls in a long 52" necklace. It also came in goldentone and in 1975 was modeled by Lee Meriweather, who starred in the TV show *Barnaby Jones*. D; $15-30. *Timeless Beauty* is a 30" chain of long links that could be used with any pendant or coupled with other chains. It was shown in the 1977 catalog with the pendant and chain on page 112. B; $8-20. *Sparkle Magic* choker from the late 1970s is a 15-17" adjustable chain with unique links attached to a bead made from imported Austrian glass stones. C; $10-25. *Sierra Choker* is an 18" length of variegated green/blue beads. It also came in red. B; $8-20. *Primrose* pendant has a large watermelon shaped red bead with goldentone tassel at the end of a 24-30" adjustable chain. This set also came with a necklace that had stationed smaller sets on a 36" chain. D; $10-25. *Courtesy of Reba Thompson*. *Lotus Blossom* pendant/necklace is on an adjustable 18-20" chain and represents lotus blossoms in a mirror reflection. This is in silvertone and very striking when worn on plain or fancy costumes. C; $15-30. *Courtesy of Reba Thompson*.

Left to right: *Candle-Glo* necklace is a 16-18" adjustable chain with a curved corner, diamond shaped goldentone pendant. In the center is tiger eye stone surrounded by six small pearl beads. B; $10-25. *Snowdrop* necklace has a pearl dangling in a teardrop shape goldentone wire on an 18" length chain. "Sarah Pendettes in Goldentone." A; $10-25. *High Society* simulated pearls feature a gold double clasp with green stone inset. C; $15-30. *Fashion Rope* chain is a solid gold rope chain for a high fashion look alone or with pendants. This 37" chain was featured in the mid to late '70s. C; $10-25.

Left to right: *Golden Rope* is an oval pendant with white inlay overlaid with a goldentone rope criss-cross effect on a 24" chain. D; $15-30. *Shangri-La* pendant is a solid teardrop shape divided into sections encrusted with turquoise sets plus clear and amethyst imported Austrian glass stones. Matching pin on page 102, matching ring on page 131, matching earrings on page 109, matching bracelet on page 128. D; $20-45. *Mandarin Magic* truly conveys "the magical look of fashion." Imagine wearing this over a sweater or dark dress in the mid-1970s for a touch of the Orient. Matching earrings on page 107. D; $15-30. *Tranquility* pendant is reversible with this tranquil setting on one side and a dark brown textured center surrounded by shiny silvertone metal on the reverse side. Matching set with earrings on page 137. C; $10-25. *Hercules* pendant is a darling goldentone dog with movable eyes and body. Many animal shapes were created by Sarah Coventry for the young-at-heart to wear anytime. D; $8-20.

Left to right: *Folklore* choker is a silvertone textured curve with a turquoise cabochon set attached to a 15-16" adjustable chain. There is one other piece with this same name, not a match. B; $10-25. *Personally Yours* initial charms were designed with one's initial in the center. They could be worn on a chain or on pierced wire earrings that usually came with the charm. B; $8-15. *Light of the East* pendant is a glass stone painted in brilliant colors of red, green, blue, and gold. It is from the late 1960s and early '70s. Matching pin on page 67, matching earrings on page 73, matching ring on page 81. A; $10-25. *Volcano* is a red imported glass stone set in an open goldentone setting on a 24" chain. The set is peaked, giving rise to the volcano name. C; $15-30. *Love Story Birthstone Ensemble* consists of a double heart shaped pendant and single heart shaped pierced earrings. The red imported Austrian glass stones are the birthstones for January. The pendant is on a 22" chain. Originally priced at $11 with the earrings priced at $8. Value now for set: $15-30. *Unidentified* is a tassel dangle marked "©SARAH COV" within the necklace clasp. There are a lot of these kind of tassels in the various catalogs, however none match exactly. Help me identify it if you can. $10-25.

Left to right: *Golden Tulip* pendant is on a 16-18" adjustable chain. The tulip blossom hanging within a thin circle of goldentone is very dainty yet bold. Matching pin on page 101, matching earrings on page 108. B; $15-30. *Polka* is the name given to this pendant of brown plastic barrels with light and dark teal bands of intricate detail. The barrels are suspended by a four-leaf clover goldentone shape. Matching earrings on page 108. C; $10-25. *Taffee Tones* pendant has three tassels of taffy colored barrels and beads with antique goldentone trim. "Artist's Palette" was the catalog caption for this unique necklace. *Venetian Treasure* is a 22" chain with red beads intricately painted with flowers stationed at the center by 1" cylinder links. "Endearing treasures from Sarah's Fashion Boutique." Matching earrings on page 107. C; $15-30.

Left to right, in original boxes: *Oriental Lanterns* necklace in embertone is a 27" chain with barrel embertone and barrel lace beads stationed throughout the goldentone chain. Matching green necklace on page 112. D; $15-30 *Springtime Choker* is a 16-18" adjustable chain with oval pearl beads stationed along the chain. It was "Delicate and close to milady's throat" in the mid-1970s. C; $20-35. *Golden Braids Choker* is exactly what the name says. A choker 16-1/2" long made of sparkling goldentone giving the impression of braids. C; $15-30.

Left to right: *Pastel Parfait* plastic beads are 37" long in hot pink and Kelly green colors. These beads can be distinguished by their grooves. Created in the early '70s, they also came in white, yellow, avocado, and lavender and were purchased with gleaming silvertone chains and white petals pin and earrings. Matching chains on page 115, matching earrings on page 19. B; $8-20. *Holiday Beads* are the red and turquoise plastic beads with a swirl effect. Other colors were yellow, lavender, white, and pink. These beads were created in the mid-70s and were attached to a goldentone chain. There were also matching dangle earrings. Matching chains on page 117. B; $8-20. *Unidentified* plastic link beads in multiple colors of yellow, orange, avocado; red, white, light blue. I was not able to confirm that these are Sarah Coventry necklaces by locating them in a catalog. They may be from very early years. Matching earrings on page 19. $8-20. *All courtesy of Dawn Michael.*

125

Bracelets

Left to right: *Fancy Free* bracelet is this wide silvertone created from shiny and textured circles connected in a free-flowing fashion. Matching earrings on page 105. B; $15-30. *Vanessa* bracelet is a goldentone mesh with a dark green stone set in the clasp, making this bracelet adjustable to any size wrist. Found in 1978 catalogs. C; $15-30. *French Links* display shiny silvertone links with cuff-link type clasp. Also came in goldentone. B; $10-25. *Simplicity* narrow bracelets are pictured in silvertone and goldentone. They are fashioned from shiny metal connected with textured fasteners and were featured in 1970. B; $10-25. *Earth-Tones* bracelet is narrow goldentone with sets ranging from browns to striped light pink. Found in 1975 catalogs, this attractive piece was pictured with other jewelry in earth colors. C; $10-25. *Partytime* bracelet is a glamorous silvertone blossom centered with multi-colored variegated stones. C; $15-30. *Pink Shadows* is a very appropriate name for this delicate bracelet of light pink stones encased in goldentone. This bracelet is from the late 1960s. A; $10-25. *Fascination* bracelet from 1977 features antiqued silvertone sections centered with a variety of shapes and colors of stones. D; $15-30. *All courtesy of Dawn Michael.*

Top row, left to right: *Star Attraction* is a silvertone hinged bracelet with star designs from 1975. C; $10-25. *Florentine* bracelet is a concave textured bracelet from 1972. Also came in silvertone. B; $10-25. *Boulevard* bracelet is a hinged cuff with rounded ends created in the late 1970s. C; $10-25. *Tailored Cuff* bracelet is a hinged cuff with overlapping round end. It came in both silvertone and goldentone in 1971. B; $10-25. **Bottom row, left to right**: *Unidentified* is a wide cuff bracelet. Many times these bracelets were in only one or two catalogs, making identification difficult. $10-25. *Milky Way* bracelet is a very slim slip-over-the-wrist type found in 1977. C; $10-25. *All courtesy of Dawn Michael.*

Left to right: *Charm Links* is a simple silvertone link bracelet made for attaching charms. I found this in 1975 and 1976 catalogs primarily because of the many charms created for the 1976 Bicentennial celebration. B; $8-15. *Blue Lady* bracelet has delicate silvertone links centered with bright blue beads. Matching ring on page 133. B; $10-25. *Northern Lights* is a sparkling row of iridescent sets light green, pink, or yellow shades. Matching earrings on page 110, matching ring on page 132. C; $15-30. *Happy Holiday* bracelet is "Color charms linked together in a delicate silvertone design you can wear anywhere, anytime. Wear with sweaters and tailored clothes or combine with pearls on dressier occasions. Multi-color charms know no season and are fashion right from morn 'til night." This bracelet is from the early 1960s cardex. Same bracelet on page 51, matching earrings on page 72. A; $15-30. *Frolic* is another variation on multi-shaped charms with various colors of stone set in silvertone. B; $15-30. *Mystique* is a delicate silvertone bracelet with amethyst rhinestones. Matching ring on page 133. C; $15-30 *Valencia* bracelet has striking goldentone links of brownish/orange bead sets. Matching earrings on page 72, matching pin on page 64 of Lindbeck book. B; $15-30. *All courtesy of Dawn Michael.*

Top, left to right: *Candlelight* bracelet from 1976 has links of textured and gleaming silvertone circles. C; $10-25. *Silver Leaf* bracelet is from the 1981 catalog. It was created in goldentone as well. Very simple yet glamorous. D; $10-25. *Talisman of Love* bracelet has alternating charms of crab design and face design in highly detailed silvertone. Matching earrings on page 107, matching pendant necklace on page 119. B; $10-25. *Minuet* bracelet has goldentone plaques encrusted with tiny pearls and glittering rhinestones. Matching earrings on page 109. B; $10-25. *Colorama* is a sleek goldentone bracelet of links with varied shapes and colors of stones. This bracelet is from 1979 and very similar to earlier bracelets. C; $15-30. *Unidentified* antiqued silver coin bracelet. $15-30. *Four Seasons* bracelet is from the early 1960s. "Another first for Sarah—a basket weave design in textured and gleaming goldentone or silvertone. Just as lively and lovely as the life you lead. Four Seasons can go anywhere you go, any time of year." A; $15-30. **Bottom, from top down**: *Textured Links* bracelet in bold goldentone was created from textured rectangles. Matching earrings on page 107, matching pendant/necklace on page 119. B; $10-25. *Turn-a-bout* bracelet from the early 1960s is reversible, with a smoother goldentone side and a rough textured reverse side. Matching necklace on page 48. A; $15-30. *All courtesy of Dawn Michael.*

Left: *New I.D.* is an oxidized silvertone bracelet that could be inscribed with your name. Came in both goldentone and silvertone. C; $15-30. **Center, top to bottom**: *Indian Maiden* bracelet is wide antiqued silvertone with three turquoise stones. C; $15-30. *Sea Star* bracelet is from the Ecology Collection. "The eternal mystery of the sea, the graceful starfish. Finely crafted, exquisite in every detail, your starfish bracelet is distinctively modern yet classically sophisticated, shimmering and warm, with the subtlety of the sea itself. *A donation has been made by Sarah Coventry to the Cousteau Society for the preservation of the environment.*" Matching choker on page 116, matching ring on page 132, matching earrings on page 104. C; $15-30. *Dolphin* bracelet is shiny goldentone with hinge closing and rounded ends. C; $10-25. **Right**: *Silver Links* bracelet is a rope shape that also came in goldentone. It could be worn plain or with charms. B; $10-25. *All courtesy of Alynda Kimbrough.*

Left to right: *Granada* bracelet has wide antiqued goldentone squares with oval multi-colored stones accenting each section. A pin and necklace with the same name are not a match. C; $15-30. *Golden Sunset* bracelet is "for those golden moments." This spiked effect in goldentone replicates a sunset glistening in the light. Matching earrings on page 109, matching necklace/pendant on page 117. C; $10-25. *Golden Shield* is an initial bracelet with a charm attached to the sturdy chain. C; $15-30. *Empress* is a wide curved band that adjusts to any size wrist. The effect gives the illusion of royalty, creating a spectacular accent for any costume. C; $10-25. *Serenade* bracelet is a beautiful combination of goldentone and bright red stones. Matching pin on page 100, matching earrings on page 105. C; $15-30.

Left to right: *Bostonian Classic* is a goldentone chain with a gleaming tassel charm dangling from the clasp. Also created in silvertone. "The tailored look of chains and pins for fashion '74." B; $8-20. *Candlelight* bracelet from 1976 has links of textured silvertone with gleaming silvertone circles. This bracelet is also like one called Disco-Tek in 1974. It is sometimes difficult to discern the differences from the catalog pictures. Check out a similar bracelet on page 127. C; $10-25. *Tailored Lady* bracelet from the late 1950s and early '60s has large heavy "S" chain links of gleaming goldentone. It could be added to the matching necklace to make the necklace longer. A; $8-20. *Counterpoint* is an appropriate name for these interwoven links of fine goldentone loops. Marked on clasp with "*Sarah*" written, not printed, engraved. Matching necklace chain on page 112. A; $10-25. *French Cuff* bracelet is created from large linked chains and has a clasp common to many of Sarah's bracelets. B; $10-25. *Chiffon* is from 1978 and comprised of multiple chains and links in goldentone. Also came in silvertone. Matching necklace/bib on page 113. B; $10-25.

Clockwise, from top left: *Austrian Lites* bracelet, one of my favorites, is created from chaton cut Austrian rhinestones of green, light pink, and burgundy or fuchsia. The smaller accent stones give added color and make this one of the most striking pieces of jewelry "for the romantic look." Matching earrings on page 104, matching pin on page 103, matching ring on page 131. C; $20-45. *Shangri-la* is a hinged silvertone bracelet encrusted with tiny turquoise beads and clear and rose pink rhinestones. The 1972 catalog shows Lee Meriweather modeling this exquisite set. Matching ring on page 131, matching earrings on page 109, matching pin on page 102, matching pendant necklace on page 123. D; $20-45. *Contessa* has antiqued goldentone links of various designs with oval and round iridescent stones of various hues in the centers of the links. Matching pin/pendant on page 98. C; $15-30. *Courtesy of a past Fashion Show Director.*

Left to right; *Strawflower* is antiqued goldentone with delicate strawflowers nestled among leaves on a narrow and yet very striking bracelet. Matching pin on page 101. C; $10-25. *Twilight* bracelet is created from large rectangular amethyst Austrian stones. "Romantic and fashionable is the look of rhinestone, lilac tones and goldentone." Matching pendant/necklace on page 120, matching set on page 137. D; $20-45. *Unidentified* is this very wide cuff bracelet of antiqued silvertone. A garden of flowers, buds, leaves, and stems grace the surface. $15-30. *All courtesy of Otheda Smith.*

Left to right: *Fashion Flip* bracelet is, as its title suggests, a reversible charm that can be flipped from this jade set to an all goldentone side. B; $10-25. *Soft Swirl* bracelet combines goldentone and white beads in dynamic contrast. Matching earrings on page 108, matching ring on page 134. B; $15-30. *Butterscotch* is a goldentone bracelet with butterscotch colored Austrian crystals alternating with open goldentone sections. B; $10-25. *Antique Rose* bracelet is highly antiqued silvertone with a rose motif repeated throughout the sections. Matching earrings on page 104, matching pin on page 101. B; $10-25. *Personal Choice* is a bracelet created to look similar to spoon jewelry. This silvertone one is oxidized for longer lasting beauty as shown by its nearly thirty years survival. Matching ring on page 133. C; $10-25.

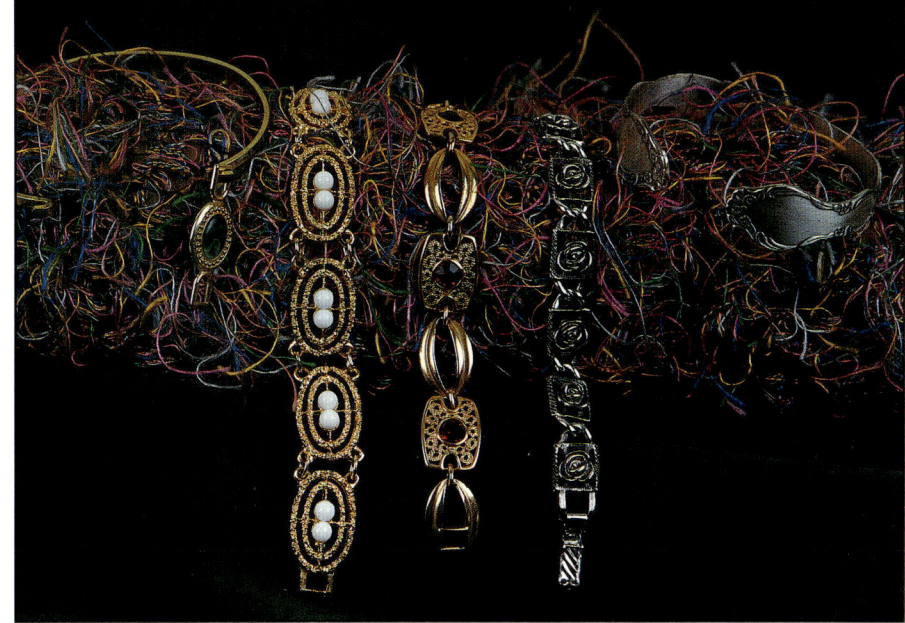

Left to right: *Melody* bracelet is a spectacular goldentone linked bracelet with delicate engravings of flowers and leaves on each section. Also created in silvertone. C; $15-30. *Nocturne* is a bracelet every owl collector will want. This cute little owl is on a slip clasp making the silvertone mesh band adjustable so it can be worn by anyone. There is a pin with this name but it is not part of the set. Matching earrings on page 104. B; $15-30. *Cosmic Wrap Around* bracelet shown here in goldentone also came in silvertone. "The new mod look of 'in' jewelry" from the early 1970s. B; $8-20. *Designer's Choice* is a hinged sculptured bracelet in silvertone. Marked in two places with "©SARAH" in raised letters. $10-25. *Jet Set* bracelet is this created from large jet black sets mounted in circular silvertone links. Matching ring on page 131, matching earrings on page 105. B; $15-30.

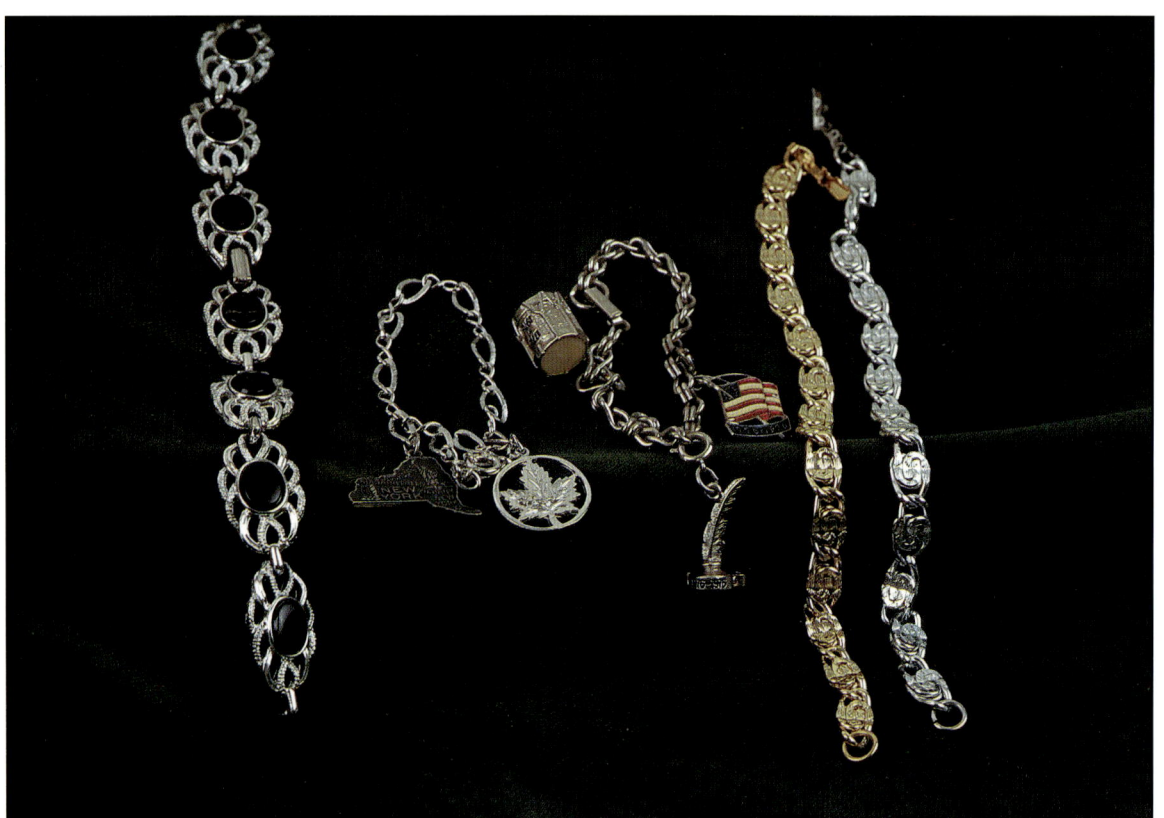

Left to right: *Black Reflections* is similar to other pieces with jet black flat stones among silvertone sections. B; $10-25. *Charm Links* bracelet is a silvertone open-link bracelet inviting the addition of charms. One charm already on the bracelet is a maple leaf representing Canada. Same bracelet on page 127. B; $8-15. *Charm Bracelet* was intended to hold the "Spirit of '76 charms" introduced to help commemorate the 1976 Bicentennial. A cannon charm was also available but not shown. C; $15-30. *Echo* bracelets in goldentone and silvertone were quite popular and inexpensive so will be easily found. A charm or pendant could easily be added to these late 1970s bracelets for a different look. They are similar to the Four Dimensions necklace on page 111. A; $8-15.

Left to right: *Designer Links* bracelet is a goldentone chain with stationed metal cylinders. Matching necklace on page 120. B; $10-25. *Mood Magic* is a silvertone double chain bracelet with stationed dark gray, medium gray, and light gray beads. Matching earrings on page 107, matching necklace on page 119. B; $8-15. *Vogue* bracelet is a colorful bracelet of red, green, black, and clear cylinder beads that when added to the matching necklace makes a 43" length necklace. Matching necklace on page 119. B; $10-25. *Wood Nymph* has brown cabochon sets stylishly set in an oval goldentone mounting. Matching ring on page 133. B; $10-25 *Sonnet* is a wide mesh goldentone bracelet highlighted by oval cabochon stones both variegated and varied in color. D; $20-35.

Rings and Sets

Top row, left to right: *Austrian-Lites* ring matches pin on page 103, matches bracelet on page 128, matches earrings on page 104. B; $10-25. *Java* ring sparkles with a center purple navette stone surrounded by smaller dark rhinestones. B; $10-25. *Love Knot* (in box) is a silvertone wire knot, very delicate and lovely. B; $8-20. *Rejoice* ring from the Lady Coventry collection has adjustable band in 12K gold filled and a genuine ruby set in sterling silver. From the late 1970s. D; $10-25. *Jet Set* from the early 1970s is marked "©SARAH COV" under the adjustable part of the ring. Matches earrings on page 105, matches bracelet on page 129. B; $10-25. **Bottom row, left to right:** *3rd Dimension Two-finger* ring is a unique piece of jewelry meant to fit two fingers. It came with three interchangeable ornaments: a large pearl, a large gold ball, and the ornament pictured. C; $15-30. *Shangri-La* ring matches pin on page 102, matches earrings on page 109, matches pendant on page 123, matches bracelet on page 128. C; $15-30. *Satin Elegance* from 1975 has a satin navette stone surrounded by clear rhinestones. B; $15-30. *Rome* from 1976 has an iridescent oval stone. B; $10-25. *Azure Skies* matches necklace on page 112, matches pin on page 102. B; $10-25.

Left to right: *Pacer* is "a ring for everything" from 1976. I wear this ring a lot because it is an "O" for my last name and one of the first rings I located. B; $10-25. *Homestead* is from 1978 and features "Imported German Glass Stones." B; $10-25. *Annette* has an "Imported German Stone" and is from the late 1970s. B; $10-25. *Cameo Portrait* from 1976 is a dazzling cameo ring. B; $15-30. *Queen's Lace* is a goldentone ring from 1978. B; $10-25. *Satin Lace* is quite different from the previous ring with its lace encircling an imported stone. B; $10-25. *All courtesy of Dawn Michael.*

Top row, left to right: *Cameo Lady* is from the early 1960s and found on the cardex. "For years Cameos have been a favorite among women with taste and wealth. Only recently have Cameos in all their delicate beauty been available at a reasonable price. You can hardly tell them from the hand carved faces of yesteryear. Soft white on gleaming black…she'll go around the clock with you and always be in good taste." A; $15-30. *Charmer* is a very appropriate name for this charming ring from 1972. C; $15-30. *Czarina* from the early 1970s matches necklace on page 98. C; $15-30. *Jan* ring is from the mid-1970s, later was a part of the hostess credit points. B; $10-25. **Bottom row, left to right:** *Lovely Lady* has an "imported German Glass Stone" in a lace-like setting. B; $15-30. *Antique Rose* matches earrings on page 104, matches pin on page 101, matches bracelet on page 129. B; $10-25. *Premiere* has another "imported German Glass Stone" in a goldentone setting. C; $15-30. *All courtesy of Otheda Smith.*

Top row, left to right: *Cleopatra* ring is a long mounting with iridescent oval set in silvertone. Look for earrings and bracelet that aren't pictured here. B; $15-30. *Jet Set* has a striking "imported Austrian Glass Hematite Stone." This name is similar to another set, but not part of it. B; $15-30. *Space Age* silvertone and goldentone rings from 1972 are wide bands with a large simulated pearl secured on top. B; $10-25. *Jet Filigree* ring from the late 1970s is simple goldentone with jet black set. B; $10-25. *Sea Star* ring identified as "SARAH" matches necklace on page 116, matches earrings on page 104, matches bracelet on page 127. See information about this set on page 104. C; $15-30. *Crimson-Lites* ring features a dark red stone surrounded by goldentone textured scroll-work. B; $15-30. *Lovely Lady* ring has an "imported German Glass Stone." Matching ring on this page. C; $15-30. *Moon Glo* ring has a "mother of pearl shell stone surrounded by an open-rope goldentone mounting." B; $15-30. **Center row, left to right:** *Sierra* is a slender ring of crème and amber swirls. C; $15-30. *Hidden Rose* has an "imported German Glass Stone" with a miniature rose hidden within. Matching earrings on page 106. C; $15-30. *Burgundy Twist* is an elongated slender ring with a swirl of goldentone in the center of the burgundy color. Marked "SARAH". C; $15-30. *Evening Cluster* ring is "never out of style…Never out of place." C; $15-30. *Ember Beauty* ring has an "Imported German Glass Stone" and is similar to Premiere, but smaller. It is from the late 1970s. B; $10-25. *Wild Honey* has a large honey colored rectangular stone set within a goldentone rope frame. Matching necklace/pendant on page 76. B; $15-30. *Egyptian* is a pearl and tiny green beaded ring of antiqued silvertone from the early 1970s. B; $10-25. *Camelot* ring was similar to some other pieces with different names. The silvertone with pearls and rhinestones combination was exquisite in the late 1960s and early '70s. "Ring your fingers in glamour." B; $15-30. *Annette* ring from the late 1970s was very popular (also shown on page 131). B; $10-25. *Ebb Tide* ring from the early 1970s was very popular and is easy to find. Marked "©SARAH COV." B; $10-25. **Bottom row, left to right:** *Elegant* is an appropriate name for this large goldentone ring covered with tiny rhinestones. C; $20-35. *Light of the East* ring was continued through the 1970s from the late '60s. It was very popular and also easy to locate. Matching pin on page 67, matching earrings on page 73, same ring on page 81. B; $10-25. *Sea Treasure* ring has a "genuine Abalone Shell Stone" mounted in antiqued silvertone. B; $15-30. *Majorca* ring has a rectangular clear red Austrian rhinestone set in an antiqued goldentone rope-like frame. *Annette* ring is shown in center row here as well. B; $10-25. *Queen's Choice* from the early 1970s is a raised ring of navette red stones set in a starfish shape and surrounded by an encrusting of tiny pearl beads. C; $20-45. *Portrait* ring resembles a portrait of red stone framed by tiny pearl beads. B; $15-30. *Northern Lights* ring has the same dazzling glass stone as the matching bracelet on page 127, matching earrings on page 110. B; $10-25. *Jet Elegance* ring with a goldentone frame was from the late 1960s into the early '70s. B; $10-25. *All courtesy of Dawn Michael.*

Top row, left to right: *Sparkling Burgundy* ring from 1974 has sparkling burgundy sets on a navette shaped open-weave goldentone mounting. B; $15-30. *Capri* is an elongated oval of silvertone with an imported blue stone. B; $15-30. *Priscilla* ring from the late 1970s has a spectacular glass stone set in gleaming goldentone. D; $20-45. *Seaswept* from 1978 has a navette shaped green imported stone set in goldentone mounting. This ring has also been identified as "Jan" in some of the catalogs—they look identical to me. B; $10-25. *Unidentified* ring, very similar to Royal Crown, but not quite the same. $15-30. *Men's Togetherness* "…the ring that says we belong together. Each ring is beautifully crafted in sterling silver expertly antiqued to bring out the fine design." The original price was $30 with a special price of $23 if two other items were purchased at the regular price. D; $20-40. **Bottom row, left to right:** *Blue Lady* from 1973-74 is a silvertone ring with blue beads. B; $10-25. *Illusive* ring was found only in one catalog from 1975. The antiqued silvertone and pearls give the illusion of not-being-there. B; $15-30. *Irish Eyes* is an appropriate name for this chaton cut emerald colored rhinestone encircled by smaller clear rhinestones mounted in silvertone. B; $15-30. *Jupiter* ring from the mid-1970s has a tiger-eye type stone mounted in a goldentone framework. B; $15-30. *Women's Togetherness* "…Each ring is beautifully crafted in sterling silver expertly antiqued to bring out the fine design. The genuine onyx stone symbolic of your genuine love." Original price was $25 with special price of $19 if two other items were purchased at the regular price. These were popular in 1972-73. D; $18-35. *All courtesy of Dawn Michael.*

Top row, left to right: *Egypt* ring: "…treasure your fingers with Sarah's brand new fashion rings at specially low, tempting prices for a limited time." A; $10-25. *Mystique* ring is marked "©COVENTRY" engraved inside. Matching bracelet on page 127. B; $10-25. *Marigold* ring from the late 1960s and early '70s has a dark amber colored rhinestone surrounded by goldentone double layered leaves. B; $10-25. *Blue Sun* is a colorful antiqued silvertone ring with turquoise-blue beads. B; $10-25. *Tutti-Fruitti* is an appropriate name for this multi-colored oval shaped stone set in an elongated goldentone frame. B; $10-25. **Bottom row, left to right:** *Happy Talk Birthstone* is a tiny ring with the "imported Austrian glass stone" for May. B; $10-25. *Ember Navette* is a wide banded textured ring with a dark amber colored navette stone mounted in prongs. Marked "©SARAH" engraved inside. B; $15-30. *Astrojet* is a jet black stone offset by silvertone circles of wire. A far-out look from 1973. Marked "©COVENTRY" engraved. B; $10-25. *LaBelle* is a very glamorous crystal rhinestone studded goldentone ring. B; $15-30. *Wood Nymph* has a brown stone prong set in a simple goldentone mounting. Marked "©SARAH COV." Matching bracelet on page 130. B; $10-25.

Top row, left to right: *Blue Buttercup* ring from the early 1970s is an antiqued silvertone portrayal of a buttercup embracing a blue bead. B; $10-25. *Bamboo* ring from the mid-1970s depicts two pieces of bamboo. A; $8-20. *Galaxy* is true to its name: "an assemblage of brilliant things," and here the brilliant things are opaque-like yet iridescent stones at the end of goldentone spikes. C; $20-35. *Rainbow Cavern* "reflects all the colors of the rainbow in this finger flattering ring with its elongated golden ovals. The romance and mystery of the famous caves are reflected in this opal-type stone." This ring was listed as a gift for any hostess who rebooked a show to be held between January 1-13, 1973 and also had eight buying guests. B; $15-30. *Papillon* is the literary word for butterfly which is reflected in this simple silvertone outlined shape. Found in the middle to late 1970s. Matching necklace on page 112. A; $8-15. **Bottom row, left to right:** *Multi-Lites* has emerald colored rhinestones prong set on this three strand silvertone ring from the mid-1970s. Marked "©COVENTRY" engraved on inside. B; $15-30. *Dusk* has dark gray and light gray simulated pearls with a rhinestone swirl connecting them on a silvertone mounting. This ring was sold during the mid-1970s and seemed to be popular as it is fairly easy to find. B; $10-25. *Blue Rose* is a large reversible stone from the mid-1970s. On this side, the rose emblem is in reverse relief. The other side is shown on page 134. B; $15-30. *Personal Choice* is a spoon shaped ring found in 1977. Identifying mark was "COVENTRY." Matching bracelet on page 129. B; $10-25. *Madame Butterfly* is a highly embellished goldentone butterfly shape. It also came in silvertone and is marked "©COVENTRY" inside. B; $8-20.

Top row, left to right: **Black Beauty** from the early 1970s has a jet black circle prong set in a silvertone mounting. There are other sets with the same name but this ring does not match any of them. B; $10-25. **Soft Swirl** ring is marked "©COVENTRY" engraved inside. Matching bracelet on page 129, matching earrings on page 108. B; $10-25. **Blue Rose** is a large reversible stone from the mid-1970s. This oval shaped variegated green setting in an elaborate silvertone mounting makes a very fashionable ring, worn one way during the day and another way during the evening. Reverse side shown on page 133. B; $15-30. **Love Story** birthstone ring is in amber for November. The imported Austrian rhinestones in a heart shape are surrounded by silvertone leaves. These rings are easily found as many enjoyed wearing their birthstone colors. Matching necklace on page 118, another ring on page 135. B; $10-25. **Morning Dew** is a double pearl set embedded in goldentone flowers. B; $10-25. **Bottom row, left to right:** **Continental** ring is a large dark red oval set in silvertone mounting. There is one set that is not a match. Matching necklace on page 116. B; $10-25. **Navajo** is a silvertone ring with cabochon beads in dark colors. B; $15-30. **South Seas** has a triangle shaped faceted "Imported German Glass Stone." Another set is called South Seas, but is not a match for this ring of the late 1970s. B; $15-30. **Lovely Lady** has the wrong set in the mounting. Many times when a set fell out replacements were not authentic. Be careful. If you haven't seen a piece of jewelry in books, etc., it may mean it isn't an authentic piece. Real ring shown on page 132. **Kari** is another example of a ring that has lost the original cameo set. The one laying beside the ring does not fit. This ring came from the late 1970s. B; $10-25.

Left to right: **Calypso** ring is an oval of goldentone dotted with gold balls and orange cabochon sets. Found in 1974 catalogs. B; $10-25. **Neptune** is an appropriate name for this navette dark blue rhinestone set at a slant on silvertone mounting. This was from the mid-1970s. C; $10-25. **Desert Flower** ring has variegated brown tones. Matching pendant on page 119. B; $10-25. **Victoria Blue** is a rectangular goldentone open-weave ring with a dark blue cabochon. Matching necklace on page 112, matching pendant on page 116, matching earrings on page 75 of Lindbeck book. B; $10-25. **Flattery** is a gorgeous green stone surrounded by scalloped silvertone. B; $10-25.

Left to right: **Flirt** is a row of amber/red rhinestones on a wide band of single threads. "Rings 'n Things for all season fashion." Marked "©COVENTRY." B; $15-30. **Satin Sand** has simple yet elegant cream colored cabochons nestled in a goldentone mounting. B; $10-25. **Honey Berries** has honey colored beads in a goldentone open-weaved setting. B; $15-30. **Golden Nest** features a simulated pearl nestled in a goldentone nest. B; $10-25. **Hazy-Daze** has a circular amber stone firmly held by the goldentone mounting. B; $10-25.

Left to right: *Imperial* ring is truly a royal one with amethyst and pearl set in a navette shape of antique silvertone. Matching pin/pendant on page 103. B; $15-30. Three *Love Story* rings in birthstone colors have imported Austrian rhinestones in a heart shape surrounded by silvertone leaves. These rings are easily found as many enjoyed wearing their birthstone colors. Matching necklace on page 118, another ring on page 134. B; $10-25 each. *Pink Champagne* is a very appropriate name for this cluster of pink rhinestones set in goldentone mountings. C; $20-35. *Reflections* is an amethyst ring of very large proportions and an unusual shape. B; $15-30. *All courtesy of Otheda Smith.*

Top row, left to right: *Lagoon* is a glamorous emerald cut light blue ring replicating a lagoon in color. C; $15-30. *Moon Beam* ring has a starburst shape with an "imported German Glass Stone." This ring was initially produced in 1975 and continued through the late 1970s. Matching pendant necklace on page 114. B; $10-25. *Catherine* is an attractive ring of antiqued silvertone with an oval amethyst center stone surrounded by four simulated pearls. Matching earrings on page 106. B; $15-30. *Eric* is "The bold man's ring made of the finest stainless steel in the Swedish tradition. Clean cut and simple in design, its beauty is enhanced by the elegant Sterling Silver insert. This sized ring will give him many years of handsome wear." Original price was $50 in 1977. $20-40.
Bottom row, left to right: To make *Old Vienna*, a "glass stone has been painted with red, blue, black and 14K gold in West Germany—after each color is applied the stone is baked for additional luster and long wear." Matching pin/pendant on page 19. C; $15-30. *Golden Lace* is a goldentone ring of lace-work found in the mid-1970s. Also came in silvery lace. A; $10-25. *Roxanne* ring was found only in 1979 as a Hostess Bonus for 2450 points. The genuine jade stone is surrounded by a goldentone frame. These gifts were only available to the hostess who met point requirements for customers, purchases, and party bookings. Usually these bonus items had been catalog items previously, however this one I could not locate earlier. The non-adjustable ring is marked "©SC". $15-30. *Wrap Around Zodiac* ring is a silvertone Gemini, adjustable—hence the term wrap around. Marked "©SARAH" engraved inside. C; $8-15.

Left to right: *Piccadilly Circle* Pendant and earrings set has "multi-color stones for a multi-fashion look." These Austrian stones are prong set in a channel of goldentone. Earrings are smaller circles of the same colored stones. Original necklace price was $13 and the earrings $13 in 1974. Current value: $25-45 set. *Maharani* set of pin and two sets of earrings was presented in the late 1960s and early '70s. This goldentone set is perhaps the most unusual of all of Sarah's designs. The top pin of turquoise cabochon sets surrounded by tiny clear rhinestones and accented with navette green sets is bold by itself. The dainty and delicate earrings to the right duplicate some of the sets and stones. "The pin or pendant dangle attach to the delicate earrings for those very special times when you want the 'bold' look of fashion." I believe this set may be hard to locate. Original cost for pendant was $8, pin was $8.50, and tiny earrings $5. Value now for any of the pieces would be $20-45 depending on quality. Full set: $55-70. *All courtesy of Dawn Michael.*

Top: **Operetta** set including pin, bracelet, and earrings came from 1973. "Paris says, 'wear rhinestones and Jet for high elegance.'" This set is a combination of silvertone triangles and diamond shapes. Original price of pin was $10, earrings $9, and bracelet $16. Current value for the set is $50-75 as this set seems to be hard to find. **Bottom row, left to right**: **New Polonaise** choker necklace with Austrian crystal rhinestones "permanently set through new methods in Austria." Prior to 1977 the same set was called Polonaise (without the word "new"). The pendant from this set is on page 98, and the matching earrings are on page 105. It is not clear what Sarah's designers were thinking when they changed the name, but kept the same design and procedure for creating it. D; $15-35. **Eleganté** pendant combines silvertone and rhinestones to create a holiday design of a decorated Christmas tree and inverted reflection. The triangle shape is replicated throughout the design. Matching earrings on page 110. C; $15-30. **Victoria** necklace (in box) was only located in 1978 under the Hostess Bonus items. This Victorian like goldentone and rhinestone necklace was available to hostesses acquiring 3400 points through customers at the party, purchases made, and other parties booked. There were matching earrings as well. $15-30 for necklace alone. *All courtesy of Dawn Michael.*

Left to right: **Golden Ice** bracelet and earrings of rhinestones and goldentone were part of a "holiday collection" in 1972 from August through December. There is another set named Golden Ice not to be confused with this one. Original cost of earrings was $10 and bracelet was $16. Current value for set: $30-45. **Debut** necklace from 1979 is very similar to the Golden Ice set. This necklace was created from "Imported Austrian Glass Stones." D; $15-30. **Enchantress** set of necklace and earrings is created from imported Austrian rhinestone crystals and SarahGlo goldentone. Another of "Sarah's After-5 Sparkling jewelry collection." This is the second set by this name. Original price of necklace was $17 and earrings was $15. Current value for set: $40-55. *All courtesy of Dawn Michael.*

Antiqued Amethyst pendant and earrings were found in the 1974 catalogs. This "Golden Collection set surrounds an amethyst stone with delicate antiqued mounting in Sterling Silver." The pierced earrings alone would never have been identifiable. The only clue to it being Sarah Coventry was the diamond tag <> on the chain. Original price is not available in the catalog. For a period of time in the mid 1970s, the pricing was in the shopping guide or order guide rather than in the catalogs. Current value: $15-35.

Heliotrope pendant and earrings set was found only in a 1972 catalog. Glamorous silvertone prong mountings give these purple faceted rhinestones secure positioning. Heliotrope is defined as "a variable color averaging a moderate purple," which is certainly seen in this striking set. I have not seen any others of this set, so it may be difficult to locate and may not be identified on each piece. Original price for necklace was $7 and the earrings $8. Current value for set: $25-40. *Courtesy of Alynda Kimbrough.*

Clockwise, from top left: **Tranquility** pendant and earring set is from 1970. Both are reversible with this tranquil setting on one side and a dark brown textured center surrounded by shinny silvertone metal on the reverse side. Same pendant shown on page 123. Original pendant with chain was $10 and earrings were $7. Current value for set: $15-30. **Twilight** set includes this pendant and bracelet. There was also a ring and a pair of large rectangular earrings. "Romantic and Fashionable is the look of rhinestone, lilac tones and goldentone." Original price in 1973 for bracelet was $15 and pendant was $12.50. Current value $25-40 for two pieces—more if set includes ring and earrings. **Blue Twilight** is a goldentone circle pin and bracelet of sapphire-blue colored rhinestones and pale blue round beads resembling turquoise. This is from "Sarah Coventry of Canada Ltd.~Port Credit Ontario." Mark on back of pin says "CANADA" and "SARAHCOV." No information about the original cost is available. Current value for set: $30-55. *All courtesy of Dawn Michael.*

Crosses

The idea of creating Limited Edition crosses started in the 1970s. From the information I have seen, I believe the first one was produced in 1973 and that they continued through 1981. Some jewelry in 1972 with the heading of "Designs from the Past Recreated for Today" may have been the inspiration for creating these collectible crosses depicting past century pieces.

In each of the years from 1973 to 1981, a cross was introduced in the spring or summer catalog. The catalog noted that the cross would only be available for sale through the end of that December, then the mold would be destroyed. Many of the employees began collecting these crosses—as did, I am sure, many customers.

Other crosses were produced during this time as well, and many of these were continued for several years. They ranged from very delicate solid goldentone or silvertone to very ornate designs utilizing pearls and stones. In the following pictures you will be able to distinguish the ones that are Limited Editions. There are several duplicates, but I chose to leave them all in because these pictures represent collections from former employees. Good luck in locating these crosses for your collection.

Top row, left to right: *Limited Edition Celtic Cross* from 1979. "Pendant is greatly reminiscent of the Celtic cultural heritage. Long admired for their intricate, web-like wire-workings, the Celts have traced this cross design through centuries of fine art and exquisite jewelry. The radiant embertone glass stone is a simulated replica of the Carngorn, the national gemstone of Scotland. It is double-cut so that it displays a brilliant array of multi-facets." This cross pendant was available for purchase from early 1979 to December 31, 1979 "at which time the mold will be destroyed." Original cost was $21.50. Current value: $20-45. *Credo Cross* pendant on a 24" chain has a goldentone center surrounded by white ceramic molding. The effect is "Old and Elegant." C; $20-35. *Crusader Pendant* cross is a silvertone open-weave cross shape accented with a clear purple cabochon in the center and simulated pearl cabochons on all four points of the cross. Created in the early 1970s, this was not a limited edition so was continued for several years. B; $15-30. **Center row, left to right**: *Today* pendant on a 25" chain has an open linked cross of silvertone surrounding a silver ball. C; $15-30. *Limited Edition Victorian Cross* "is a masterpiece of design taken from the pages of early Victorian artisans. These techniques have been interpreted by Sarah's master designers and craftsmen This beautiful Victorian Cross is a Sarah Coventry Limited Edition and cannot be purchased after December 31, 1973. The mold will then be destroyed." This cross was also "Specially gift boxed." C; $15-30. *Limited Edition Peace Cross* is a 24" antiqued chain and cross with a center of simulated pearl. This was "Sarah's Limited Edition in 1975. Available for purchase through Dec. 31, 1975 at which time the mold will be destroyed." D; $20-35. **Bottom row, left to right**: *Solitude Cross* pendant is a 16-1/2 to 18-1/2" adjustable chain—notice the "o" ring two inches from the end of the chain use to shorten the necklace. The center stone is an imported Austrian glass stone. B; $10-25. *Serenity Cross* pendant is a goldentone cross on a 16-18" adjustable chain. Also made in silvertone. C; $8-20. *All courtesy of Helen Knapp.*

Left to right: *Victorian Cross* is the same limited edition cross from 1973 shown on page ___. C; $15-30. *Florentine Cross* was "Sarah's Limited Edition for 1974." Created in silvertone with a 24" silvertone chain, it was "Available for purchase through Dec. 31, 1974 at which time the mold will be destroyed." C; $15-30. *Peace Cross* was a limited edition from 1975. D; $20-35. *Majestic Cross* is a 23" chain attached to the top points of this cross. "Sarah Coventry's Limited Edition Cross intricately detailed in goldentone and touched by the delicate luster of simulated pearls and deep royal blue enamel is marked by the same quality elegance and grace that was so admired by the French kings. The cross culminates in a royal crown bearing three simulated pearls connoting the Trinity and symbolic of purity. " This cross was available the whole year of 1977 "until Dec. 31, 1977 at which time the mold will be destroyed." D; $20-35. *Limited Edition Mythology Cross* was Sarah's 1978 Limited Edition on a 24" goldentone chain. "Inspired by the ancient craft of hand painted porcelain, Sarah Coventry brings you this most distinctive cross. The Grecians were noted for perfecting the concept of showing jet black fields with painted or etched designs, and it is with this that Sarah's cross was designed in direct response to the early revolution of ceramics. Enhanced by the beauty and hand polished luster of the 18KT gold leaf pattern, this genuine porcelain cross uniquely combines the skill of this ancient craft with the art of modern jewelry design." As with the others, it was available only through Dec. 31, 1978 at which time the mold was broken. D; $20-45. *Celtic Cross* was a limited edition from 1979. D; $20-45. *All courtesy of Dawn Michael.*

Left to right: *Romanesque Cross* necklace from the late 1970s is a highly antiqued/blackened silvertone open-weave pendant on an similarly colored 24" chain. This is not a limited edition so was continued for several years. D; $15-30. *Today Pendant Cross* on a 25" chain has an open linked cross of silvertone surrounding a silver ball. It is from the mid-1970s and also shown on page 138. C; $15-30. *Golden Splendor Cross* is a geometrically designed cross shape pendant of solid textured goldentone with an adjustable 22-24" chain attached at the top corners. This cross is quite different from any of the others. C; $15-30. *All courtesy of Dawn Michael.*

Left to right: *Crusader Cross* is a silvertone open-weave cross shape accented with a clear purple cabochon in the center and surrounded by simulated pearl cabochons on all four points of the cross. It is also shown on page 138. This was created in the early 1970s but not as a limited edition so was continued for several years. I found it in a limited edition box. People do tend to put things in wrong boxes, so BEWARE. B; $15-30. *Marriage Cross* pendant is a simple, traditionally designed cross with a criss-cross of goldentone rope no doubt symbolizing the unity in a marriage vow. The chain is 20-24" adjustable and the cross can be worn with either side out. D; $15-30. *Tudor Cross* drop is reversible with scrolled and highly antiqued silvertone on one side and Roman holiday stones inlaid in antiqued silvertone frame mountings on the main side. Matching earrings on page 106, matching Roman Holiday pendant on page 116. B; $15-30. *Unidentified* cross of antiqued silvertone is very similar to other pendants and sets, but not exactly the same. The necklace does has the identifying <> shape tag, but the pendant may not be a Sarah Coventry item (customers may have purchased the chain and added a non-Sarah pendant). $8-20. *18th Century Cross* was Sarah's Limited Edition Cross for 1976. "The unusual deep grey linen textured finish is achieved through modern methods and enhances the hand engraving, which outlines the blue-green color." Again this cross was available for only one year with the mold being destroyed on Dec. 31, 1976. D; $15-30.

1972 Catalog

The following 1972 catalog is courtesy of Helen Knapp, who located it among her many pieces of jewelry. Viewing this catalog is almost like being at a real Sarah Coventry party!

143

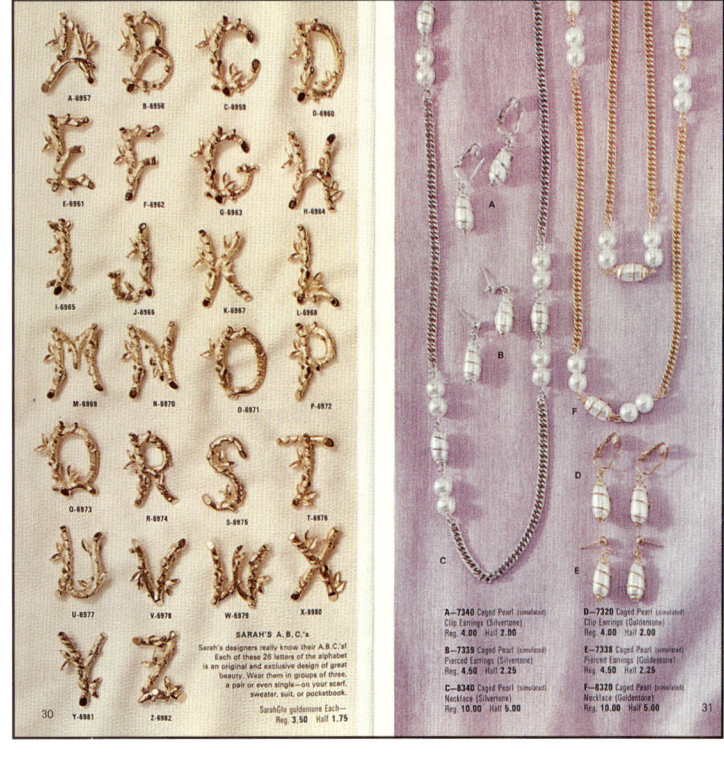

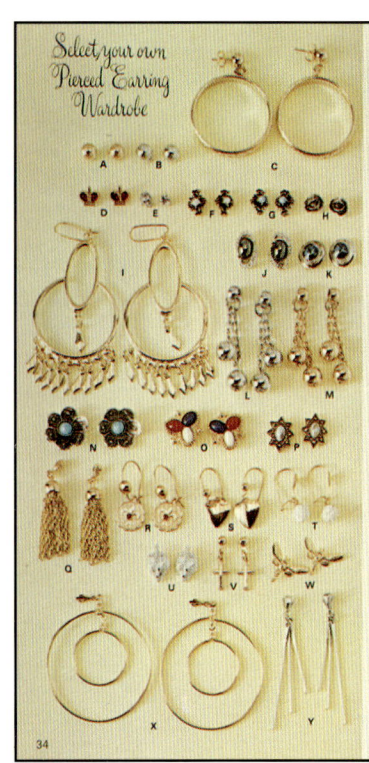

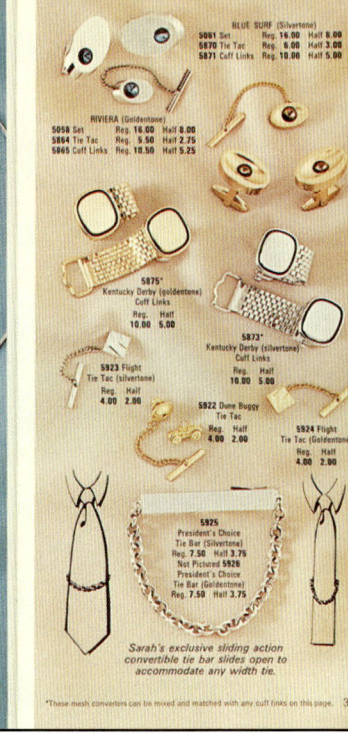

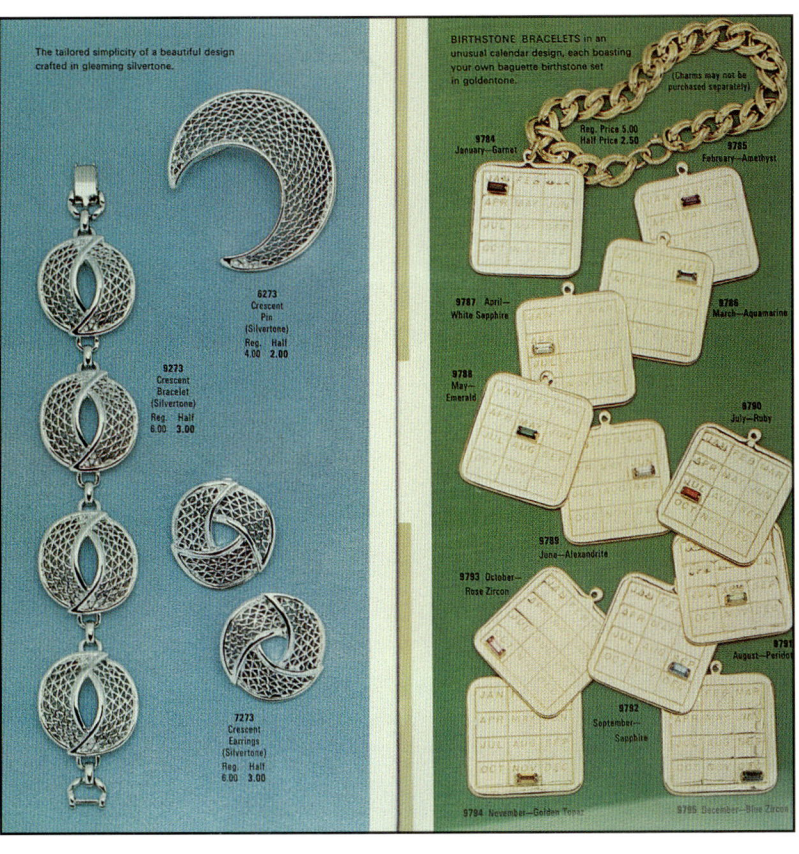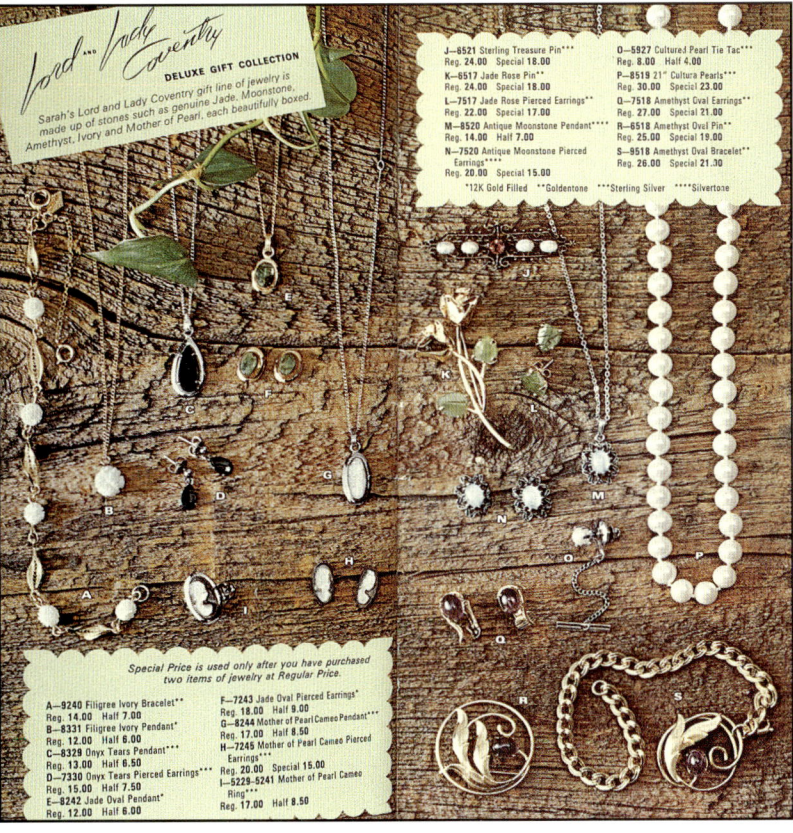

Chapter Five

The 1980s

Several of the former Sarah Coventry employees I interviewed commented that "All good things must end" and ultimately that is what happened to a company that had survived for over thirty years. As the 1980s began, the company—like many others in the late 1970s and early '80s—was making plans for a new decade. Sarah Coventry's plan was called "Direction 80." This new direction included adding "the new" to all Sarah Coventry advertising and sales catalogs from 1981 through 1984. A great deal of diversity was instituted into the direct sale party line, such as luggage, watches, perfume and a multitude of other items. One Fashion Show Director commented that carrying six catalogs to the parties became overwhelming.

Who would have thought that what should have been a bright directional arrow pointing to a very prosperous future would turn into an anchor thwarting progress and ultimately—in 1984—capsizing the company altogether. Many of the people you have met so far continued through to the very end—losing insurance, back bonuses, a total livelihood.

Much of Sarah Coventry jewelry in the 1980s was very similar in pricing to those pieces from the '70s, with some of the popular pieces held over. However, to compete with the "real gold" items being promoted by jewelers, Sarah Coventry added a line of 14K gold and diamonds that were quite pricey. They even had wedding ring sets, expensive charms, and Black Hills Gold items. There were still inexpensive items, but some of the 14K gold pierced earrings ranged from $55 to $225. Many of these earrings and pieces were not marked; they will therefore be most difficult to identify as Sarah Coventry jewelry of the '80s.

Sarah Coventry also introduced "The Most Precious Of Precious Metals…PLATINUM" in 1983. Promotional information describes it as the "Strongest…longest enduring…rich and lustrous…Grows ever more beautiful with wear." Platinum chains and charms ranged from $100 for a 7" to $1800 for a 24" French rope and from $150 for a 1 gram to $575 for a 5 gram platinum ingot drop in 14K gold frame.

Change is inevitable and as for many companies today, the direction that change took within Sarah Coventry was devastating. Yet nowhere else have I found so many former employees who have such positive feelings about a company. The skills and self confidence that were ingrained in these people certainly carried them to new heights in other companies and gave them courage to strive for security in other endeavors.

Shown on the following pages are specific pieces of jewelry I was able to identify from the 1980s. There are also many of the late 1970s pieces that were continued into the '80s, but only placed in one section.

The 1980s jewelry represented a wide variety, from large and chunky to dainty and petite—whatever fit the occasion, the costume, and the wearer. This picture shows a sample of jewelry pieces from this era, including (left to right) **Exclamation** and **Mural** bracelets, **Bronze Glo** pendant, and a pair of **Unidentified** earrings. *All courtesy of Otheda Smith.*

Necklaces

Top to bottom: **Lariat Necklace** is a 38-1/2" linked lariat with a slip loop bearing a greenish/brown cabochon stone. Marked with "©SARAH" engraved on back of slip piece. D; $15-30. **Twisted Knot Lariat** is a fine goldentone chain of 38" with twisted goldentone knots on each end of the chain. When worn, a loop could be fashioned at any length. D; $10-25. **Fashion Basic Chain** is shown in tow different lengths: 30" and 45". These chains were often combined with pendants in the 1970s, but were continued without pendants in the '80s when plain was in vogue. C; $10-25.

Top to bottom: **Valerie Choker** is a simple pendant attached to a 15-17" adjustable goldentone chain. C; $10-25. **Oxford Pendant** has a dainty imported glass stone in this removable goldentone drop. D; $10-25. **Regency** necklace included this pendant on a 29" goldentone chain along with a set of white beads 36" long. The total set was originally priced at $26 in 1980. C; $15-30. **Jubilee** necklace is a 34" goldentone chain with attached tiny heart glass stones encased in goldentone frame. This necklace also had a removable tassel drop created from the same glass hearts and open heart shapes. Very delicate yet fanciful. Necklace and tassel originally cost $25. C; $10-25 (for just the chain).

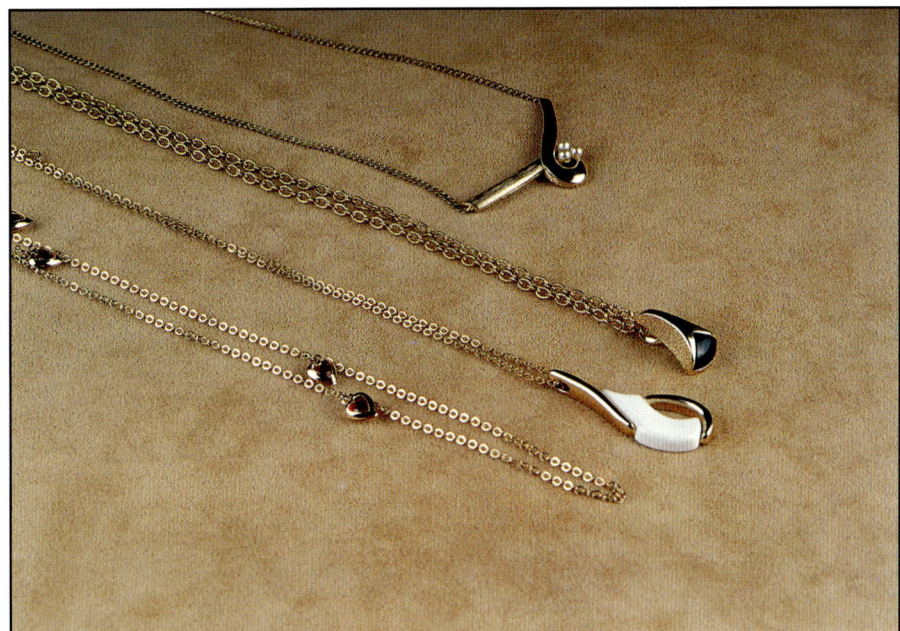

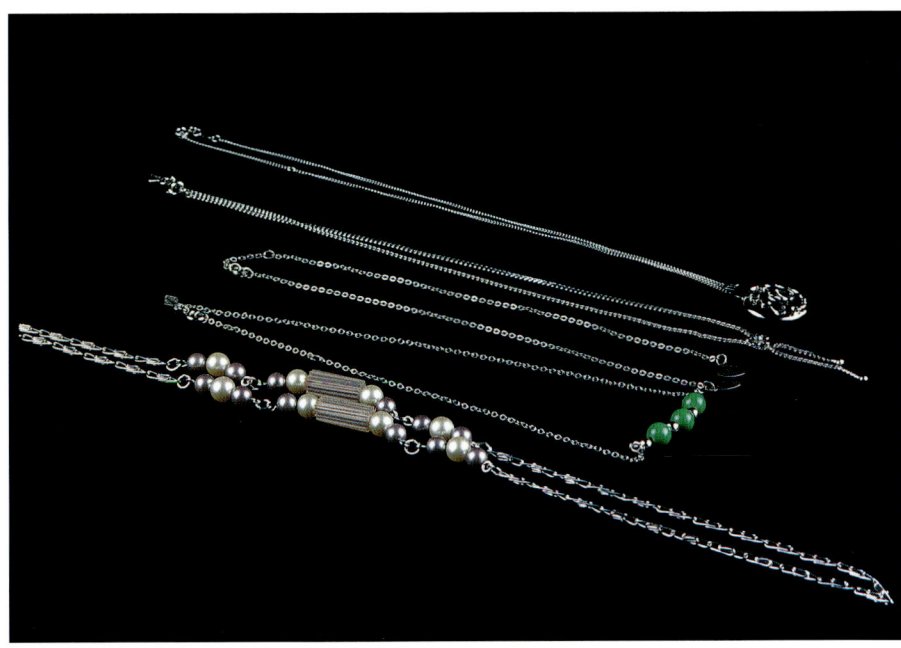

Top to bottom: **Silvery Zodiac** pendant is Gemini for May 21 to June 21 birthdays. This dainty chain and pendant was originally from 1974 and continued for several years. C; $10-25. **Sara Lariat** is a 17-1/2" fine chained lariat with a glass stone slide. There was a miniature matching ring. D; $10-25. **Flirting Heart** is a delicate double heart pendant attached to a fine 15-16" adjustable silvertone chain. B; $5-12. **Spring Melody** necklace was originally a silvertone two chain set. This one is a 15-17" adjustable chain with the stationed beads in the center; the other chain has a single green bead stationed throughout the 37" length. Original price for full set was $22.50. C; $10-25 (for one chain). **Springtime Lilac** necklace is a 36" silvertone chain with stationed lilac cylinder beads plus darker lilac and white beads. There was also a 33" matching chain necklace priced at $26.50. D; $10-25 (for just this chain).

Left to right: *Granada* necklace is a combination of 37-1/4" dark blue beads and 29-1/2" silvertone chain with stationed beads and filigree spacers. D; $15-30. *Unidentified* pearl and embertone beaded necklace has a highly textured goldentone dangle pendant. I am not certain that this is a 1980s necklace but have included it here. $15-30. *Bittersweet* necklace is a combination of two chains (31" and 36") with different colored and shaped stationed beads. This set began in the mid-1970s and continued through the early '80s. D; $15-30. *White Magic Choker* was identified as "White 'n Bright" and is a 16-1/4" choker with multi-sized white bead sections worn close to the throat. C; $15-30. *All courtesy of Dawn Michael.*

Left to right: *Castaway Choker* is a hinged 16" goldentone choker with inlaid dark enamel, introduced with the following: "You, the women of the 80s, are sure of yourselves, able to dress confidently in fashions that you feel most comfortable in. Boutique works with you to reflect your inner style with distinctive dimensions, designs and colors. Make your fashion statement." D; $15-30. *Broken Heart* pendant is a 30" silvertone chain secured to a silvertone open heart pendant. Hang tag is a rounded corner rectangle with "SARAH COV" engraved. C; $10-25. *Orchid Pin/Pendant* was originally on a 24" black cord. It is removable and can easily be placed on a chain. There is no marking on the back of this pin/pendant. C; $10-25. *Seaswept choker* is this shiny and very realistic goldentone pendant on chain with the oval Sarah Coventry tag. Marked "SARAH COVENTRY®" on back of shell. D; $10-25.

Left to right: *Herringbone Chain* is a 16" chain of herringbone design from the early 1980s. C; $15-30. *French Rope* chain is 18" in length with matching bracelet that could be added to increase the length. Matching bracelet on page 152. C; $10-20. *Stretched Cable* truly provides a stretched look to be worn with other chains, necklaces, or beads. C; $10-25. *Twisted Rope* chain from 1980 was 28" goldentone. Also came in silvertone. Matching necklace chains on pages 117, and 151, matching bracelet on page 152. D; $10-25. *Curtain Call* chains 25" in length were introduced in the mid-1970s and continued throughout the '70s and early '80s. They were coupled with multi-colored beads for variety and versatility. B; $10-25 each.

Left to right: *French Rope Chain* in both goldentone and silvertone. Matching chain on page 150, matching bracelet on page 152. C; $10-20. Two versions of *Twisted Rope* are shown here, one with a larger link than the other. Chains in a variety of sizes, lengths, and uses were abundant in the 1980s. Matching chain on page 150. D; $10-25.

Left to right: *Sweetheart Choker* was introduced in the 1979 catalogs and continued throughout the '80s. This glamorous heart shape of "Imported Austrian Glass Stones" is on a 14-16" adjustable silvertone chain. Marked "SARAH" in raised letters on the back edge. C; $15-30. *Spellbound Choker* is not identified with a marking tag. "The bold duo-tone with a touch of starlight to steal his heart away" featured both links of goldentone and mounting for the imported glass stones of silvertone. Original price was $37.50. Matching earrings on page 153. D; $20-45. *Unidentified* diamond shape open goldentone pendant may not be Sarah Coventry, but it was on this chain identified by a <> tag. Help me out with name. $8-15. *Two-Tone Butterfly* pendant was actually two layered butterfly designs—one silvertone, one goldentone. Only the goldentone survived. The chain is goldentone 15-17" adjustable and was common in the late 1970s and early '80s. Marked with a rounded corner rectangle hang tag with "sarah cov" engraved. D; $8-15.

Pins, Bracelets, Earrings, and Rings

Top: *Porcupine* pin is a realistic portrayal of a porcupine with colored glass stone eyes. Marked "©SARAH" in raised letters. B; $10-25. **Bottom row, left to right**: *Conch Shell* pin is a part of the late 1970s and early '80s. This simple conch design could be worn with simple or elaborate costumes. Marked "©SARAH" raised on back. C; $10-25. *Canary* pin is an elongated goldentone pin with yellow enameling. Striking yet very simple. Marked "©SARAH" in raised letters. B; $10-25. *Antique Scroll Bar* is an antiqued goldentone pin bar to be worn on coats, sweaters, dresses, jackets, or any costume in the early '80s. Marked "SARAH" engraved. B; $8-20. *Contour* pin is a shiny silvertone plain pin, very striking, yet very simple. B; $8-20.

Left to right: *Rope Chain* bracelet was very popular in the late 1970s and early '80s. B; $8-15. *French Rope* chain bracelet was also very classic in both silvertone and goldentone. Matching necklace chain on page 150. B; $8-15.

Left to right: *Twisted Rope* bracelet in goldentone has a Balboa charm attached. The matching necklace chain is on page 117. B; $10-25. *Mesh Links* bracelet has a clasp that says "SARAH" and was located in a catalog from 1980. B; $8-20. *M'Lady* bracelet in the box is a glamorous bracelet of goldentone links with a caged-like pearl. B; $10-25. *Headliner* bracelet is a goldentone beaded bracelet, glamorous yet simple. D; $12-25.

Left to right: *Unidentified* earrings in a rope design embracing a pearl-like bead also sport a splotch of red and blue on either side of the pearl. This pair is pierced but is marked "SC©" on the back. Help me out with the name. $10-25. *Spellbound* earrings are "The bold duo-tone with a touch of starlight to steal his heart away." They featured both a link of goldentone and mounting for the imported glass stones of silvertone. These earrings are pierced and therefore do not have an indicating mark. Matching necklace on page 151. D; $10-25. *Bouncy* earrings were first featured in the mid 1970s but were continued through the early '80s. Marked "©SARAH" engraved. A; $10-25.

These earrings were included in a large assortment of Sarah Coventry jewelry that I purchased. They are not marked because they are wire hoops and pierced; also, many pieces in the later years did not have identifying marks. Without access to all of the 1980s catalogs, I have been unable to identify specific names for these. If you can provide me with names or documentation, please let me know.

Top row, left to right: These rings were sized, with some coming only in three sizes while others were full range. *Night Lights* sparkles with imported glass stones surrounded by black epoxy on goldentone. E; $15-30. *Twinkles* is an imported crystal stone set in the center of a black inlaid heart shape on goldentone. E; $15-30. *Spice* is a delicate ring with a tiger-eye type glass stone mounted in a goldentone open pod. E; $15-30. *Escapade* is a silvertone puffed heart shape. There were several of these puffed heart shapes with different names. D; $15-30. *Genuine Jade* ring is, as its name implies, a navette shaped genuine jade stone set in offset goldentone. Marked "SARAH" on back of ring set. E; $15-30. *Unidentified (Part of the Ultra-Fashion Collection)* ring has crystal sets alternating with green stripes. Although I don't have any information about this collection, I am assuming that the sets could be semi-precious or actual diamond chips. No original cost is known. Current value: $20-45. **Bottom row, left to right**: *Kathleen* is not a 1980s ring, but is from the early 1960s. "Sparkling, fiery rhinestones paved in a sunburst design and centered around a brilliant emerald-type stone make a truly glamorous evening ensemble." This ring was adjustable, not sized. Matching pin on page 27, matching earrings on page 84. A; $20-45. *Autumn Haze* is an emerald cut red/amber rhinestone set in a goldentone frame. This ring was not sized, but adjustable under the stone. C; $15-30. *Reflections* ring is from the late 1970s and continued into the early '80s. The prong set emerald cut imported German glass hematite stone is surrounded by tiny imported glass stones framing a silvertone ring. B; $15-30. *Shrimp* ring is a goldentone solid shrimp shape. D; $15-30. *Viva* is an appropriate name for this chaton cut green stone surrounded by an antiqued silvertone mounting accented with simulated pearls on each point. "Have a Ring Fling." B; $20-35. *All courtesy of Dawn Michael.*

1982 Catalog

This 1982 catalog is courtesy of Dawn Michael. Notice "the new" title on this catalog.

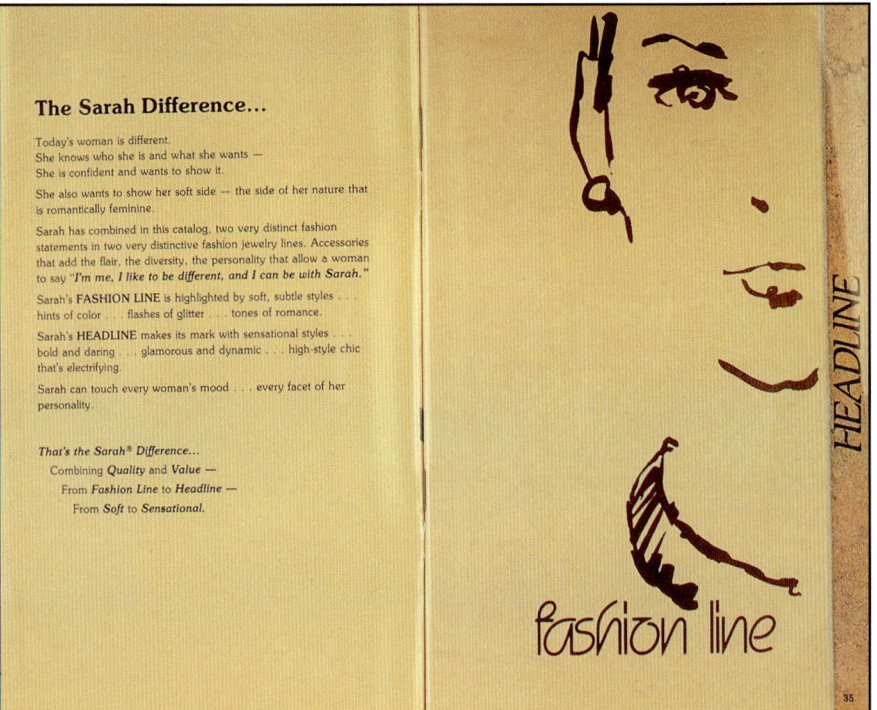

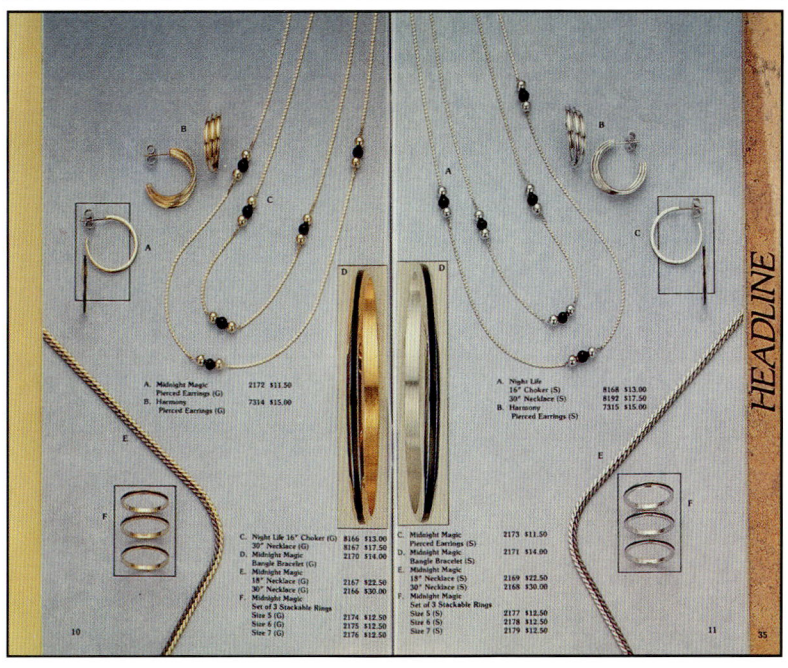

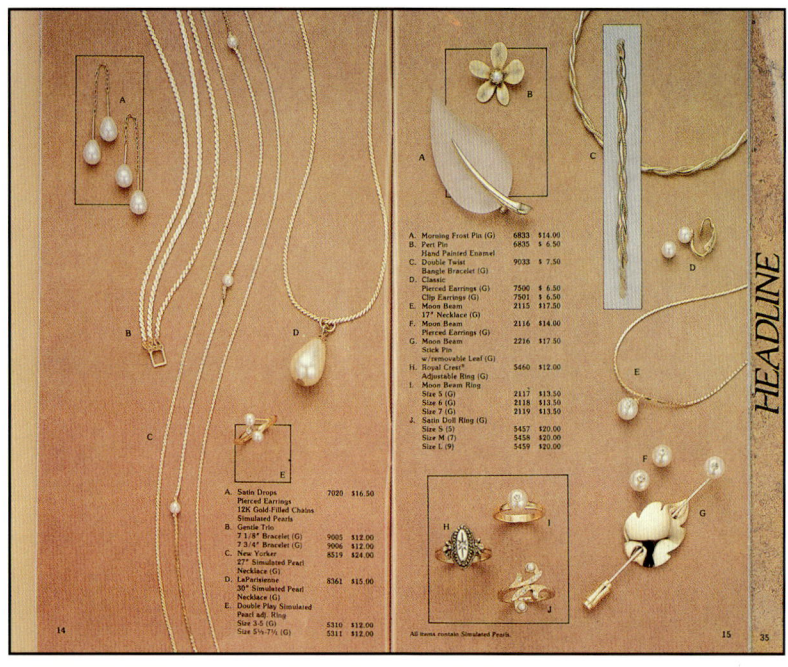
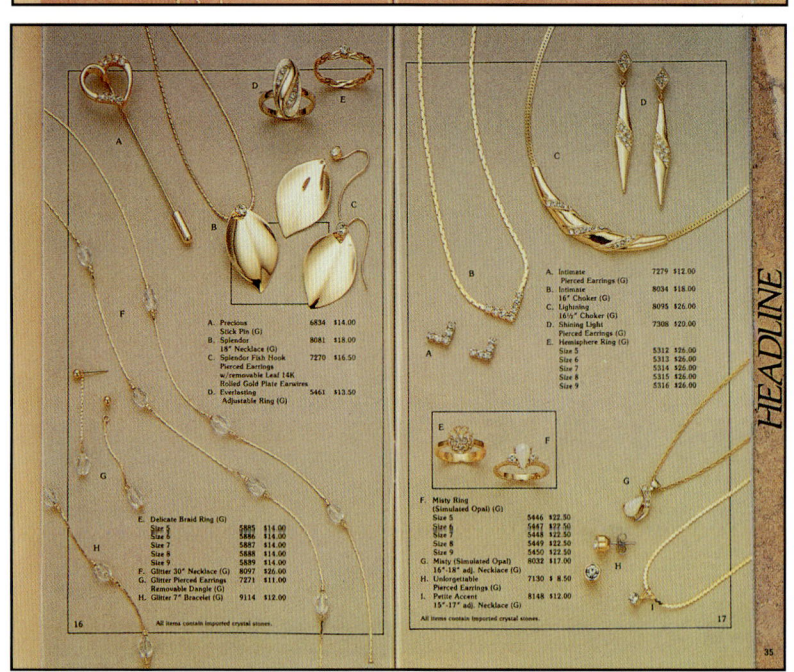

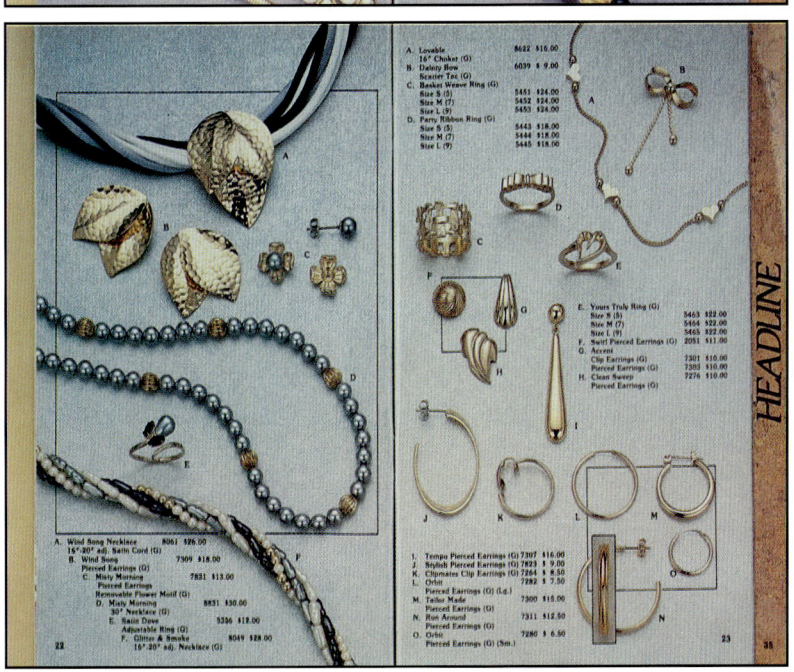

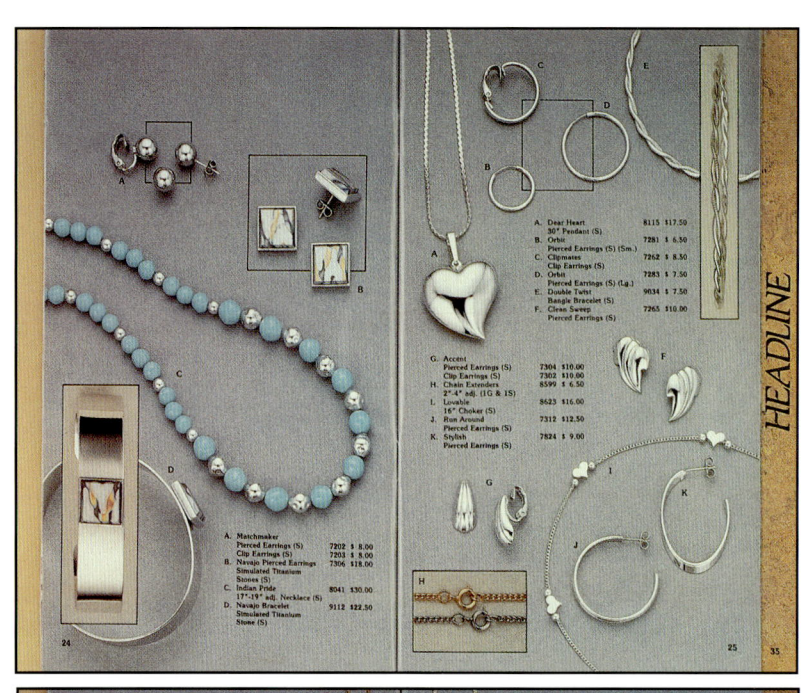
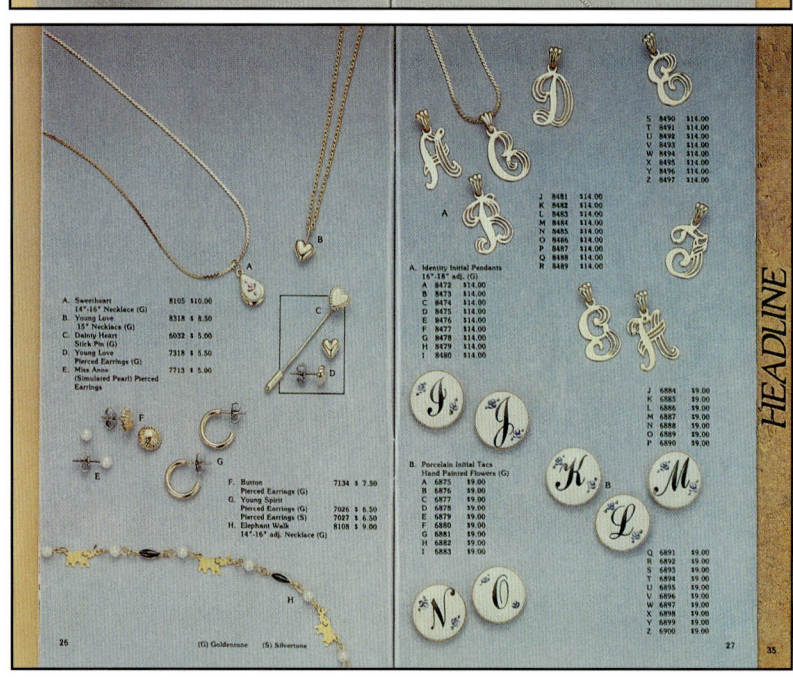

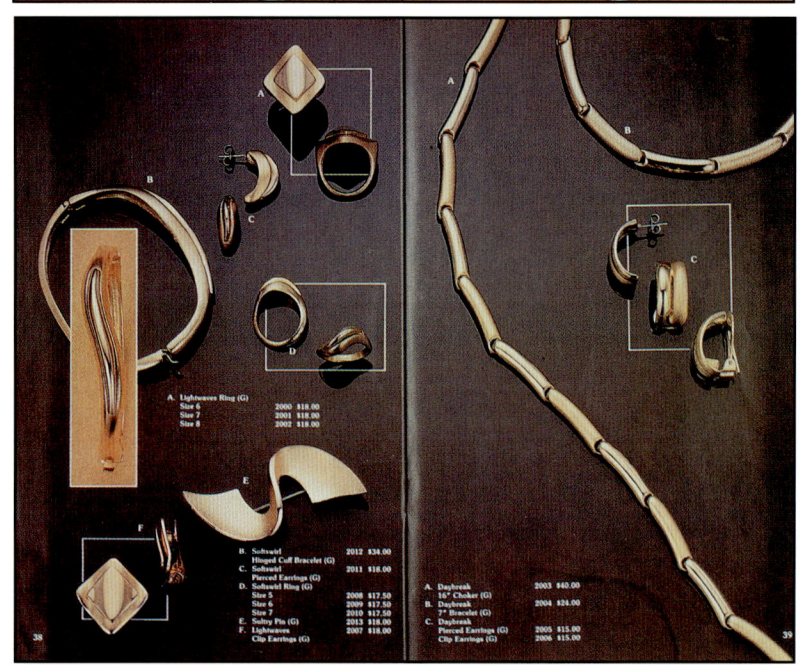
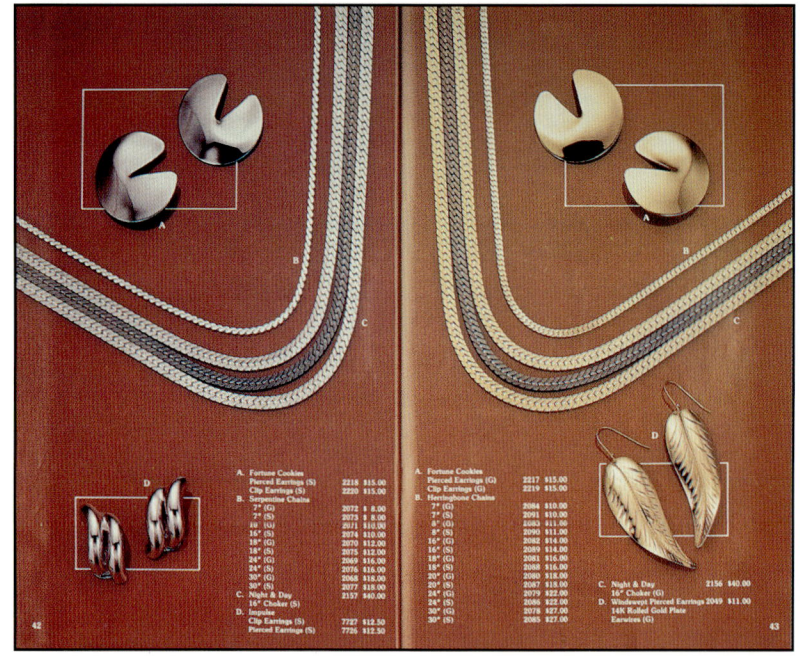

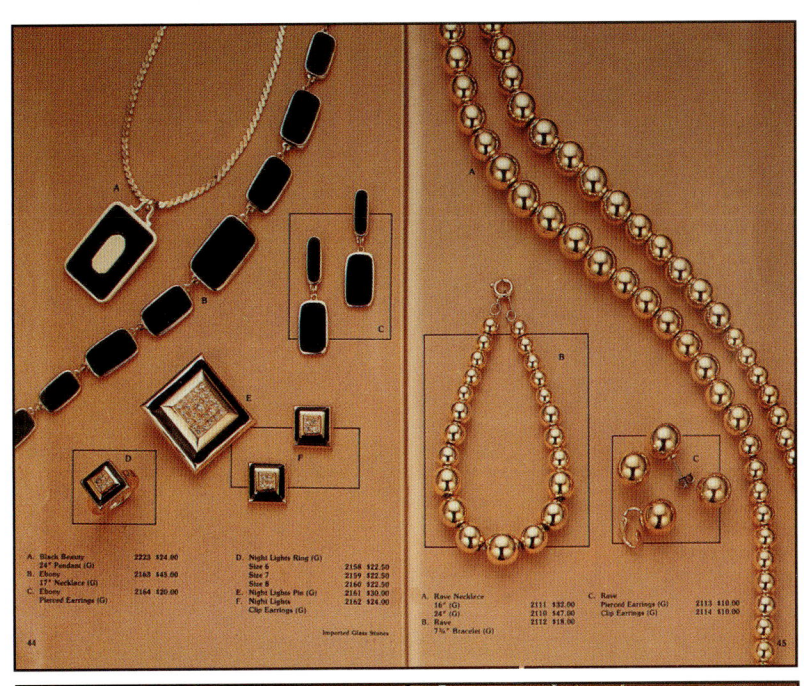

A. Black Beauty		
24" Pendant (G)	2223	$24.00
B. Ebony		
17" Necklace (G)	2163	$45.00
C. Ebony		
Pierced Earrings (G)	2164	$20.00
D. Night Lights Ring (G)		
Size 6	2158	$22.50
Size 7	2159	$22.50
Size 8	2160	$22.50
E. Night Lights Pin (G)	2161	$30.00
F. Night Lights		
Clip Earrings (G)	2162	$24.00

A. Rave Necklace		
16" (G)	2111	$32.00
24" (G)	2110	$47.00
B. Rave		
7½" Bracelet (G)	2112	$18.00
C. Rave		
Pierced Earrings (G)	2113	$10.00
Clip Earrings (G)	2114	$10.00

Imported Glass Stones

A. Gateway®		
Pierced Earrings (G)	2231	$16.00
Clip Earrings (G)	2230	$16.00
B. Crescent		
Pierced Earrings (G)	2052	$18.00
Clip Earrings (G)	2053	$18.00
C. Living Places		
Pierced Earrings (G)	2039	$18.00
D. Falling Leaves		
Pierced Earrings		
14K Rolled Gold Plate		
Earwires (G)	2050	$14.00
E. Around In Circles		
Pierced Earrings (G)	2043	$20.00
F. Cleopatra		
Pierced Earrings (G)	2046	$17.50
Clip Earrings (G)	2047	$17.50
G. Favorites Pierced Earrings (G)	2044	$20.00
(S)	2045	$20.00
H. Impulse Pierced Earrings (G)	7724	$12.50
(S)	7726	$12.50
I. Round About		
Pierced Earrings (G)	7317	$20.00

A. Creamy Shell		
30" Pendant (G)	2227	$27.50
B. Starfish		
30" Pendant (G)	2224	$18.00
C. Sea Shell		
Pin/Pendant Drop	2025	$20.00
D. Sea Shell		
Pierced Earrings (G)	2026	$10.00
E. Gentle Breeze		
30" Pendant (G)	2225	$26.00
F. Highlight		
Hinged Cuff Bracelet (G)	2028	$22.50
G. Highlight		
Pierced Earrings (G)	2027	$10.00

(G) Goldentone (S) Silvertone

A. Caress Necklace		
22" & 23" Strands (G)	2101	$125.00
Glass Beads		
B. Seabreeze Pierced Earrings	2121	$16.00
14K Rolled Gold Plate		
Earwires (G)		
C. Seabreeze Pin (G)	2120	$18.00
D. Caress		
7½" Bracelet Glass Beads (G)	2102	$48.00
E. Sea Treasures		
Pierced Earrings (G)	2107	$20.00
Clip Earrings (G)	2108	$20.00

A. Captive Ring (G)		
Size 6	2103	$20.00
Size 7	2104	$20.00
Size 8	2105	$20.00
B. Captive Pin (G)	2109	$18.00
C. Captive		
Pierced Earrings (G)	2106	$22.50
D. Tara Necklace		
Glass Beads (G)		
16"	2098	$30.00
18"	2097	$32.00
24"	2096	$38.00
28"	2095	$42.00
E. Tara 7" Bracelet		
Glass Beads (G)	2099	$18.00

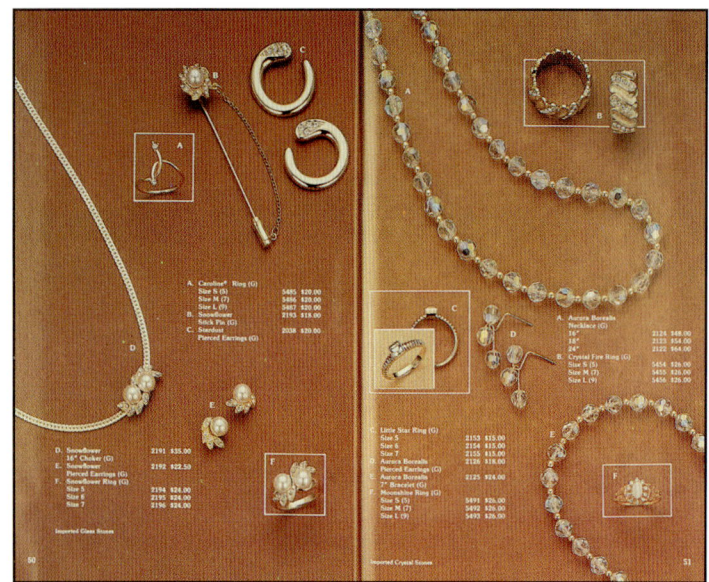
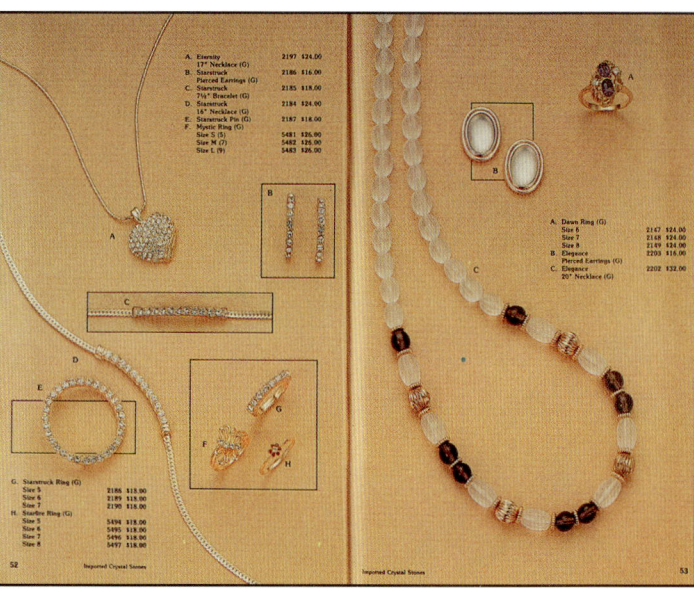

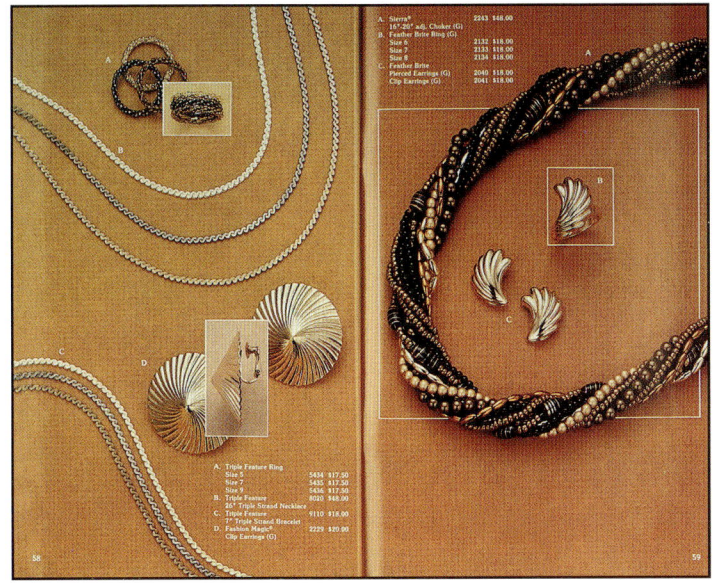

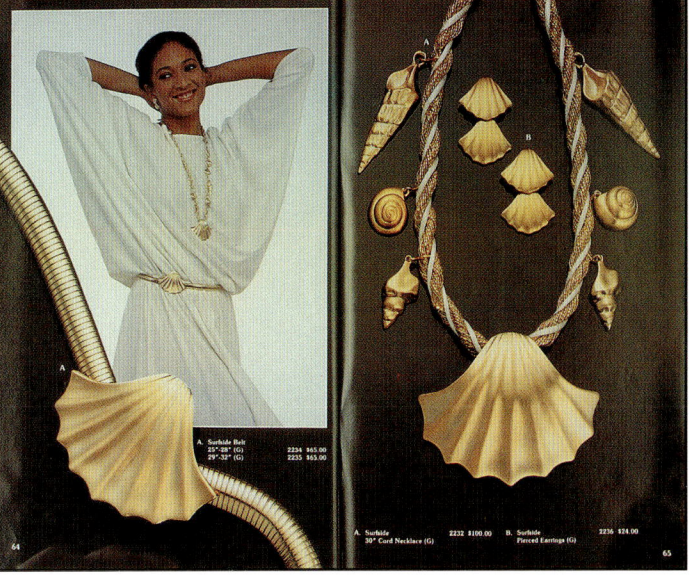

Chapter Six

Men's Jewelry and Accessories

Men's Jewelry

The jewelry craze during the era of Sarah Coventry was not only for women, children, and teens, but also for men. In the early Sarah Coventry years, the dress code for men was very formal with suit and tie; therefore, tie bars and cuff links were popular. You will view many of these sets in the following pictures. When the special collection of Lady Coventry jewelry began in the late '60s, the counterpart Lord Coventry collection also used semi-precious stones. As men's clothing trends changed in the 1970s and 1980s, the Sarah designers changed their direction for men's jewelry selections. Casual trends led to casual jewelry—bracelets, necklaces, and rings.

Promotional materials for men's jewelry also included some slides used for training. Dawn Michael located some of these slides and one of them is shown at right.

Among the promotional materials provided to the Fashion Show Directors were slides that could be used for trainings or for parties. This slide was one used for introducing a line of men's jewelry offered during the company's later years. *Courtesy of Dawn Michael.*

As mentioned earlier in Chapter One, men were an important part of the direct sales force in the field along with women. And, a high percentage of the men were part of husband and wife teams. Besides the company awards and the monetary rewards, many men received personally made items. One of these is pictured below; it's a pillow made for John Knapp, courtesy of his wife Helen. The pillow was created from John's ties, each depicting a part of his life. Of particular significance is the Lord Coventry label. John and Helen worked with the Sarah Coventry company for nearly thirty years, staying right up to the end.

Among the awards/gifts given to Sarah Coventry employees were those items made by friends and families to commemorate special holidays—birthdays, anniversaries, etc. This pillow was created from some of John Knapp's ties, with each piece depicting a part of his life. Notice the Lord Coventry label in the upper left corner. *Courtesy of Helen Knapp.*

There weren't as many men's items designed and sold as there were women's, so fewer will be available for your collection. Therefore, the ones you find will be very desirable and make your collection even more special. Good luck in your quest!

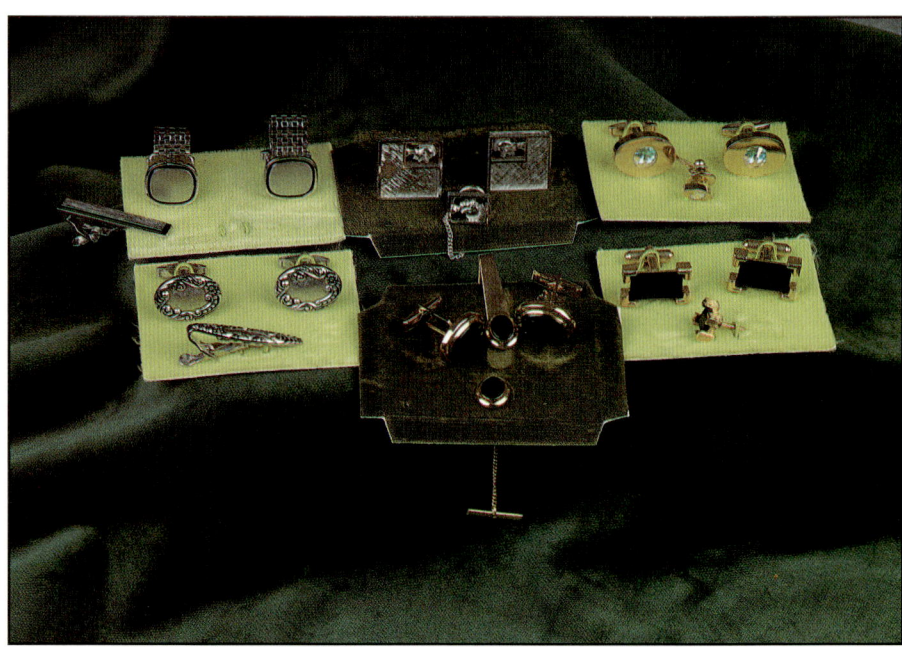

Top row, left to right: *Kentucky Derby* set in silvertone includes cuff links and tie bar. D; $10-25. *Heraldic* cuff links and tie tac in goldentone. D; $10-25. *Riviera* cuff links and tie tac have a goldentone background paired with iridescent Austrian glass stones. D; $15-30. **Bottom row, left to right:** *Antiqued Classic* set of cuff links and tie bar is antiqued silvertone. C; $10-25. *Male Elegance* is a four piece set of cuff links, tie tac, and tie bar with jet black stones in goldentone mounting. C; $15-30. *Bold Knight* set is from the late 1950s and early 1960s. "This midnight black glass stone, encased in a real tailored frame, makes a men's set of great dignity and beauty. The matching tie tac completes a set women will love to buy and men will love to wear." B; $15-30. *All courtesy of Dawn Michael.*

Top row, left to right: These sets were very popular in the early and mid-1970s. *Switzerland* set of cuff links and tie tac is goldentone plain design. D; $15-30. *Germany* set of cuff links and tie tac is silvertone with a cabochon hematite stone in each. D; $15-30. *Denmark* set of cuff links and tie tac has goldentone interlocking diamond shapes. D; $10-25. **Bottom row, left to right:** *Paris* cuff links are glistening goldentone with iridescent Austrian stones for a Parisian look. C; $10-25. *England* set of cuff links and tie bar is antiqued silvertone with a highly detailed design on the bar and around cuff links. D; $15-30. *Italy* set in goldentone has an interlocking link style of cuff links and tie tac. C; $10-25. *All courtesy of Dawn Michael.*

Top row, left to right: *Unidentified* set of cuff links and tie tac in solid goldentone with a lightly textured surface. $10-25. *Venus* cuff links are silvertone with blue glass stones in the corners. B; $10-25. *Genuine Jade* cuff links and tie tac are from the Lord Coventry collection and feature genuine jade stones. C; $15-30. **Bottom row, left to right:** *Neptune* set of cuff links and tie tac is goldentone with crystal aurora rhinestones. D; $15-30. *Mosaic* set of cuff links and tie tac matches the women's mosaic set so he and she could match. Matching women's pieces on pages 105 and 112. C; $15-30. *Mercury* set includes silvertone cuff links with wrap-around mesh and tie bar with black enamel channel around the edges. D; $10-25. *All courtesy of Dawn Michael.*

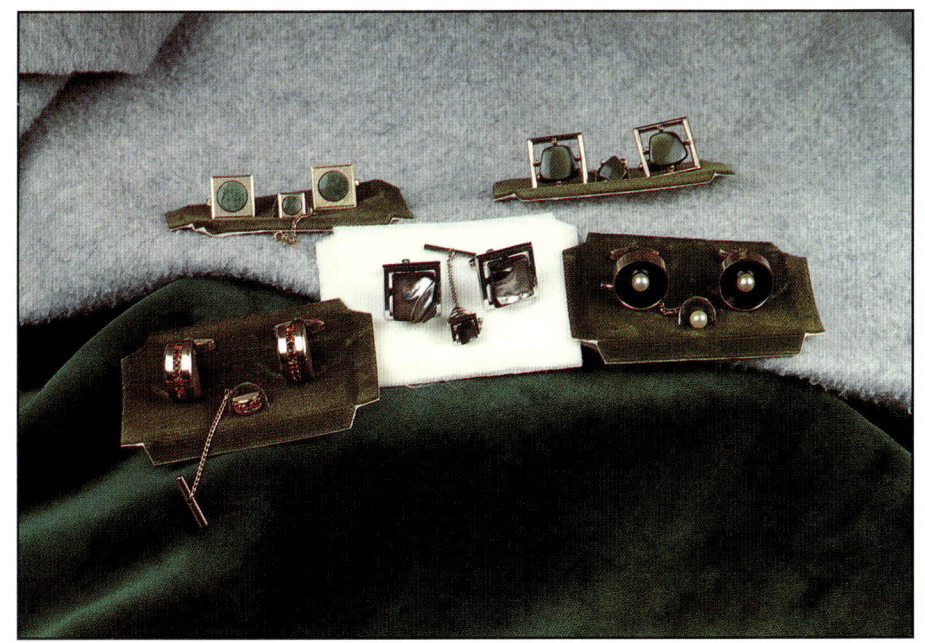

Top row, left to right: *Royal Jade* are genuine jade cuff links and tie tac from the late 1960s. D; $15-30. *The New Yorker* cuff links and tie tac are "A smart looking set for any man from New York to San Francisco who likes to be well dressed…The olivine color of the stone is enhanced by the rich silvertone background." This set is from 1966. B; $15-30. **Bottom row, left to right:** *Mars* cuff link and tie tac are goldentone drum-like shapes with red crystal rhinestones. D; $15-30. *Tahitian Pearl* cuff links and tie tac are silvertone with genuine Tahitian pearl stones. This set is part of the Lord Coventry collection. D; $15-30. *Unidentified* set of cuff links and tie tac is made of simulated pearls. There are many sets with simulated pearls, however, this specific one was not in any of my catalogs. Many times these pieces were in only one catalog and since I have been unable to locate every catalog, I may have missed this specific set. Help me out with it. $15-30. *All courtesy of Dawn Michael.*

Left to right: *Duke Choker* is 18" of silvertone regular links interspersed with wider links to create a choker that could be worn alone or with a charm or drop. C; $10-25. *Daytona Choker* of multi-colored elongated beads with goldentone is 18-1/2" long and could be worn with this sand dollar drop or another drop. E; $15-30. *Gentry* chain is an antiqued goldentone chain handsome alone or with a masculine drop. B; $10-25. *Calvary Cross* could be worn by either men or women and was most handsome on this 16-18" adjustable goldentone chain. B; $10-25. *Italian Horn* with genuine pewter drop on a stainless steel 24" chain could be worn by any age man. C; $10-25. *Slicker Chain* is a goldentone linked chain with a refined rather than a bold look. Any drop could be added for more elegance. B; $10-25. *Embraceable Chain* is a 16" goldentone chain that also came in silvertone for versatility. It could be worn alone, with zodiac pendants, or with any other drop. B; $10-25. *All courtesy of Dawn Michael.*

Top left: *Explorer* bracelet for men is made of oxidized silvertone. B; $8-15. **Bottom row, left to right:** *Leather Cuff* bracelet has a genuine leather back and was actually made for boys or men with small wrists. B; $10-25. *Dare Devil* bracelet is made of oxidized goldentone. C; $15-30. *Brute* bracelet is also oxidized goldentone. It came in oxidized silvertone as well. C; $10-25. *New I.D.* is an oxidized silvertone bracelet just waiting to be engraved with his or her name. These were popular in the mid-1970s. C; $15-30. *Kojak* bracelet is a flat linked goldentone bracelet from 1976. B; $10-25. *Third Gear* adjustable bracelet is made from a combination of oxidized silvertone, goldentone, and solid copper. C; $10-25. *All courtesy of Dawn Michael.*

Left to right: *Regimental* cuff links and tie tac are silvertone red sets with a black strip. They are from the late 1960s. C; $15-30. *Men Runner Pendant* is a part of the Sportsman's Collection. "All pendants are fashioned from stainless steel and are 18-20" adjustable. These action pendants will tell the whole story as your men gear up for an active life. Summer will see men on the golf course, swinging a tennis racket and jogging their miles. Winter will find men taking a ski jump or bowling a perfect 300. Your men will want to be fashionable as well as rugged so choose from our action-filled Sportsman's Collection and help them on their way." These were from the early 1980s catalogs. C; $10-25. *Men's Zodiac* charm is a solid goldentone symbol of the zodiac. Zodiac charms were very popular in the 1970s and were designed in a variety of forms, from these solid shapes to coin-like shades to very detailed and elaborate disks. This is Capricorn for December 22 to January 20. C; $10-25. *Dune Buggy* tie tacs were part of a set created in the early 1970s. Others were Skee-Doo, Free Wheeling, and Big Red. These were designed to give men a symbol to wear representing their interests or hobbies. B; $8-20.

Top row, left to right: *Cultured Pearl* tie tac was a part of the Lord Coventry collection and is pictured here in goldentone. B; $10-25. *Tailored Elegance* tie bar is "…elegant in its simplicity of design, striking in its use of the linen, or textured finish contrasted with the satin finish. Will he prefer the goldentone or silvertone, this is your only question, you know he will love the design." From the late 1950s or early '60s. A; $10-25. *Genuine Onyx* cuff links of silvertone were part of the Lord Coventry collection as the box indicates. Note the tag distinguishing the genuine onyx. B; $15-30. **Center, top to bottom**: *Cultured Pearl* tie tac in silvertone was also part of the Lord Coventry collection. B; $10-25. *Charcoal Classic* from the late 1950s and early '60s has "An artificial hematite glass stone used to create this unusual masculine tie bar and cuff link set. The charcoal gray is enriched by the gleaming silvertone finish. A set designed by a man for real men, this set can be worn with almost any color in your wardrobe." A; $15-30.

Accessories

As can be seen throughout the catalogs, Sarah Coventry's designers were fascinated not just with jewelry but also with accessory items; these ranged from belts to key rings to scarf clips. Whatever was in vogue at the time, Sarah was right there. Shown in this section are just a few of these many accessories.

You will see that watches are included here. I have not seen watches advertised in any of the catalogs. However, it is my understanding that watches were part of the award gifts. One FSD mentioned that watches were part of the diversification that was instituted during the early 1980s. After the company name was sold in 1984, the purchasing company did manufacture watches, which were sold in regular department stores such as Dillards and discount outlets like Wal-Mart and K-Mart. Some of the watches pictured here may be award items. If you have specific information about these, please let me know.

Left to right: *Scarf Keeper* in goldentone is "The new mod look of 'in' jewelry." These coins with dangles came in both goldentone and silvertone to provide options for wear with various scarves popular in the early 1970s. A; $10-25. *Golden Gypsy*: "Links of 'Gypsy gold' make up this exciting and dashing sautoir necklace or belt. Thirty-three inches of unusual large chain which gives you miles of versatile fashion ideas." This was from the late 1950s to early '60s. Matching earrings on page 42. B; $15-30. *Key to My Heart Key Ring* of silvertone is a key ring made of heart-shaped metal. In the late 1970s, several of these type accessories were created to add variety to the Sarah Coventry line. Marked "SARAH" engraved on the inside edge. A; $8-15.

Top to bottom: *Continental* belt is "A golden band of sleek charm and distinction…around your waist, by night, by day. Perfect with basic dresses, and suits, it adds a dashing accent to casuals too. This golden mesh is a compliment-getter, a conversation piece wherever it goes." From the late 1950s and early '60s. B; $10-25. *Twist About Belt* was from 1978 and came in a stretch goldentone material to accommodate 26-1/4" to 33-1/2". E; $15-30. *Courtesy of Alynda Kimbrough.* *Four Seasons* belt in silvertone was from the early 1960s and described as "another first for Sarah—a belt to fit all waists from 21 inches to 36 inches and a belt that can also span the seasons. A basket weave design in textured and gleaming goldentone or silvertone and to complete your look of fashion—a matching bracelet. Just as lively and lovely as the life you lead. Four Seasons can go anywhere you go, any time of year." Matching bracelet on page 127. B; $15-30. *Courtesy of Nancy Isgrigs.*

Although I have not seen watches displayed in any of the catalogs I've located, I did learn that after the company name was sold in 1984, the purchasing companies manufactured watches for distribution through department and discount stores. In this picture, the watch on the far left with the diamond chip may have been an award given to employees while the others may be some of those sold in stores after 1984.

Epilogue

    As I complete this manuscript I am still locating and purchasing pieces of Sarah Coventry jewelry. Some pieces are ones I've not seen before, so I eagerly search for their names and dates. Could this be addicting?

    If you are lucky enought to meet an original Sarah Coventry dealer or Fashion Show Director who identifies a piece as Sarah Coventry, even though there are no identifying marks, most likely it *is* Sarah jewelry. I have located several such pieces in this way.

    I know there are many Sarah Coventry pieces out there awaiting you. So identify, collect, wear, trade, display, and— most importantly—cherish these wonderful gems from the past.

Glossary

Amethyst. A natural gemstone in shades from lavender to purple. Costume jewelry used imitation rhinestones in these same shades.

Aurora Borealis. A name derived from the colorful aurora lights seen in the northern latitudes. The glass rhinestones have actually been treated with metals—layers of different materials vacuum plated to glass—which gives the iridescent effect. Introduced especially for Sarah Coventry by Swarovski.

Baguette. A gemstone elongated, faceted, and straight on the side.

Baroque Pearl. A large, bumpy, misshapen pearl, real or man-made.

Bib. A necklace of three or more strands of chain, beads, or simulated pearls in concentric lengths. See Chiffon-Bib, page 113, for an example.

Black Diamond. A smoky colored rhinestone, a simulated not real diamond.

Cabochon. A dome shaped round or oval cut with no facets. Usually flat on the underneath side.

Channel setting. A groove or channel with the upper flange bent over to keep the stones secure; could also be a metal track holding baguette stones securely in place.

Charms. As used by costume jewelers, the term refers to the small decorative ornaments fastened on a chain, bracelet, necklace, or today even on earrings.

Chatelaine. Originally, this referred to a chain hanging from the belt of a household employee on which articles like keys, a watch, a comb, or coin purse were secured. Later it became a term used for describing a pair of pins that were connected by a chain or perhaps several chains. The two pieces could be worn separately or together. Sarah Coventry had several of these in the late 1950s. See Chit-Chat, page 32.

Chaton cut. The most popular cut for rhinestones. An octagon shaped center with eight trapezoid faces from the octagon to the outside edge of rhinestone. The top is a flat surface, the bottom of the stone comes to a point. See Aurora Blaze set, page 83.

Clip. A spring clasp at the back of earrings.

Cluster setting. Small rhinestones clustered around a larger, central rhinestone.

Costume Jewelry. Jewelry not containing precious jewels or metals. Some Sarah Coventry jewelry does not meet this definition because of semi-precious stones used. See Semi-Precious Turtle, page 87.

Cultured Pearl. A pearl cultivated in a controlled environment, allowing for a uniform size and color.

Demi-parure. Sometimes used in descriptions or other books, referring to a set of two matching pieces of same design. Much of Sarah's jewelry fits this category.

Double cut. A cut often used to create added brilliance because it has twice as many facets as a standard cut.

Drop. A small decorative object or ornament suspended from a brooch, necklace, hoop, or earring. May also be described as a dangle.

Enamel. A process in which a paint or lacquer is painted on a metal surface and hardens to resemble the old enameling techniques.

Engraving. Etching of a pattern or figure into a metal surface using a sharp tool. Also used for applying the marking of company name.

Epoxy. Paint applied by hypodermic needle and air pressure.

Facets. Cuts made to shape a rhinestone and allow for enhanced light refraction, thus creating the sparkle.

Faux. French word for false or not genuine. Also means counterfeit, copied, or simulated.

Filigree. Ornamental work that looks lacy, intricate, and delicate because it is created from intertwining gold, silver, brass, or other fine wires. Queen's Lace ring, page 131, is an example.

Findings. The functional parts of jewelry, including catches, hooks, jump rings, springs, clips, screws, wires, bolts, caps, loops, rings, stones, beads, and more, which can be collected to fix costume jewelry.

Foil. A thin leaf of bright metal secured behind a glass or crystal stone which adds to the brilliance of the stone and enhances the color.

Gold filled. A lesser metal sandwiched between two layers of gold, identified as 18K g.f. or 24K g.f.

Goldentone. A gold-like finish used for costume jewelry, created by covering metal with an alloy of gold. Similar to SarahGlo with high luster.

Graduated strand. Identifies the graduating sizes of pearls or beads from smaller in the back to larger in the middle front. See Perfection Necklace, page 113.

Intaglio. A design cut or carved into a gemstone, piece of glass, or plastic. Intaglio is the opposite of cameo, which is a relief design (raised). See Thea Pendant, page 112.

Jabot. A scarf-like accessory (a pleated frill of cloth or lace attached down the center front of a woman's blouse or dress) worn in the early 1950s. One of Sarah's descriptions uses this term.

Jet. A coal fossil lignite of glossy black color. It is usually a cabochon rather than a black glass rhinestone. Sarah's Jet Set, page 129, is a good example.

Lariat. A long necklace without a clasp giving the open ends the opportunity to be knotted, looped, or held together with a clasp, ring, or pin.

Marked or Signature. Refers to when the designer's or manufacturer's mark is identified on the back of the piece of jewelry, either engraved or a raised carving. Sarah Coventry jewelry has a wide variety of such markings.

Moonstone. A pearl, bluish opaque, cabochon stone. Sarah Coventry used these stones in the Lady Coventry set.

Navette or Marquise. A rhinestone cut in a canoe shape with points at both ends.

Necklace lengths. Various names used, depending on length, as noted below.

    Choker. 14" to 16" in length; could be a necklace or ribbon worn close to the throat.

    Princess. 16" to 20" in length; usually used for beads, chains, or combinations

    Matinee. 20" to 26" in length; used by Sarah Coventry in the early years for beads, chains with stationed beads, and later for chains.

    Opera. 28" to 36" in length; could be left as a single strand or coiled twice around neck.

    Rope. 40" or longer in length; generally a length given to the many early popular beads.

Parure. The French name given to a matching set of jewelry consisting of more than two pieces, usually consisting of necklace, bracelet, earrings, pin, and ring. Many of Sarah's sets included all of these pieces.

Paved or pave. Tiny rhinestones placed very close to each other giving the jewelry the effect of literally being paved with rhinestones. On costume jewelry these rhinestones were glued in place.

Pear or Teardrop. A popular rhinestone cut in an oval with a point at one end.

Prong set. Metal fingers or prongs used to hold a stone securely in place. Many of Sarah's first pieces were hand set with prongs: later they were glued in for faster production.

Reverse carving. A carving from the underneath side of the piece.

Rhinestone. A cut stone of glass that uses light refraction to create sparkle and could be iridescent. Often backed with foil for additional brilliance. The term comes from the area near the Rhine river in Austria where these glass stones were originally produced. Sarah Coventry used many of these imported Austrian and German stones.

Rhodium. A whitish-gray silvery metal that is a part of the platinum family. It is very hard and resistant to corrosion and is electroplated in costume jewelry. Sarah Coventry used a lot of rhodium in the earlier years to create longer lasting pieces.

Rosette. A group of closely placed rhinestones arranged in a circular shape around a center stone.

SarahGlo. High luster finish achieved by a process of covering metal with an alloy of gold.

SarahSheen. High luster finish achieved by a process of covering metal with rhodium.

Sautoir. A long open-ended necklace of chains, pearls, beads, or even cording with tassels, drops, or other ornaments at the end. See Fashion Parade, page 45.

Silvertone. A finish used for costume jewelry, in which metal is covered with rhodium for a lasting finish. Similar to SarahSheen with high luster.

Simulated. An imitation or counterfeit of something that is genuine. Simulated pearls are an example.

Stationed. To assign to or set in a station or position. See Frosted Ice, page 122.

Topaz. A gemstone in a yellow to orange color. See Golden Embers, page 76.

Bibliography

Baker, Lillian. *Fifty Years of Collectible Fashion Jewelry 1925-1975*. Paducah, Kentucky: Collector Books, A Division of Schroeder Publishing Co., Inc., 1986.
Clements, Monica Lynn and Patricia Rosser Clements. *Sarah Coventry Jewelry: An Unauthorized Guide for Collectors*. Atglen, Pennsylvania: Schiffer Publishing Ltd., 1999.
Lindbeck, Jennifer A. *Fine Fashion Jewelry From Sarah Coventry*. Atglen, Pennsylvania: Schiffer Publishing Ltd., 2000.
Rezazadeh, Fred. *Costume Jewelry, A Practical Handbook & Value Guide*. Paducah, Kentucky: Collector Books, A Division of Schroeder Publishing Co., Inc., 1997.
Simonds, Cherri. *Collectible Costume Jewelry: Identification and Values*. Paducah, Kentucky: Collector Books, A Division of Schroeder Publishing Co., Inc., 1997.

Appendix

Personal Collection Sheets

To document your purchases, I recommend the use of Personal Collection Sheets like the sample below. You can reproduce this chart onto any size paper, then carry with you on your treasure hunting trips to keep track of your finds. Happy collecting!

—Kay

Description (Name)	Purchase Price	Purchase Date	Reference Information

Index

This index has been designed to assist you in identifying pieces in your collection. To be as user friendly as possible, the index is primarily organized by type of jewelry, e.g., Necklaces, Earrings, Bracelets, etc., with an alphabetical list of individual items beneath the headings. Sets have also been identified by individual pieces, to help in locating just one piece. You will find general information about the company under Overview, and a list of Unidentified jewelry near the end of the index.

The numbers in parentheses after each piece are the original company code numbers (when known). Keep in mind, however, that these numbers may have changed when pieces were reproduced at a later time. Also, note that individual items within sets often have the same last three numbers, with the initial number indicating the type of piece, i.e., 6=brooches, 7= earrings, etc.

Accessories, 169
   Belts, 115, 169
      Continental, 169
      Fashion Wrap (8797), 115
      Four Seasons (5960), 169
      Golden Gypsy (8945), 169
      Twist About (8016), 169
   Key Chains
      Key to My Heart (5971), 169
   Scarf keepers (6295), 169
   Shoe Clips
      Moonlight Madness, 54
   Watches, 169

Awards. See Employees

Birthstones
   Birthstone Pendant Lady Coventry (8156), 88
   Children's Birthstone Ring, 88
   Happy Talk Birthstone Ring (5405-5416), 133
   Love Story Birthstone Pendants (8881-8892), 118
   Love Story Rings (5469-5480), 82, 88, 134, 135
   Love Story Set (6887, 7887), 124
   Miss Sarah Birthstone Pendant (8911-8922), 88
   Mother's Pin (5044-5054), 88
   Sarah Coventry's Family Bouquet, 88
   Sarah's Mother Rings (5570-5582), 88
   Sterling Silver Charms (9083-9093), 89

Bracelets, 50-52, 79-80, 126-130
   Acapulco (9275), 79
   Alaskan Summer, 53
   Antique Garden (5064), 80
   Antique Rose (9439), 129
   Aurora Swirl, 55
   Austrian Lites (9633), 128
   Black Reflections (9507), 130
   Blue Hawaii (9914), 50
   Blue Lady (9636), 127
   Bostonian Classic (9028-G, 9029-S), 128
   Boulevard (9631), 126
   Butterscotch (9064), 129
   Camelot (9647), 79
   Candlelight (9276), 127, 128
   Carousel, 26
   Celebrity (9878), 50
   Celestial Fire, 55
   Chantilly Lace, 54
   Charm Bracelet (9231, charms 9232-9236), 130
   Charm Links (9284), 127, 130
   Chiffon (9445), 128
   Circle Charm (9557), 80
   Colorama (9003), 127
   Contessa (9936), 128
   Continental (9597), 79
   Cosmic Wrap Around (9383), 129
   Counterpoint (9598), 128
   Crescent (9273), 80
   Crystal Snowflake (9277), 83
   Delightful (9986), 50
   Designer Links, 130
   Designer's Choice, 129
   Disco-Tek (9875), 128
   Dolphin (9537), 127
   Earth Tones (9131), 126
   Echo (9046), 130
   Egyptian Temptress, 51
   Empress (9539), 128
   Enchantress (9728), 83
   Exclamation (9998), 148
   Fancy Free (9412), 126
   Fascination (9057), 126
   Fashion Cuff (9593), 79
   Fashion Flip (9249), 129
   Florentine (9466), 126
   Four Seasons (9883), 127

   Four-Dimensions (8107), 111
   French Cuff (9426), 128
   French Links (9777), 126
   French Rope (9716), 152
   Frolic (9542), 127
   Frozen Lace, 54
   Golden Cuff (9767), 79
   Golden Ice (9550), 136
   Golden Shield (9960),128
   Golden Sunset (9855), 128
   Gracious Lady (9906), 52
   Granada (9495), 129
   Grecian (9671), 113
   Happy Holiday (9826), 51, 127
   Harmony (9983), 50
   Harvest Wheat, 51
   Headliner (9053),152
   Hearts and Flowers (9606), 51
   Heritage (9697), 79
   Indian Maiden (9823), 127
   Indian Treasures (9888), 50
   Jet Set (9312), 129
   Lady of Spain (9830), 51
   M'Lady (9730), 52
   Mademoiselle (9905), 51
   Melody (9586), 129
   Mesh Links, 152
   Midnight Magic (9605), 83
   Milky Way (9577), 126
   Minuet (9506), 127
   Monte Carlo (9831), 52
   Mood Magic (9988), 130
   Moon-lites (9287), 80
   Multiple Strand, 80
   Multi-Swirl (9930), 50
   Mural (9727), 148
   Mystique (9030), 127
   New I.D. (9796), 127
   Nocturne (9484), 129
   Northern Lights (9576), 127
   Operetta (9828), 136
   Parisienne Nights (9847), 52
   Party Pastels (9594), 79
   Partytime (9872), 126
   Pearl Flattery (9936), 51
   Pearl Swirl (9615), 80
   Personal Choice (9129), 129
   Pink Shadows (9213), 126
   Plain and Fancy (9673), 52
   Pyramid Treasures, 80
   Rope Chain (9450), 152
   Royal Ballet, 54
   Royal Highness (9899), 51
   Sea Star (9349), 127
   Serenade (9354), 128
   Shangri-La (9526), 128
   Silver Links, 127
   Silvery Cascade (9749), 80
   Silver Leaf (9077), 127
   Simplicity (9322-S, 9321-G), 126
   Simply Elegant (9894), 51
   Soft Swirl (9567), 129
   Sonnet (9937), 130
   Star Attraction (9190), 126
   Strawflower (9194), 129
   Tailored Cuff (9288), 126
   Tailored Lady (9943), 128
   Talisman of Love (9560), 127
   Textured Links (9112), 127
   Tortoise Fashions (9802), 80
   Turn-a-bout, 127
   Twilight (9827), 129, 137
   Twisted Rope (9332), 152
   Valencia (9291), 127
   Vanessa (9932), 126
   Versaille, 52
   Vogue (8196), 130
   Whispering Leaves (9724), 80
   Wood Nymph (9344), 130
   World's Fair (9947), 51, 84
   Woven Classic (9939), 51
   Young and Gay (9733), 50
   Young Charmer (9681), 79

Brooches, 27-33, 65-70, 98-103, 153.
See also Brooch/Pendant Combinations
   Acapulco (6275), 68
   Accent (6640), 68
   Acorn (also known as Golden Acorn), 102
   Alaskan Summer, 53
   Allusion (6208), 69
   Amber Jet (6881), 28
   Amber-lites, 32
   American Beauty (6837), 33
   Americana (6387),100
   Antique Rose (6439), 101
   Antique Scroll Bar (6005), 152
   Aurora Blaze (6725), 66, 83
   Austrian Lites (6633), 103
   Autumn Haze (6511), 28
   Autumn Splendor (6601), 103
   Azure Skies (6575), 102
   Baroque Goddess (6256), 67
   Bird of Paradise (6534), 29
   Birds in Flight (6704), 69
   Bittersweet (6868), 28
   Black Beauty (6734), 29
   Black Beauty (6863), 30
   Black (Imitation) Diamond (5011), 70
   Black Saturn (6813), 31
   Blue Champagne (6708), 32
   Blue Lagoon (6991), 83
   Blue Note (6732), 29
   Blue Snowflake (6659), 102
   Burgundy (6485), 101
   Camellia (6909), 30
   Cameo Lace (8848), 32
   Canary, 152
   Candy Land (6557), 102
   Carousel (6532), 99
   Celebrity (8878), 29
   Celestial Ice, 32
   Ceylon (6409), 98
   Chit-Chat (6771), 32
   Circulet (6825), 103
   Conch Shell (6089), 152
   Contour (6045), 152
   Coraline (8924), 103
   Covered Wagon Award, 70
   Crescent (6273), 67
   Criss-Cross (6388), 100, 101
   Crystal Snowflake (6277), 83
   Daisy (6919), 32
   Daisy Mae, 31
   Daisy Time (6385), 68
   Dazzling Aurora, 17
   Deep Burgundy (6613), 66
   Delicious (6292), 99
   Demi-Flower (6249-G, 6250-S), 67
   Designer's Choice, 27
   "Dogwood" White (6222), 68
   Ember Flower (6513), 99
   Ember Light (6702), 103
   Endearing (6564), 67
   Evening Accent, 31
   Evening Comet (6573), 69
   Evening Snowflake (6926), 27
   Evening Splendor (6750), 69
   Evening Star (6629), 68, 83
   Fantasy (6705), 30
   Fantasy (6887), 68
   Fashion Flower, 69
   Fashion Flower (6834), 28
   Fashion in Motion (6251), 68
   Fashion Leaf, 31
   Fashion Parade Stick (6203), 67
   Fashion Petals (6738, 6742, 6741), 65
   Fashion Round (6315), 70
   Fashion Splendor, 98
   Fashion Twist Stick (6676), 101
   Feather Bright (6642), 102
   Feather-Brite (6735), 67
   Feather Fantasy (6765), 31
   Festival (6122), 101
   Filigree Clover (6461), 70
   Fire 'n Ice (6829), 102

   Flair (6351), 99
   Fleurette (6990), 100
   Flirtation, 102
   Flower Flattery (6743-6745), 69
   Frenchie (6626), 69
   Frosted Leaves (6516), 27
   Galaxy (6880), 30, 68
   Garland (6209), 66
   Golden Acorn (also known as Acorn) (6639), 102
   Golden Brocade, 32
   Golden Cherries (6507), 29
   Golden Maple, 27
   Golden Mum (6219), 67
   Golden Swirl, 32
   Golden Trillium (6253), 70
   Golden Tulip (6903), 101
   Granada (6995), 100
   Harvest Time, 30
   Harvest Wheat, 70
   High Fashion (6892), 30
   Holiday Ice (6230), 83
   Honeybunch, 31
   Hooter (6353), 100
   Inca (6879), 102
   Inca Fire (8368), 19
   Ivy (6783-S, 6782-G), 66
   Jade Garden (6642), 67
   Jonquil (6184), 103
   Jubilee (6185), 100
   Kathleen (6511), 27, 84
   Lady Bug (6598), 31
   Leading Lady (6355), 21, 83, 84
   Light N' Bright (6216), 69
   Light of the East (6212), 67
   Lime-light, 31
   Lotus Blossom (6866), 28
   Madame Butterfly (6441-S, 6442-G), 101
   Magic Moods, 101
   Maharani (6284), 135
   Masterpiece (6497), 100
   Masterpiece Stick (6498), 99
   Midnight Magic (5066), 83
   Mini Fleur (6207), 29
   Moonflower (6584), 66
   Moonlight (6841), 101
   Moon-lites (6287), 99
   Mosaic, 84
   Mountain Flower (6210), 70
   Mr. Sea Gull (6908), 100
   Multiple Choice (6298-6323), 99
   Mystic Blue (6281), 67
   Mystic Swirl (6641), 70
   Nature's Choice (6933), 28
   Nocturne (6614), 66
   Ocean Star (6799), 68
   Old Vienna (8123), 19
   Operetta (6828), 136
   Orbit (6348), 101
   Patches (6278), 14
   Peace (6406), 99
   Pearl Bloom (6518), 28
   Pearl Elegance (6929), 30
   Pearl Flight (6641), 32, 55
   Pearlized Perfection (6569), 67
   Peking (6548), 101
   Persian Princess (6386), 98
   Peta-Lure (6911), 28
   Petite (6627), 68
   Pink Ice, 31
   Pinwheel (6886), 27
   Placid Beauty (6680), 69
   Polynesian (6668), 31
   Porcupine (6047), 152
   Precious (6857), 28
   Primrose (6910), 30
   Professor (6192), 100
   Promise (6700), 67
   Radiance (6932), 99
   Raspberry Ice, 30
   Remembrance (6798), 67, 99
   Remembrance Stick, 99

   Ribbonette (6421), 98
   Royal Hawaiian, 68
   Royal Plumage, 32
   Royal Velvet (6553), 100
   Sabu (6512), 102
   Sarah's ABC's (6957-6982), 30
   Sarah's Angel (6760), 69
   Sarah's Circles (6520-G, 6582-S), 66
   Satin Flame (6778), 31
   Satin Petals (6952), 66
   Saucy (6504), 53
   Saucy (6510-S, 6511-G), 100
   Scented Traveler (6280), 68
   Scepter, 31
   Scepter Stick, 31
   Sea Sprite (6509), 99
   Sea Whispers (6890), 28
   Serenade (6354), 100
   Shangri-La (6526), 102
   Siam (6908), 33
   Sign of Spring (6038), 103
   Silent Spring (6341), 99
   Silvery Maple (6679), 69
   Silvery Mist (6407), 99
   Silvery Nectar (8121), 102
   Silvery Nile, 33
   Silvery Splendor (6953), 29
   Silvery Sunburst (6255), 100
   Silvery Swirl (6460), 99
   Simplicity (6612), 69
   Slick Chick (6283), 99
   Snow Flower, 27
   Song of India (6576), 67
   Space-Age (6342), 103
   Sparkle Lites, 100
   Splendor, 27
   Split-Trick (6836), 102
   Spring Bouquet, 27
   Springtime (6493), 98
   Star Fire (6720), 66
   Starburst (6838), 67
   Star-lit Trio (6853), 33
   Strawberry Festival (6640), 69
   Strawberry Ice (6736), 66
   Strawflower (6194), 101
   Stunning (6458), 27
   Summer Magic (6586), 1960s; called New Summer Magic in 1970s (6290), 30
   Sun Flower (6645), 70
   Sun Flower, 33
   Sunflower (6228-S, 6227-G), 66
   Suzette (6424), 100
   Tahitian Flower Blue (6226), 68
   Tailored Swirl (6723-G, 6722-S), 66
   Tangerine (6638), 103
   Temple-Lites (6254), 67
   Tic-Tac-Toe (6706), 69
   Touch of Elegance (6326), 100
   Tracery (6955), 101
   Trellis (6826), 103
   Tropicana (6873), 29
   Venetian (6279), 100
   Vienna, 84
   Water Lily (6587), 66
   Westminster (6529), 100
   Whispering Leaf (6701), 67
   White Petals (6462), 101
   White Velvet (6430), 98
   Wind Flower (6924), 28
   Windsong, 33
   Wings of Fashion (6033), 103
   Wisteria, 21, 53
   Wizard of Oz, 14
   Wooded Beauty (6753), 67
   Woodland Flight (6696), 70
   Woven Classic (6939), 31
   Zebra (6229), 31

Brooch/ Pendant Combinations, 19, 29, 83, 98-100, 103, 148, 150
   Adam's Delight (6820), 29
   Black Charmer (8381), 98

Bronze Glo (8027), 148
Celebrity (8878), 29
Contessa (6936), 98
Coraline (8924), 103
Imperial (8940), 103
Inca Fire (8368), 19
Jet Set Versatile (8312), 99
Masterpiece (6497), 100
Midnight Magic (8605), 83
Old Vienna (8123), 19
Orchid (8320), 150
Sunset Elegance (8013), 98

Cardex Views, 50

Catalog Pages, 85, 90-95, 140-147

Children's Jewelry
Primrose Pendant (8536), 13
Shaggy Dog Pin (6324-S, 6325-G), 13
Funny Face Necklace, 13
Myrtle Pendant (8543), 13
Pixie Pets (8345), 120

Christmas Charms, 13

Crosses, 87, 114, 138-139, 167
18th Century Cross-Limited Edition (8649), 139
Calvary Cross (8915), 114
Celtic Cross-Limited Edition (8063), 138
Calvary (8692), 167
Credo Cross (8277), 138
Crusader Cross (8403), 138-139
Florentine Cross-Limited Edition (8044), 138
Golden Splendor Cross (8037), 139
Majestic Cross-Limited Edition (8437), 138
Marriage Cross (8019), 139
Mythology Cross-Limited Edition (8506), 138
Peace Cross-Limited Edition (8130), 138
Romanesque Cross (8270), 139
Serenity Cross (8109), 138
Solitude Cross (8099), 138
Tiger Eye Cross (Lady Coventry), 87
Today Cross (8834), 138, 139
Tudor Cross (8834), 139
Victorian Cross-Limited Edition (8870), 138

Earrings, 34-44, 71-75, 104-110, 153
Acapulco (7275), 72
Adam's Delight (7820), 36
A-Go-Go (7660), 72
Alaskan Summer, 53
Allusion (7208), 36
Aloha (7041), 104
American Beauty (7837), 41
Americana (7387), 104
Antique Garden (7064), 107
Antique Rose (7439), 104
Antiqued Amethyst (7693), 136
Aquarius (7360), 104
Aura (7928), 107
Aurora Blaze (7725), 72, 83
Aurora Swirl, 55
Austrian Lites (9633), 104
Autumn Haze (7511), 36
Autumn Splendor (7601), 110
Bewitchery (7731), 72
Bird of Paradise (7534), 71
Birds in Flight (7704), 73
Bittersweet (7868), 36
Black Beauty (7863), 35
Black Beauty (7734), 75
Black Diamond (Imitation) (7011), 74
Black Saturn (7813), 38
Blue Hawaii (7914), 36
Blue Lagoon (7991), 83
Bold and Beautiful (7725), 35
Bouncy (7854), 153
Burgundy (7485), 106
Butterfly Lace (7913), 41
Button Pearl (7588, 7646), 106
Café Society Fashion Swingers (7662), 73
Caged Pearl (7340), 74
Camellia (7909), 40
Camelot (7647), 74
Cameo Lace (7648), 38
Candlelite (7463), 110
Candy Land (7557), 104
Caramelftone (7850), 107
Career Girl, 41
Carnival (7313), 19
Carousel (7762-7766), 73
Carousel, 26
Casual Classic (7425), 43
Catherine (7525), 106
Celebrity (7878), 35

Celestial Ice, 41
Ceylon (7409), 105
Chain-Ability (7453-S, 7454-G), 107
Chain-o-lites (7220), 72
Chantilly Lace, 54
Charisma (7650), 105
Chit-Chat (7771), 42
Circulet (7608), 108
Color Frame (7282-7283), 75
Color Spray (7816), 41
Confetti (7710), 41
Cool Surrender (7671), 36
Crescent (7273), 72
Crystal Navette (7927), 35
Crystal Snowflake, 44
Crystal Snowflake (7277), 83
Daisy (7919), 42
Daisy Mae, 38
Dancing Jet (7604), 74
Dancing Magic (5016), 75
Dawn to Dusk (7671), 71
Dazzling Aurora, 17
Deep Burgundy (7613), 71
Demure (7752), 39
Designer's Choice, 40
Diamonice (7263), 104
Ebb Tide, 39
Egyptian Temptress, 41
Elegantè (7551), 110
Embassy (7198), 108
Ember Tears (7272), 109
Emerald Ice (7786), 44
Enchanted Forest (7699), 71
Enchantress - 1960s (7728), 75
Enchantress - 1970s (7416), 136
Endearing (7564), 37
Evening Accent, 44
Evening Splendor (7750), 74
Evening Star (7629), 37, 83
Exotic, 37
Fancy Free (7798), 40, 105
Fanfare (7899), 110
Fan-Fare (7756), 40
Fantasy, 37
Fashion Flirt (7703), 42, 71
Fashion Flower (7703), 73
Fashion Flower (Dainty and Daring) (7875, 7834), 35
Fashion Leaf, 40
Fashion Loops (7872), 71
Fashion Parade (7941), 35
Fashion Petals (7737-7742), 73
Fashion Round (7315), 74
Fashion Splendor (7286), 106
Fashion Swingers (7662-7663), 73
Fashionette (7597), 71
Fashion-rite (7541), 105
Feather Fantasy (7765), 43
Feathered Fashion, 40
Fiesta (7183), 19
Filigree Clover (7461), 75
Flair, 105
Free Fall (7003), 107
Frosted Feathers, 40, 41
Frozen Lace (7565), 54
Galaxy (7880), 35
Garland (7209), 43, 73
Goddess of Fashion (7885), 71
Golden Avocado, 84
Golden Bangle (7568), 71
Golden Cherries (7507), 72
Golden Coin (7237), 109
Golden Embers (7643), 74
Golden Gypsy (also known as Gypsy) (7945), 42, 72
Golden Ice - 1970s, 136
Golden Ice (Holiday Collection) (7550), 110
Golden Lace (7484), 106
Golden Lanterns (7523), 107
Golden Maple, 40
Golden Petals (7400), 105
Golden Sunset (7946), 109
Golden Tassel (7349), 106, 109
Golden Trillium (7253), 75
Golden Tulip (7903), 108
Goldenrod (7997), 106
Gypsy (also known as Golden Gypsy) (7603), 72
Happy Holiday, 72
Harvest Wheat, 75
Heirloom Treasure (7800, 7801), 75
Heliotrope (7547), 137
Hi-Lo Elegance (7478), 105
Hi-Swinger (7664), 73, 75
Hidden Pearl (7903), 34
Hidden Rose (7669), 106
Holiday (7590, 7622, 7620, 7619, 7621), 73
Holiday Circles (7647), 19
Holiday Ice (7230), 73, 83
Hong Kong (7362), 83
Hulabaloo (7658, 7659), 19
Inca (7879), 107

Indian Princess (7954), 38
Ivy (7783), 37
Jet Ice (7832), 107
Jet Set (7312), 105
Kathleen (7511), 84
Lady of Spain (7830), 36
Lazy Daisy (7649), 43
Leading Lady (7355), 21, 83
Light N' Bright (7216), 39, 73
Light of the East (7212), 73
Lotus Blossom (7866), 34
Lotus Blossom (7935), 108
Love Story (red) (7887), 124
Mademoiselle (7905), 41
Maharani (7284), 135
Mandarin Magic (7991), 107
Matchmaker (7717), 109
Matinee Elegance (7855), 36
Midnight Magic (7605), 83
Ming Garden (7521), 105
Minuet (7506), 109
Mirage (7285), 109
Modern Leaf (7201), 37
Molten Topaz (7928), 42
Monte Carlo (7831), 39
Mood Magic (7829), 41
Mood Magic (7992), 107
Moonflower (7584), 41
Moonlight Madness, 54
Moon-lites (7287), 106
Mosaic - 1960s, 84
Mosaic - 1970s, (7522) 105
Mountain Flower (7210), 74
Mystic (7922), 40
Mystic Blue (7281), 75
Nature's Choice (7933), 35
New Mode (7358), 105
New York (7361), 37
Night Garden (7589), 107
Night N' Day (7727), 37
Nocturne (7614), 104
Northern Lights (7576), 110
Ocean Star (7799), 72
On Stage (7499), 72
One N' Only (7726), 34
Operetta (7828), 136
Oriental (7443), 110
Paris (7363), 84
Pastel Parfait (7580), 19
Pearl Bloom (7518), 34
Pearl Contour (7920), 42
Pearl Elegance (7929), 71
Pearl Flattery (7936), 40
Pearl Flight (7684), 55
Pearl Showers (7851), 41
Pearl Swirl (7615), 42, 75
Pearl Wardrobe (7851), 22
Pearlized Perfection (7569), 72
Peking (7548), 106
Peta-Lure (7911), 35
Petite (7627), 37
Piccadilly Circle (7989), 135
Pierced Classics (7528), 42
Pink Ice, 37
Pinwheel (7886), 34
Placid Beauty (7680), 43
Plain and Fancy (7673), 39, 43
Polka (7043), 108
Polonaise (7644), 105
Polynesian, 74
Powder Puff, 38
Precious (7857), 34
Princess (7900), 110
Pyramid Treasure (7503), 105
Pyramid Treasures, 74
Radiance (7932), 39
Rain Flower (7287), 74
Raspberry Ice, 37
Remembrance (7266 or 7798), 72, 104
Rhapsody in Blue (7856), 40
Romanesque (7270), 110
Royal Ballet (7796), 54
Royal Hawaiian, 71
Royal Highness (7899), 39
Royal Plumage, 38
Royal Velvet (7553), 106
Sabrina (7294), 105, 109
Sarah's Circles (7582 S, 7520 G), 73
Sara-Zade (7293), 42
Sassy (7120), 108
Satin Flame (7778), 40
Satin Petals (7952), 73
Saucy (7841), 41
Saucy (7504), 53
Saucy Swingers (7746), 72
Sea Sprite (7509), 105
Sea Star (7349), 104
Sea Whispers (7890), 35
Serenade (7354), 105
Serene (7648), 37
Shangri-La (7526), 109
Showtime (7422), 109
Siam (7908), 36
Silvery Cascade (7749, 7761), 75

Silvery Maple (7689), 73
Silvery Mist (7407), 105
Silvery Nile (7814), 110
Silvery Splendor (7953), 34
Silvery Tassel, 41
Simply Elegant (7894), 42
Slim 'N' Trim (7860), 39
Slim Line, 37
Snow Flower (7723), 40
Snow Princess, 39
Snow White, 39
Soft Swirl (7567), 108
Song of India (7576), 73
Sophisticated (7605), 71
South Seas (7781), 81
Sparkle Lites, 106
Spellbound (7104), 153
Splendor, 40
Star Fire (7720), 72
Starburst - 1960s (7838), 36
Starburst - 1970s (7040), 108
Strawberry Festival (7640), 71
Strawberry Ice (7736), 36
Stunning (7458), 34
Sultana (7768), 73
Summer Festival (7762), 74
Summer Frost (7727), 36
Summer Frost (7616), 38
Summer Magic (7586; called New Summer Magic in 1970s (7290), 34, 73
Sun Flower, 41
Sun Flower (7645), 75
Sunflower (7228-S, 7227-G), 74
Symphony (7279), 74
Tailored Swirl (7723-G, 7722-S), 37, 73
Talisman of Love (7560), 107
Tangerine (7638), 110
Taste of Honey (7951), 104
Tawny Shadows, 55
Temple-Lites (7254), 75
Textured Links (7112), 107
Three Cheers (7579-W, 7631-R, 7632-B), 107
Times Square (7408), 106
Touch of Elegance (7326), 105
Town and Country (7757), 38
Tranquility (7319), 137
Trellis (7826), 108
Trio (7902), 43
Tudor (7607), 106
Turn-a-bout, 37
Two-Timer (7482), 106
Ultima (7211), 38
Umber Tones (7042), 108
Valencia (7291), 72
Venetian (7274), 106
Venetian Treasure (7939), 107
Versaille, 39, 71
Vienna (7376), 84
Vienna Nights, 44
Watusi (7585), 107
Wayside (7442), 106
Westminster (7529), 106
Whispering Leaf (7701), 72
Whispering Leaves (7724), 38
White Petals, 104
White Satin (7682), 74
Wind Flower (7924), 41
Windsong, 37
Wisteria - early 1960s (7592), 21, 53
Wisteria - 1970s (7134), 109
Wooded Beauty (7753), 72
Woodland Flight (7696), 74
World's Fair, 84
Woven Classic (7939), 40
Young and Gay (7733), 36

Emmons Jewelry, 16

Employees
Awards/Celebrations, 8, 10, 11, 18, 70, 165
Clothes, 8
Fashion Show Directors
Helen, 24
Dawn, 64
Alynda, 96
Promotional Materials, 8, 10, 89, 164
Props, 9, 25, 12

Glossary of Terms, 171-172

Lady Coventry, 85-89
Bracelets
Amethyst Oval (9518), 86
Antique Treasure (also called Opal Treasure) (9296), 86
Filigree Ivory (9240), 87
Filigree Jet Onyx (9674), 86
Jade Oval (9242), 87
Lady Coventry Bracelet (8519), 89
Onyx Tears (9329), 86
Brooches

Amethyst Oval (6518), 86
Diamond Classic (5097), 88
Flower of the Month (6775), 88
Flowered Circle (5091), 87
Jade 'n Pearl (6750), 87
Jade Oval (6328), 87
Jade Rose (6517), 87
Onyx Tears (6329), 86
Semi-Precious Turtle (6248), 87
Tiger Eye Butterfly (6751), 87
Earrings
Amethyst Oval (7518), 86
Aqua Treasure (7433), 86
Carved Tiger Eye (7694), 87
Diamond Classic (5097), 88
Diamonice (7263), 104
Flowered Circle (7091), 87
Genuine Jade (7414), 87
Genuine Sodalite (7412), 87
Genuine Tiger Eye (7110), 87
Jade Oval (7242), 87
Jade Rose (7517), 87
Lady Coventry (pearl) (7551), 88
Lovers Knot (7366), 88
Mother of Pearl Cameo (7245), 88
Onyx Tears (7329), 86
Satin Drops (7020), 88
Necklaces
Antiqued Amethyst, 88
Aqua Treasure (8433), 86
Carved Tiger Eye Pendant (8694), 87
Cultural Pearls (8519), 89
Diamond Accent (8173), 88
Filigree Ivory Pendant (8331), 88
Filigree Jet Onyx (8674), 86
Genuine Jade (8414), 87
Genuine Tiger Eye Choker (8843), 87
Jade n' Pearl (8750), 87
Jade Oval (8242), 87
Lady Coventry Birthstone (8156), 88
Mother of Pearl Cameo (8244), 88
Onyx Tears (8329), 86
Silvery Moonstone (8069), 88
Sodalite, 88
Tiger Eye Cross (8694), 87
Rings
Genuine Opal (5880), 88
Genuine Sodalite (5714), 87
Genuine Tiger Eye, 88
Horizons, 88
Initial, 88
Lord or Lady Coventry (5695-5713), 88
Lord or Lady Initial, 88
Rejoice (5462), 88

Limited Editions, 96, 138, 139
Christmas Charms, 96
Crosses, 138-139
1973 Victorian Cross (8870), 138
1974 Florentine Cross (8044), 138
1975 Peace Cross (8130), 138
1976 18th Century Cross (8649), 139
1977 Majestic Cross (8437), 138
1978 Mythology Cross (8506), 138
1979 Celtic Cross (8063), 138

Men's Jewelry, 164-168
Bracelets
Brute (9795), 167
Dare Devil (9995), 167
Explorer (9293), 167
Kojak (9705), 167
Leather Cuff (9767), 167
New I.D. (9796), 167
Third Gear (9427), 167
Cuff Links
Genuine Onyx, 168
Paris (5934), 166
Venus, 166
Necklaces
Calvary Cross (8692), 167
Daytona Choker (8433), 167
Duke Choker (8054), 167
Embraceable Chain (8909-8910), 167
Gentry Chain (8518), 167
Italian Horn (8664), 167
Men Runner Pendant (8209), 168
Men's Zodiac drop (8007), 167
Slicker Chain (8299), 167
Rings
Togetherness (5355), 133
Sets
Antiqued Classic (5750-5751), 166
Bold Knight (5977-5978), 166
Charcoal Classic (5953-5954), 168
Denmark (5079), 166
England (5075), 166
Genuine Jade, 166
Germany (5077), 166
Heraldic, 166
Italy (5080), 166

Kentucky Derby (5062), 166
Male Elegance (5998-5999), 166
Mars (5914), 167
Mercury (5820), 166
Mosaic (5081), 166
Neptune (5916), 166
Regimental (5909), 168
Riviera (5058), 166
Royal Jade (5094), 167
Switzerland (5076), 167
Tahitian Pearl (5911-5912), 167
The New Yorker (5979-5980), 167
Tie Bars/Tie Tacs
  Dune Buggy (5922), 168
  Cultured Pearl (5927), 168
  Tailored Elegance (5969), 168

Necklaces (many named because of pendants, 45-49, 76-78, 111-125, 149-151. *See also* Brooch/Pendant Combinations
Acorn Treasures (8934), 48
Allure (8678), 116
Aloha (8041), 119
Antique Lady (8207), 78
Antiqued Amethyst (8693), 136
Antiqued Chains (8343), 122
Applause (8136), 115, 117
Athena (8648), 116
Aura (8928), 120
Autumn Mist (0886), 113
Azure Skies (8524), 112
Big Apple, The (8114), 112
Bittersweet (8275), 111, 150
Blaze (8346), 117
Blue Champagne (8708), 48
Bold and Beautiful (8725), 45
Broadway (8500), 116
Broken Heart, 150
Bronze Glo Pendant (8027), 148
Cameo Fashions (8195), 115
Candle-Glo (8527), 123
Candlelite (8464), 118
Carameltone (8850), 119
Caravan chain (8017), 122
Carefree Choker (8712), 113
Carousel Fashion (8765-8766), 76, 77
Castaway Choker (8188), 150
Casual Classic (8425), 116
Celebrity (8878), 45
Celestial Fire, 55
Chain O' Fashion (8867-G, 8876-S), 45
Chain-Ability (8453-S, 8876-S), 115
Chain-o-lites (8220), 77
Chantilly Lace, 54
Charisma (8650), 113
Chiffon-Bib (8445), 113
Chinatown (8703), 116
Christina Locket (8135), 111
Classic Pendant, 47
Classic Partners Chain (8418), 117
Colleen, 78
Color Spray (8816), 49
Contempo (8205), 120
Contessa (Pearl) (8595), 77
Continental (8242), 116
Cool Surrender (8671), 46
Counterpoint Choker (8598), 112
Coventry Square Chain (8534), 112
Crystal Navette, 46
Crystal Snowflake (8277), 83
Cultured Pearls, 89
Cupid's Touch (8384), 115
Curtain Call (8842), 150
Czarina (8404), 98
Dancing Magic (5016), 46
Danish Modern, 48
Danish Mood (8994), 115
Dawn to Dusk (8671), 49
Debut (8407), 136
Delicate Twist Chains (8332-G, 8498-S), 118
Delightful (8986), 45
Desert Flower (8032), 119
Designer Links (8658), 120
Double Choice (8128), 118
Dream Boat Locket (8856), 118
Elegantè (8551), 136
Ember Tears (8272), 115
Emberwood (8271), 114
Emeraude Drop (8050), 98
Empress (8515), 112
Enchantress - 1960s (8728), 83
Enchantress - 1970s (8416), 136
Encounter (8128), 116
Evergreen Pendant (8832), 121
Exclusive (8501), 115
Exquisite Lady (8612), 115
Fancy Free (8798), 117
Fanfare (8899), 119
Fantastic Chain (8682-S, 8683-G), 118
Fashion (Pearls) (8298), 121
Fashion Basic chain (8851), 149
Fashion Circle (8904), 48

Fashion Duet (8950), 121
Fashion Flair (8051), 116
Fashion Flirt (8703), 77
Fashion Loops (8672), 77
Fashion Melody (8209), 119
Fashion Parade (8941), 45, 76
Fashion Rope Chain (8942), 123
Fashion Wrap (8797), 115
Fashion Zodiac (8857-8868), 119
Fashionette (8596-8597), 76
Filigree Lady (8847), 123
Fire-Lite (8398), 112
First Love (8399), 118
Flight (8115), 120
Flirting Heart Choker (8279), 149
Floral Locket (8256), 111
Flutter Byes (8199), 117
Folklore (8420), 118
Folklore (8541), 124
Four-Dimensions (8660-G, 8107-S), 111
French Rope (8717), 150, 151
Frosted Feathers, 47
Frosted Ice (8046), 112
Goddess of Fashion (8885), 77
Golden Avocado, 84
Golden Braid (8647), 49
Golden Braids Choker (8953), 125
Golden Cascade (8896), 113
Golden Chains (8842), 120
Golden Dove (8201), 117
Golden Embers (8643), 76
Golden Ice (8550), 119
Golden Nile (8452), 120
Golden Nugget (8530), 113
Golden Petals (8400), 114
Golden Rope Pendant (8396), 123
Golden Sunset (8855), 117
Golden Teardrop (8872), 111
Golden Tulip (8903), 124
Golden Wardrobe, 49
Granada (8996), 122, 150
Grecian (8671), 113
Heirloom (8471), 117
Heirloom Treasure (8800), 76
Heliotrope (8547), 137
Hercules (8360), 123
Herringbone Chain (8466), 150
Hidden Rose (8668), 114
High Society (8066), 123
Hi-Lo Elegance (8478), 112
Holiday Beads (8097-8099, 8895-8897), 125
Holiday Chain (8220-G, 8219-S), 117, 118, 120
Holiday Garden (8374), 111
Holiday Ice (8230), 83
Inca Fire (8368), 19, 117
Instant Fashion (8204-G, 8205-S), 48
Interlude (8836), 116
Jamie Choker (8576), 118
Jet Elegance (8206), 76
Jet Streamer (8854), 117
Jubilee (8153), 149
Juke-Box, 47
LaBelle (8983), 117
Lariat (8024), 149
Legend (8289), 114
Light of the East (8212), 124
Lilac Time (8208), 114
Limbo (8592), 114
Liquid Lites (8382), 47
Lotus Blossom (8935), 123
Love Story Birthstone Ensemble (6887), 124
Mademoiselle (8840), 117
Mandarin Magic (8990), 123
Matinee Elegance (8898), 48
Melon Holiday Garden (8377), 111
Ming Garden (8521), 78
Molten Topaz (8928), 47
Monte Carlo (8831), 48
Mood Magic (8988), 119
Moon Beam (8594), 111
Moonlight Madness, 54
Mosaic (8522), 112
Multi-Fashion (8684), 77
Nature's Treasures (8290), 121
Navajo Pendant (8651), 121
New Mode (8358), 117
New Polonaise (8956), 136
New Seasons (8874), 111
Night Garden (8589), 118
Nite-Owl (8871), 116
Omega (8448), 116
On Stage (8499), 77, 98
Oriental Lanterns (8411), 112, 125
Over the Rainbow (8427), 118
Oxford Pendant (8254), 149
Pandora (8404), 114
Papillion (8591), 112
Pastel Glo (8402), 117
Pastel Parfait (8485), 115, 125
Patrician (8118), 118

Pearl Swirl (8615), 78
Pearl Wardrobe (8851), 22
Perfection (8502), 113
Personalized Pearls, 49
Personally Yours (8957-8982), 124
Phoenix (8694), 117
Piccadilly Circle (6989), 135
Polka (8043), 124
Polonaise (8644), 119
Pompeii (8952), 19, 121
Primrose (8536), 123
Princess (8900), 122
Pyramid Treasure (8451), 121
Rain Flower (8287), 48
Rajah Pendant (8405), 121
Regency, 149
Rock-Trio (8419), 113
Roman Holiday (matches Tudor) (8637), 116, 122
Romanesque (8270), 122
Rose Cameo (8653), 76
Rose-Marie (8317), 112
Royal Ballet (8796), 54
Royal Highness (8899), 47
Sabrina Fair (8699), 47
Safari (8984), 115
Safari (8954), 119
Sara Lariat (8255), 149
Sassy (8120), 119
Satin Beauty Choker (8561), 111
Scarlet Tears (8822), 122
Seaswept Choker (8198), 150
Sea Star Hoop (8349), 116
Secrets Locket (8535), 117
Serenade (8826), 118
Serene (8648), 78
Serpentine Chain (2069), 120
Shangri-La Pendant (8526), 123
Sierra Choker (8548), 123
Silver Chains (3875-3879), 122
Silvery Cascade (8749), 46, 113
Silvery Zodiac (8154-8165), 149
Simply Elegant (8894), 48
Snowdrop (8359), 123
South Seas (8781), 51
Spangle-Bangles (8923), 19
Spanish Moss (8475-G, 8476-S), 118
Sparkle by the Yard (8620), 113
Sparkle Chain (8473), 120
Sparkle Magic (8636), 123
Spellbound Choker (7104), 151
Spinner Choker (8690), 122
Spring Melody (8253), 149
Springtime Choker (8203), 125
Springtime Lilac (8094), 149
Star Shower, 47
Starburst (8040), 119
Stone Age (8443), 113
Stretched Cable (8364), 150
Stunning Plus (8935), 47
Sultana (8768), 46
Summer Flirt (8604), 118
Summer Magic (8955); called New Summer in 1970s (8290), 46
Sunset Elegance (8013), 98
Swan Lake (8540), 115
Sweetheart Choker (8663), 151
Swingalong (8494), 77
Swingalong Chain, 120
Taffee Tones (8179), 124
Talisman of Love (8560), 119
Tassel Magic (8629), 19
Taste of Honey (8951), 115
Tawny Shadows, 55
Textured Links (8112), 119
Thea Pendant (8425), 112
Tiger Fish (8606), 115
Timeless Beauty (8559), 112, 123
Timely (8341), 114
Tortoise Fashions (8802), 76
Tradewinds (8245), 117
Tranquility (8319), 123, 137
Trapeze (8949), 122
Tricia Choker (8410-G, 8411-S), 117
Triple-Treat (8873), 19
Turn-a-bout (8110), 48
Twilight (8827), 120, 137
Twisted Knot Lariat (8134), 149
Twisted Rope Chain (8258), 117, 150, 151
Two-tone Butterfly, 151
Ultra-Versatile (8596), 114
Valerie Choker (8939), 149
Venetian Treasure (8023), 124
Versatility Chain (8779-S-8780-G), , 78
Victoria (0809), 149
Victoria Blue (8202-Pendant 8197), 112, 116
Vienna (8196), 119
Vogue (8196), 119
Volcano (8191), 124
Whispering Leaves (8724), 49
White Magic Choker (8394), 150
White Satin (8642), 49

Wild Honey Pendant (8356), 76
Wisteria (8592), 114
World's Fair (8947), 46, 84
Young and Gay (8733), 46, 78
Zodiac (8300-8311), 114

Overview, 6-23
Current Value Information, 22
Get your charm, 23
Markings, 13, 15-18
Original Pricing, 22

Rings, 53-55, 81-84, 131-137, 153
Annette (5788), 131, 132
Antique Rose (5377), 132
Astrojet (5404), 133
Austrian Lites (5392), 131
Autumn Haze (5507), 153
Azure Skies (5371), 131
Bamboo (5403), 133
Bewitching (5153), 81
Birthstone (5144-5146), 82
Black Beauty (5124), 134
Blue Buttercup (5292), 133
Blue Lady (5393), 133
Blue Rose (5536), 133, 134
Blue Sun (5264), 131
Burgundy Twist (5039), 132
Calypso (5487), 134
Camelot (5224), 132
Cameo Lady (5821), 132
Cameo Portrait (5617), 131
Capri (5505), 133
Catherine (5387), 135
Celebrity (5123), 53
Charmer (5338), 132
Cleopatra (5329), 132
Continental (5765), 134
Crimson-Lites (5380), 132
Czarina (5261), 132
Deep Burgundy, 81
Desert Flower (5517), 134
Dusk (5514), 133
Ebb Tide (5263), 132
Egypt (5385), 131
Egyptian (5223), 132
Elegant (5172), 132
Ember Beauty (5768), 132
Ember Navette (5401), 133
Eric (5682-5694), 135
Escapade (5351), 153
Evening Cluster (5785), 132
Fashion Parade (5137), 82
Flattery (5506), 134
Flirt (5459), 134
Gala (5157), 82
Galaxy (5750), 133
Genuine Jade (5865), 153
Golden Embers (5161), 82
Golden Lace (5483-S, 5484-G), 135
Golden Nest (5569), 134
Golden Nugget (5183), 82
Happy Talk Birthstone (5405-5416), 133
Hazy-Daze (5599), 134
Hidden Rose (5679), 132
Homestead (5503), 131
Honey Berries (5528), 134
Illusive (5530), 133
Imperial (5503), 136
Irish Eyes (5374), 133
Jan (0893), 132
Java (5511), 131
Jet Elegance (5182), 81, 132
Jet Filigree (5855), 132
Jet Set (5723), 131, 132
Jonquil (5184), 82
Jupiter (5523), 133
Kari (5776), 134
Kathleen (5151), 153
LaBelle (5716), 133
Lagoon (5496), 135
Light of the East (5216), 81, 132
Love Knot (5221), 131
Love Story (5375), 82, 88, 134, 135
Lovely Lady (5650), 132, 134
Madame Butterfly (5658), 133
Majorca (5189), 82, 132
Marigold (5357), 133
Moon Beam (5748), 135
Moon Glo (5850), 132
Morning Dew (5398), 134
Multi-Lites (5395), 133
Mystic Blue (5218), 81
Mystique (5504), 133
Navajo (5399), 134
Neptune (5524), 133
New Bermuda Blue (5255), 82
Night Lights (2158), 153
Night N' Day (5120), 82
Northern Lights (5388), 132
Old Vienna (5567), 135
Pacer, 131
Papillion (5499), 133
Parisienne Nights (5118), 81

Personal Choice (5527), 133
Pink Champagne (5516), 135
Portrait (5456), 133
Premiere (5755), 132
Priscilla (5860), 133
Queen's Choice, 132
Queen's Lace (5171), 131
Rainbow Cavern (5389), 133
Reflections (5466), 135, 153
Rejoice (5462), 134
Rome (5564), 131
Rose Cameo (5162), 82
Roxanne, 135
Sabrina Fair (5114), 53
Satin Elegance (5513), 131
Satin Lace, 131
Satin Sand (5490), 134
Sea Star (5771), 132
Sea Treasure (5733), 132
Seaswept (5717), 133
Shangri-La (5372), 131
Shrimp (5348), 153
Sierra (5859), 132
Soft Swirl (5390), 134
South Seas (5789), 134
Space-Age (5168), 132
Sparkle Mountain (5489), 81
Sparkling Burgundy (5397), 133
Spice (2141), 153
Symphony (5186), 82
Third Dimension-Two Finger (5256), 131
Togetherness (Woman's and Man's) (5355M, 5342W), 133
Trulove (5174-5180), 82
Tutti-Fruitti (5522), 133
Twin Jades (5160), 82
Twinkles (5571), 153
Victoria Blue (5597), 134
Viva (5498), 153
Vogue (5158), 82
Wild Honey (5166), 132
Woody Nymph (5339), 133
Wrap Around Zodiac (5618-5629), 135

Sets, 53-55, 81-84, 131-137, 153
Alaska, 53
Antiqued Amethyst, 136
Aurora Blaze, 83
Aurora Swirl, 55
Blue Lagoon, 83
Celestial Fire, 55
Chantilly Lace, 54
Crystal Snowflakes, 83
Enchantress, 83
Enchantress, 136
Evening Star, 83
Frozen Lace, 54
Golden Avocado, 84
Golden Ice, 136
Heliotrope, 137
Holiday Ice, 83
Kathleen, 55
Leading Lady, 83
Maharani, 135
Midnight Magic, 83
Moonlight Madness, 54
Mosaic, 84
Operetta, 136
Pearl Flight, 55
Piccadilly Circle, 135
Royal Ballet, 54
Saucy, 53
South Seas, 81
Tawny Shadows, 55
Tranquility, 137
Twilight, 137
Vienna, 84
Wisteria, 53
World's Fair, 84

Signet Examples, 20, 23, 56-63

Swarovski Crystals
All Birthstone pieces, 82, 88-89, 118, 124, 133-135
Charm, 18

Unidentified Pieces
United States
  Bracelets, 13, 51, 79, 126, 127, 129
  Brooches, 13, 30, 32, 33, 55, 70, 102
  Crosses, 14, 139
  Earrings, 14, 18, 19, 21, 42-44, 55, 75, 105, 148, 153
  Necklaces, 14, 55, 78, 121, 122, 124, 125, 150, 151
  Men's, 152, 166, 167
  Rings, 133, 153
  Sets, 14, 26, 55
  Ultra-Fashion Collection, 18
Canadian, 15, 33, 137
Great Britain, 15, 83